The English Folly
The Edifice Complex

The English Folly

The Edifice Complex

Gwyn Headley and
Wim Meulenkamp

Published by Liverpool University Press on behalf of Historic England, The Engine House, Fire Fly Avenue, Swindon SN2 2EH
www.HistoricEngland.org.uk

Historic England is a Government service championing England's heritage and giving expert, constructive advice.

The views contained in this book are those of the authors alone and not Historic England or Liverpool University Press.

First published 2020

ISBN: 978-1-78962-197-6 cased
ISBN: 978-1-78962-212-6 limp

British Library Cataloguing in Publication data
A CIP catalogue record for this book is available from the British Library.

Typeset in Georgia Pro Light 9/11

Edited by Sarah Enticknap
Page layout by Carnegie Book Production

Printed in the Czech Republic by Akcent Media Limited

Contents

This book is dedicated to the memory of
Vernon Gibberd, Architect (1931–2019)

Foreword

Follies were always built by eccentrics. Or so we would like to think. True, many of them were. And if not, at least the follies themselves are eccentric – or is that only our perception? In *On Liberty* John Stuart Mill (1806–1873) remarked: 'The amount of eccentricity in a society has generally been proportional to the amount of genius, mental vigour and moral courage it contained. That so few now dare to be eccentric marks the chief danger of the time'.

Nowadays there are even fewer of them left. For some reason (climate, diet, lie of the land, who knows) England has always abounded in eccentrics. Other peoples and countries have had their fair share, but eccentrics appear to have thrived exceedingly well in the English environment.

So did the architectural folly. Who would deny that Lord Berners, 'Mad Jack' Fuller, William Beckford and George Durant were anything but true eccentrics, half wise/half mad at the best of times, some even quite insane. Most of them built more than one folly and made a splendid show of it. Sixteenth century squire Sir Thomas Tresham would have been hugely disappointed if you called his three architectural essays in piety and religious obsession – the Triangular Lodge, the Market House in Rothwell or Lyveden New Bield – follies. But they're all included here.

On the other hand, the begetters of arguably the most absurd and delightful 18th century collection of follies, at Barwick Park in Somerset, John and Grace Newman, appear to have been solid, rather sedate folk.

And how about perhaps the maddest of them all – another 'Mad Jack' – Shropshire's John Mytton (1795–1834)? He never built a folly in his short and energetic life. Yes, this hunting-mad squire lived in the right age and possessed the peculiarities and proclivities (riding a bear in his parlour, setting fire to his night shirt while still in it to get rid of the hiccups, keeping 2,000 hounds) specific to the Class 1 eccentric. But not an architectural folly in sight.

Eccentricity and follies aren't necessarily boon companions, but it certainly helps.

WIM MEULENKAMP

Acknowledgements

The authors would like to thank Yvonne Headley and Moni Engel for their constant encouragement, correction and support.

Karen Lynch has demystified the North of England for us, and her passion and enthusiasm for the subject, as shown in her Folly Flâneuse blog posts, have been a source of lasting motivation. The Gazetteer has been greatly improved by her suggestions, along with the remarkable input provided by Alan Terrill and Paul Brooker during the enforced Coronavirus lockdown.

It is pleasant to record that members of the Folly Fellowship are still talking to us after all these years, and we would like to single out Mary Bright and Iain Gray for their enduring constancy.

We would also like to thank John Hudson of Historic England, Alison Welsby and Patrick Brereton of Liverpool University Press and Rachel Chamberlain of Carnegie Book Production for their patience and forbearance.

Our thanks are due to every one of them.

Introduction

In the 19th century the population of London exploded from one million in 1800 to 6.7 million in 1900. People needed to be housed, and London was soon swathed in terraces of houses with a faintly Gothic aspect. How did this come about? Why the Gothic?

It was because Victorian architects were influenced by 18th-century Gothic follies. A folly is a misunderstood building, which can take any size, shape or form. The first Gothic Revival building in England was a folly. The first Greek Revival building in England was a folly. It would not be too far-fetched to claim that the general architectural face of England has been influenced more by the folly revivalist style than by anything else.

But first every writer on follies has to pay homage to the pioneering work of artist Barbara Jones (1912–1978) (Fig 0.1). Her 1953 book *Follies & Grottoes* was the first full-length book on the subject and certainly triggered our interest in it. The present writers have gone on together and separately to write seven printed books and 40 ebooks on follies. Enough, one might say, but over time we realised that our pleasure and delight in revealing previously unrecorded examples was little more than simple cataloguing, and an investigation into what drove people to build them was called for. So this book is about people and attitudes as much as it is about 'glass, bones and a hank of weed', Jones's matchless illustration of the spirit of folly.

Such an investigation of necessity takes the form of potted biographies, and here's where fact trounces fiction every which way. If this were a novel, the tales of astounding wealth, sexual perversion, murder, munificence, rape, insanity, brutality, slavery, religious mania, selfishness, snobbery, charity, suicide, generosity, theft, madness, smelliness, wickedness, failure and eccentricity that will unfold in these pages would be too concentrated to allow for the willing suspension of disbelief. All these sins and virtues, and more, are displayed by the characters in this book, some exhibiting several of them simultaneously.

Yet, given the fact that there are nigh on 2,000 folly sites in England, we clearly cannot hope to cover them all here. At the end of each chapter we have provided a gazetteer of the follies of that type to be found across the country, and Heritage Ebooks have published a highly illustrated series of ebooks on the *Follies of England*, each one featuring a different county, and available to download from heritage.co.uk.

An interest in follies does not have to be a solitary obsession. The Folly Fellowship, a registered charity set up in 1988 to preserve, promote and protect follies,

Fig 0.1

Barbara Jones, the doyenne of folly writers. [© Tony Raymond/ fotoLibra]

grottoes and garden buildings, publishes the quarterly *Follies Magazine*, which covers many of the differing viewpoints on the subject, and the Folly Fellowship website, which among other delights has mapped virtually every folly site in Britain.

If you have opened this book in a Pollyanna spirit of freedom and optimism, anticipating a delight of diversity and inclusivity, then we are afraid that we will disappoint you. Most of the people celebrated here are dead white males. What they have in common is an edifice complex. They loved to build; in some cases were simply driven to build. It is a rare drive, and one that is seldom shared by women. Of course, there are some glorious exceptions such as the Winchester House in California, endlessly built by the heiress to the Winchester Rifle Company in expiation of the thousands killed by her husband's company's products, but in the main, follies are built by men. The most obvious reasons are money, land and time, properties until quite recently held exclusively by men. Another argument is that women are far too sensible to bother with such fripperies. Both have an element of truth.

In England, we can count the number of female folly builders (excluding grottoes, of which more later) on one hand. They are Lady Anne Clifford of Cumbria, Bess of Hardwick, the Parminter cousins of Devon, Sarah Losh of Cumbria and Annie Lawrence. We will encounter them by and by.

We have no excuse for being so pale, male and stale. That's the way it was, and it is not our remit to rewrite or reinterpret history. What we must realise and accept is that the people who populate this book are nothing like us. They do not share our dreams, our thoughts, our ambitions. They do not share our loves and our laughter. They are not us in fancy dress. They thought differently, they acted differently, they behaved differently. If one of them escaped to live in today's world he would probably be seen as a sociopath. Novelist L P Hartley summed it up in his most famous saying: 'The past is a foreign country: they do things differently there'.

Probably the single most remarkable difference between them and us is sympathy. In our welfare-cushioned world we have a safety net to catch the helpless and hopeless; in former days there was nothing. No benefits, no National Health, no dole. We look on them as pitiless autocrats; they would see us as pathetic, dependent, sentimental, self-pitying cry-babies. In the past if you weren't working you were starving. Abandon hope all ye who enter here. Charity, private enterprise's version of the welfare state, cold as it was, could only do so much, and it could be withdrawn on a whim. The gap between rich and poor was staggering; perhaps not as much as it is today, between a Bezos, Gates or Zuckerberg and a couple of humble architectural writers, but back then it was unbridgeable.

Descendants of these cruel, proud lords will always rush to their defence when confronted with the tangible evidence of their folly – 'It was built to relieve unemployment!' And in some cases it was, but these prodigious feats of building seldom included what we would now call affordable housing. The odd almshouse may have been donated to the village, the local church refurbished, rebuilt or aggrandised, but the people who had the money kept it, and tended to spend it on themselves. If you've driven past Woburn Abbey (which has a lovely Chinese Dairy and a very early grotto by Isaac de Caus but no great follies of note) you will have followed mile after mile – nine in all – of best red Bedfordshire brick wall. If it isn't the longest private wall in England, we'd like to know what is. Of course, it was built to relieve poverty and unemployment – the concept of paying someone to sit on their backside and do nothing was incomprehensible to our ancestors. If they worked, for example, in helping to build a nine-mile wall, then they would be paid. And the Duke's overseer decided how much they would get – no minimum wage promises then.

Most of us enjoy a little self-indulgence, but these people made it their life's goal. With great wealth came great privilege and great power, but not always what they really wanted – and what they all really wanted was a title. A title brought social acceptance, and this is one aspect where they are not so different from us – we all want to be loved and admired. Today we want more followers, more likes, more BFFs; an aristocratic title has long slipped into irrelevancy. But you can't buy a house on likes alone. When there was only one source of true wealth, land – well, two, if you count plunder – the driving force was to acquire as much good land as possible because, as Mark Twain sagely pointed out, 'they're not making it any more'. Other sources of money were limited or risky: the professions were circumscribed, the Church had suffered since Cardinal Wolsey attracted the attention of Henry VIII with his spectacularly ostentatious new palace at Hampton Court, business barely existed; land was the only credible source of wealth. Looking at the men we shall meet here, up to the turn of the 20th century all the folly builders bar half a dozen or so were substantial landowners. And, this being England, they were all white men. Many of course were the descendants of immigrants, fortune hunters who came over with William the Conqueror, which explains the inordinate number of Norman village names among the English aristocracy – Beauchamp, Glanville, Grosvenor, de Courcy, Melville, Beaumont, Giffard, Delaval, Beaufort, Montagu etc. – and they were very much the wrong sort of immigrants; not the *Express* and *Mail* sort who arrive and immediately start claiming benefits, but the sort who killed you and stole your land, something that is frowned upon today.

You cannot consciously build a folly. The title is an honorific to be bestowed by others. We cannot call ourselves Sir Gwyn Headley or Baron van Meulenkamp – at least, not yet. As we said, follies are misunderstood buildings. You can build a church, a castle, a house or an office, but you can't set out to build a folly. It's an honorarium; only other people may grant your monstrous erection the title of folly. For you, as a genuine folly builder of course, it has to be a perfectly sensible, logical, affordable structure. Modern folly builders in England are, if not necessarily moneyed, then educated and connected, unlike their contemporaries in, say, America, who have no idea that anyone has ever done anything remotely similar to what they're doing now – in the heartlands of America there is little awareness of elsewhere.

For centuries people built what they wanted where they wanted. As the population grew and trod more heavily upon the land, this became a problem. When Queen Elizabeth II was born there were two billion people on the planet. Today there are an unsustainable 7.7 billion. The Town and Country Planning Association was founded in 1899 to promote garden cities and improved housing, and local councils began to take an interest in what was being built in their realms. The pressure was intensified by ribbon developments, which began to appear in the 1930s and which appealed to developers because they wouldn't be responsible for supplying and paying for roads and services. Town planners felt that 'without a planning system everyone could construct buildings or use land in any way they wanted, no matter what effect this would have on other people who live and work in their area' and it is noticeable how few follies have been built since the rise of the council planning departments. The concept of a folly is inconceivable to the council mind, which is the antithesis of folly. They look on follies as a dog looks at typography, with total incomprehension and an utter lack of interest, and with incomprehension comes the urge to destroy, as any dog will tell you.

Local government in England is notoriously inchoate and chaotic. We used to have counties and shires: Hampshire, Oxfordshire, Northamptonshire, Warwickshire, Leicestershire, Derbyshire, Yorkshire, the backbone of England. Now there are 353 spineless local authorities, including non-metropolitan counties, unitary authorities, metropolitan boroughs, metropolitan counties, London boroughs, The Greater London Authority, The City of London Corporation, and non-metropolitan districts, each one a petty fiefdom run by exceptionally well-paid anonymous people wielding a disproportionate amount of power. In 2020 there were over 500 council officers who were earning more than the prime minister, despite the councils' income having been slashed by government austerity programmes. Their services were cut, but not their salaries. Within these giant bureaucracies few ply more power, are more reviled, or are more poorly rewarded than the Planning and Conservation officers. Desperate to retain their jobs, their safest option is to prevent or hinder any planning application involving a listed building, citing anything from bats, archaeologists, neighbours, heritage or lady's slipper orchids as obstacles to renovation. People who follow the prescribed route through planning applications when restoring listed buildings in England are frustrated at every turn, so much so that many are forging ahead without consultation, figuring the risk of getting caught is preferable to trying to cope with the bureaucracy. Belief in and support for the planning system is collapsing, putting our entire heritage conservation at risk. The removal of VAT on listed building repairs and a coherent nationwide conservation policy would dramatically improve the situation, but increasingly our successive governments only appear to be able to deal with one subject at a time, and as for getting a tax reduced or removed, the likelihood is on a par with politicians' promises being kept.

The first great folly of the 20th century and the last before planning consent was introduced was the 1908 Ashton Memorial in Lancaster (Fig 0.2). The newly installed system wasn't severely tested until 1934 when Lord Berners applied for planning permission to build a folly on Folly Hill in Faringdon. Inevitably permission was refused, but Berners saw the council for what they were, simply went over their heads, and obtained government approval from a friend at the Ministry of Health. Planning officers are now better educated, less ideological and more aware of the environment in which follies have their place. As a result, more follies have been granted planning permission so far this century than in the whole of the last, although, ideological purists that we are, we feel that if you're asking for planning permission for a folly, then it cannot be a folly.

Another factor is individuality. Follies are personal and personable. Committees, councils and governments can commit follies, but they shouldn't build them. Follies are above all fun, and we don't elect governments to have fun. During his tenure as Mayor of London, Boris Johnson spent £52 million of public money on plans for The Garden Bridge, a scheme to put a new pedestrian bridge across the Thames, championed by Joanna Lumley and designed by

Fig 0.2

The Ashton Memorial was probably the last folly to be built without planning permission.

[© Sue Burton LRPS/fotoLibra]

Thomas Heatherwick. Not a brick was laid and all those millions disappeared into the pockets of friends of friends. The only casualties were London ratepayers, but that was just collateral damage. Is that folly, or grand larceny?

In our several books on follies in the past we have focused mainly on the architecture and the anecdotes. Here we are investigating the lives of the builders, the people who thought it would be a good idea to erect that teetering tower on top of the tor, to tunnel their way through the city, to build the façade of a castle on a distant ridge. What went through their minds?

What were their motives, what did they want to achieve? Did they seek admiration? Approval? Respect? Awe? Or was the urge to build simply too strong to resist?

Come with us, and we will find out.

1 | Bones of the ancients: druids, hermits and pharaohs

Liths

One of the great mysteries about England is that its most famous prehistoric monument wasn't mentioned until the 12th century, when Geoffrey of Monmouth (c 1095–1155) wrote his *Historia Regum Britanniae*. The Romans must have passed Stonehenge thousands of times; their Road 44 from Old Sarum to Mildenhall runs within a mile, but they never commented on it. Geoffrey relates that giants from Africa erected a stone circle on a hill in Ireland, and Merlin went over with 15,000 men to take possession of them. However, the men couldn't budge the stones, 'and when they were all weary and spent, Merlin burst out laughing and put together his own engines. At last, when he had set in place everything whatsoever that was needed, he laid the stones down so lightly as none would believe'. They shipped the stones back to Britain and erected them on the Mount of Ambrius as a cenotaph to the earls and princes whom Ambrosius Aurelianus had lost in his battles with Hengist.

The first book to be written specifically about Stonehenge was published in 1740 by the Revd William Stukeley (1687–1765), doctor, clergyman, Freemason and antiquarian. Bishop Warburton (1698–1779) wrote, '[T]here was in him a mixture of simplicity, drollery, absurdity, ingenuity, superstition and antiquarianism … I have often heard him laughed at by fools, who had neither his sense, his knowledge, or his honesty'. Stukeley more or less unifies the follies we are concerned with in this chapter. His life was dedicated to an obsession with megaliths and stonehenges through to the Druids and the simple hermit. In every smallish house garden he ever owned (Grantham, Stamford, Barnhill and Kentish Town) he saw to it that at least one hermitage was built and a henge delineated in the turf. There were lapidariums of Roman antiquities, pilfered medieval glass in the hermitage walls, and he even laid an embryo, his wife's miscarriage, and (as in ancient Egypt) a cat to rest in these garden shrines. We may find such behaviour bizarre, but Stukeley was completely serious. Every sham Stonehenge, each hermitage and even every pyramid one finds in England comes equipped with the ghost of Dr Stukeley.

The vogue for ancient Druidic monuments started in the 17th century with, among others, Inigo Jones (1573–1652), who thought he had found the key to Stonehenge's purpose and plan: the Romans had built it as a temple. John Aubrey (1626–1697) was a bit more level-headed, and he proposed the Druids as originators. This last label stuck, and started a fashion for mock megaliths which lasted well into the 19th century.

Stone circles, sarsen stones and assorted megaliths rose up all over the country, mainly in the north, at Styall, Alderley Edge, North Brierley, Weston Rhyn (which even has Ogham-like inscriptions to add to its authenticity), Stonor Park, Park Place in Henley, Alton Towers (a fanciful construction called the Druid's Sideboard), the Ilton Stonehenge, Cobham Park in Kent, and on Pocklington's Island in Derwentwater.

Park Place/Walpole

The first substantial piece of megalithomania in England has Horace Walpole (1717–1797), that archetypal 18th-century man, as its godfather. The now demolished Temple Combe house, part of **Park Place**, Remenham, was built by General Henry Seymour Conway (1721–1795), a career soldier and politician who ended up as a Field Marshal. The *Dictionary of National Biography* noted that 'he was a better soldier than he was a general, a better general than he was a statesman'. He had tremendous presence, genuine popularity and, no doubt because of Walpole's sustained assistance, success and great office were inevitable. It is unlikely, however, that a simple manly soldier would have been greatly concerned with the amelioration of his estate with architectural conceits and fripperies, and we suspect that the 'improvements' of Park Place and the surrounding area owe not a little to Cousin Horace. The 45 standing stones make a cromlech or dolmen, a sacred burial place. This one was imported – it is the genuine article, a leaving present from Jersey where Conway was governor at the time (1785) and re-erected at Park Place in early 1788. Others get a clock or a watch; the general got a burial chamber. And Walpole was as pleased as Punch with the prospect of seeing it, according to a letter of 11 November 1787:

> I shall be wonderful glad to see little master Stonehenge at Park-place: it will look in character there; but your own bridge is so stupendous in comparison, that hereafter the latter will be thought to have been a work of the Romans. Dr. Stukeley will burst his cerements to offer mistletoe in your temple – and Mason, on the contrary, will die of vexation and spite that he cannot have Caractacus [a famous poem by William Mason of 1759] acted on the spot … he would immortalize you, for all you have been carrying on in Jersey … Inigo Jones, or Charlton, or somebody, I forget who, called Stonehenge *chorea gigantum* [title of Walter Charleton's book on Stonehenge, 1663, meaning 'the giant's dance'] – this will be the chorea of the pigmies … Pray do not disappoint me, but transport the cathedral of your island to your domain on our continent. I figure unborn antiquarians making pilgrimages to visit your bridge, your daughter's bridge, and the druidic temple.

The first bridge referred to here is the so-called 'Ragged Arch', in the Cyclopean style, apparently built from the ruins of the medieval Reading Abbey to the design of Thomas Pitt, first Lord Camelford (1737–1793), Walpole's equally gay neighbour in Twickenham, and something of an accomplished architect, and engineered by Humphrey Gainsborough (1718–1776), inventor and engineer, as well as a nonconformist minister at Henley and brother of Thomas G, the painter. Walpole at the time, in the guise of a Chinese prince, Mi Li, in the *Hieroglyphic Tales* (written in the 1760s, but published 1785), also commented upon it: 'the vale was terminated by a stupendous bridge, that seemed composed of the rocks which the giants threw at Jupiter's head, and had not a drop of water beneath it'. There is a lot more in and near the grounds of Happy Valley, a grotto, tunnels and a rebuilt Chinese pavilion. It is, however, private.

Druid's Temple/Danby

The ultimate sham Stonehenge, however, still stands on the edge of the moors in Yorkshire: the so-called **Druid's Temple** (Fig 1.1), built by William Danby (1752–1833) of Swinton Hall, a local squire from an old Masham family. He seems to have devoted his life to his personal cultural and antiquarian interests, and is said to have been very benevolent to the local populace. In the 1760s he had the old mansion rebuilt by the ubiquitous Yorkshire architect John Carr (1723–1807), and a further building campaign followed in the 1790s (John Foss) and again in the 1810s (also Foss, with drawing room designed by James Wyatt), while a series of castellations and turrets and a rather spectacular and hefty round tower by Robert Lugar were added in the 1820s. Lugar's speciality was the picturesque Gothic, as shown in his work at Culzean Castle of the same date.

An 1822 tourist guide to the surroundings gives an impression of Swinton Hall and its singular inhabitant:

> Swinton, the seat of William Danby, esq. whose house boasts a fine collection of Pictures, both by ancient and modern masters: an excellent assortment of Ores, Minerals, &c. properly classified; and whose grounds, which are open for public inspection, are well deserving of a visit from the lover of landscape Gardening, being laid out with that true taste, that perfect adaption of art to the wants of nature.

The poet Robert Southey, who met Danby in 1829 (but may have been an acquaintance from Danby's trip to the Lake District in 1785; see below), says he had 'a very large fortune', and rather took to him. Danby was also a man of letters, possessing a well-stocked library and going in for self-publishing on a grand scale. Strangely enough, his first three books were printed in far-off Exeter by Edward Woolmer, who also published the leading

Fig 1.1
William Danby's Druid's Temple
in the Yorkshire Dales.
[© Peter Crump/fotoLibra]

local newspaper. This connection with Devon may have resulted from Danby knowing the divine Charles Caleb Colton of Tiverton, whose chief and most popular work, *Lacon* (1820), Danby expanded upon in the second edition of his own *Thoughts, chiefly on serious subjects* (1821 and 1822). In fact, it may have been Colton who gave him the idea for so many of his 'Thoughts' collections, as Colton had published his *Lacon: or, Many Things in Few Words* (with a second volume in 1822) a good few months before Danby started his series of books. Then, in 1827, came Danby's *Ideas and Realities*, a book he gave to Southey, followed by Danby's extracts and translations from the works of Cicero (1829). The last book emanating from Exeter was *Travelling Thoughts* (1831), while in the same year he published in London (the printer this time was the well-known Rivington) *Thoughts on Various Subjects*, as well as his *Poems*, in Edinburgh. Finally, a year before Danby's death in 1833 came his *Extracts from Young's Night Thoughts*. Danby seems to have been besotted by Young's *Night Thoughts*, which he mentions often and enthusiastically.

To readers dozing through so much bibliographic detail we can only say that Danby's writing and self-publishing reveals much of his personality: a man who believed his thoughts were worth sharing again and again, who in the same period was constantly rebuilding his house, and apparently was something of a mineralogist and fossil-hunter as well. The productive zenith of his life appears to have been his late sixties and seventies, and he kept on building and publishing until the year of his death at 81. So it cannot have been pure whim to establish the country's largest imitation henge at Ilton/Masham Moor, commonly known as The Druids' Temple or the Ilton Stonehenge. Usually a specific reason is provided for this undertaking: Danby wanted to alleviate unemployment in the area. His benevolence to the surrounding populace seems to have been great and genuine. But surely this cannot be the main reason for having dozens of men carting great big boulders around the countryside. He may have been urged to conduct an experiment on how people would build a henge. His interest in antiquity bears him out on this. Apparently, the monument owes its existence to a trip Danby made in 1795 to the Lake District. According to the late David R Coffin, Danby was inspired by Richard Payne Knight's *The Landscape: A Didactic Poem*, the second edition (1785) of which Danby had in his library. Payne Knight seems to have influenced Danby with his anti-Capability Brown stance and his championing of the rough-and-ready landscape to be found in the North. Unsatisfied with the existing Brownian park at Swinton, Danby must have decided upon roughening up the landscape again. And now we may add our own speculations: Danby must have seen Pocklington's Island in Derwentwater, an early tourist development from 1778 onwards by Joseph Pocklington, who besides mock forts, batteries and a sham church, decided to build a Druid's Circle as a tourist attraction. Most has gone now (Southey applauded the destruction of 'these deformities'), but there we have a precursor of the Ilton Stonehenge. Another of Payne Knight's books, *A Discourse on the Worship of Priapus* (1787) (an earlier edition with a different title, was published in 1786), may have been the origin of the phallic stones at Ilton.

But, there it is – a replica, or rather a fanciful recreation of what was Danby's idea of a Druid's circle, or to be precise, a Druid's oval. There also is a persistent story, surfacing in 1910, that he hired an ornamental hermit to sit among the none-too-comfortable stones. The traditional stipulations were no shaving nor speaking. Food was provided, and a subsequent annuity awaited him after his tenure of the also traditional seven years. This particular hermit kept at it for four and a half years until he gave up. Several are said to have followed in his footsteps, none of them successful.

The Ilton Stonehenge looks like the forecourt of a prehistoric dealer in prêt-a-porter megalithic monuments: Menhirs-R-Us. There is a cromlech, there are sarsen stones, altars, sundry standing stones – several of them phallic – and all the megalithic paraphernalia one could wish for. It is certainly impressive; the best mock henge in the country, nowadays surrounded by Forestry Commission trees, and, as another mood-changer, Leighton Reservoir in the valley. The visitor does well to imagine this in its original setting: the moors, no trees, and without the debris of beer cans, bottles and food wrappings left by insensitive visitors.

Nearby are three or four more of Danby's creations, all dating from his later years. The picturesquely sited castellated Quarry Gill Bridge of 1822 by John Foss; the Speculum Seat nearby (1832), with the rather touching inscription

THIS SEAT
OVERLOOKING SOME OF THE
BEAUTIFUL WORKS OF THE CREATOR
WAS BUILT WITH A GRATEFUL MIND
BY WILLIAM DANBY ESQ A.D.1832

and the Monkey Seat, of similar design, further off. There is also the 1824 Arnagill Tower, round, with arched entrance and windows, again by Foss, on Masham Moor.

A final word on the possible inspirations for the Ilton Stonehenge: the Druid's circle at Pocklington's Island has been mentioned here, but the rough-and-ready primitive and rustic buildings of the mid-18th-century folly garden at Hackfall were only a few miles away, and an even more direct Druidical connection was presented by the Brimham Rocks or Crags, seven or eight miles off, which have always been paraded about as, *dixit* the afore mentioned 1822 tourist guide to the area, 'these celebrated Druidical Monuments'.

Egyptiana

Bonomi

The full-blown Egyptian style is a relative *rara avis* in the Western world, perhaps because, however mistakenly, apparently only the Greeks and Romans are regarded as our spiritual forefathers, forgetting by the way our true begetters, the Celts, the Germanic peoples and other tribes. We authors don't object to the scarcity of certain styles; the rarer they appear, the dearer they are to us. Familiarity breeds contempt, scarcity awakens our lust for more.

To be a Bonomi may seem to be a prerequisite for building in the Egyptian manner in England. There were three of them: Joseph Bonomi Sr (1739–1808) and his sons Joseph Jr (1796–1878) and Ignatius (1787–1870). Senior, by the way, appears to have sired his two sons rather late in life. Joseph Sr arrived in England from Rome in his late twenties, employed by the brothers Adam. He busied himself with designing a fair few country houses and kept away from follies except for one grand edifice, the **mausoleum at Blickling Hall**, Norfolk, for John, 2nd Earl of Buckinghamshire and his two consecutive wives. It is in the shape of a 45ft pyramid, which certainly owes something to the famous Cestius pyramid (*c* 12BC) in Rome. But Bonomi added side windows and a massive entrance porch. Its date is 1794 which is late when compared to the full flourishing of pyramid building on the Continent during the whole of the 18th century, often with Masonic overtones.

His son Ignatius was also an architect but appears to have limited himself to country houses in Durham, Cumbria and Derbyshire. It fell to Joseph the Younger to champion the Egyptian style which his father had kicked off. But he was no architect, more of an architectural designer, besides his official professions as artist, sculptor, Egyptologist and curator. From the 1820s up to the 1840s Joseph made several lengthy journeys to Egypt and the Near East, usually accompanying scientific expeditions for which he provided the artwork, recording the temples and artefacts. In 1861 he was appointed curator at Sir John Soane's Museum.

His work was mainly academic, but anyone who named the house where he lived with his brother Ignatius in Wimbledon – The Camels – must have had a sense of the ridiculous. Sadly, no illustrations seem to survive of their abode. He first tried his pen on a design by William Hosking (1800–1861) for the 1839–1843 entrance to Abney Cemetery, Stoke Newington, London. By 1840 Joseph Bonomi was involved by providing the hieroglyphic text that should have read 'The Gates of the Abode of the Mortal Part of Man', but he somehow muddled up his ancient Egyptian. For all-out funerary Egyptian one must, however, visit Highgate Cemetery's splendid and eerie Egyptian Avenue of *c* 1840 by James Bunstone Bunning (1802–1863). But Bonomi was the go-to person for a bit of Egypt-in-England. The **Egyptian Spring** of 1850 at Hartwell House, Buckinghamshire, shows a squarish wellhead-cum-seat of three compartments, with a hieroglyphic inscription telling that it was built in the thirteenth year of the reign of Queen Victoria, Mistress of the Waves. This time the text was composed by someone with a steadier hand in ancient Egyptian. Hartwell House was the property of Dr John Lee, a wealthy antiquarian and devotee to things Eastern.

But the glory of Bonomi was and is the Egyptian **Temple Mills** in the Holbeck district of Leeds (Fig 1.2). Exoticism in industrial factory country – what could possibly go wrong? It didn't, except for a brief occupation by angry strikers led by Chartists in 1842, the so-called Plug Riots. It had nothing to do with architectural criticism though, but with workers' conditions. A contemporary source describes the event:

> [T]he vicinity of the new mill in Marshall Street was completely crammed with an excited mob, many of whom were armed with bludgeons, stones &c. The yard door leading to the boilers of the new mill was strongly defended by Mr J. G. Marshall, and a number of workmen; but the mob by repeated efforts forced down the door, and rushed into the yard. They could not find the plug [hence the name of the riots] of the boiler, and consequently did not succeed in stopping the mill. They left the premises without having done any serious mischief, and then proceeded to the mill of Messrs. Titley, Tatham and Walker, Water Lane.

Not that the workers at John Marshall's Temple Mills had much to complain about. The factory owner was a patriarch who looked after his 2,600 labourers. They received schooling and a reasonable wage, hygiene was considered important, and there was, of course, a strong Temperance influence. The mill itself, with cast iron pillars of an Egyptian design, was opened in 1841, but most famous are the offices of 1842–1843. It is trapeziform with winged emblems above the entrance and a portico with huge lotus flower capitals. Bonomi drew his inspiration from the temples at Edfu, Dendera and Philae after spending eight years in Egypt – and he left visual proof of his field studies incised on an inner wall of the Temple of Hatshepsut at Medinet Habu in Luxor. It reads:

> Js. Burton.
> Cs. Humphreys.
>
> Jh. Bonomi.
> 1825

with the middle name erased – why? Almost each member of the Hay expedition in the 1820s, James Burton, Charles Humphreys, and Bonomi, appears to have bought himself a woman at the Cairo slave market. Robert Hay, the leader, even ended up marrying a Greek slave girl. Bonomi himself turned out to be something of a cad – he acquired the woman Fatima, with whom he begat two sons, but whom he eventually left penniless.

Another of John Marshall's improvements was the lighting of his flax mill – he needed daylight to percolate to the factory floor, and so had 66ft-tall conical leaded-glass domes, somewhat in the shape of Indian teepees, installed on the flat roof. Never one to miss a chance of providing something useful to his workers, he had grass sown on the roof, in between the domes, for his workers to enjoy a healthy walk on the roof. This created a problem, however, as the grass had to be mowed, and again he had an idea: Marshall had a flock of sheep hoisted to the roof by hydraulic lift. Everything went well until one of the sheep clambered onto a glass dome end and fell through, killing one of Mr Marshall's employees at his machine in the process.

Nowadays the Grade I listed Temple Mills is threatened by severe neglect; surely one of Leeds's – no, one of the nation's – most interesting, innovative and exotic buildings must be looked after. There are plans to make the building a northern outpost of the British Library.

Foulston and Others

The south-west of England produced another strain of Egyptiana, flourishing in the 1820s and 1830s, and these bore some strange fruits indeed. Delightful and quirky, these commercial productions belong to another concept of the style. John Soane (1753–1837) and his collaborator Joseph Gandy (1771–1843), though adept at introducing rather severe Egyptian themes in their neo-classical buildings, hated that style being used for 'many of our shop fronts'.

Devonport had always been plain Plymouth Dock until, by the 1820s, the inhabitants argued there was more to it, so the town that had developed around the dockyards was named Devonport and decked out with suitable municipal buildings on a new layout. The architect was John Foulston (1772–1842). Huddled in a corner of Ker Street we have the severe Doric Town Hall (now Guildhall), and placed in an asymmetrical position the 125ft **Column** (an engraving shows it crowned with the statue of George IV, but because of financial difficulties that never happened), and a third building is in the Egyptian style: **Odd Fellows Hall** (Fig 1.3). There was, however, a fourth partner in the ensemble: the phantasmagoric Mount Zion Chapel (demolished 1902), in the 'Hindoo' style. All four were built between 1821 and 1824 (though the column was only finished in 1827, sans statue, so our illustration is a fantasy).

By 1838 Foulston found time to self-publish his *The public buildings erected in the West of England as designed by J. Foulston F.R.I.B.A.*, and in it he stated:

> Notwithstanding the grandeur and exquisite proportions of the Grecian orders, the author has never been insensible to the distinguishing beauties of the other original styles; and it occurred to him that if a series of edifices, exhibiting the various features of the architectural world, were erected in conjunction, and skilfully grouped, a happy result might be obtained. Under this impression, he was induced to try an experiment, (not before attempted) for producing a picturesque effect, by combining, in one view, the Grecian, Egyptian, and a variety of the Oriental … in Ker-Street, Devonport.

THE TOWN-HALL, COLUMN, & LIBRARY, DEVONPORT.

Fig 1.3

John Foulston was given a free Egyptian hand in Devonport ... [Gwyn Headley collection]

Foulston appears to have been something of an oddball. His successor in the Plymouth practice was George Wightwick (1802–1872), himself quite an original, who left a description of Foulston's own house and park, 'Athenian Cottage', Townsend Hill, Plymouth:

> [He] lived a pleasing amateur life for some years, decorating his pretty cottage and grounds in the suburb, and seeking to rival, in little, the famed falls of Niagara, by an artistic spreading of the Plymouth watercourse, or leet, over some yards of spar and rockwork, greatly enhancing the beauty of his shrubbery ... The vehicle wich served him as a gig ... was built in the form of an antique biga, or war-chariot; ... and he looked like Ictenus [the architect] of the Parthenon, 'out for a lark'.

Originally the Classical and Mathematical Subscription School until 1827, morphing into a library after that, finishing up in 1867 as the Odd Fellows Hall, Foulston's building is in the most gaudy Egyptian style, although its interior was always more restrained. Pevsner mentions it as 'the craziest of Foulston's buildings'. It certainly is. Its façade is a play on the pylon theme, the entrance is guarded by two lotus-capitalled pillars, and the windows are in a quite minute trellis-like grid. The lintel above the first of its two floors shows Egyptian heads and droopy wings. The lettering 'ODD FELLOWS HALL' was added later.

Penzance holds yet another **Egyptian House**, in Chapel Street, *c* 1834–1837 (Fig 1.4). It even out-Egypts Devonport's splendid creation by Foulston. A

three-storied façade with lotus columns, pylon-shaped windows and surrounds, William IV's coat of arms and topping that, an eagle spreading its wings. Again, it still retains its original intricate trellis-gridded windows. It is decked out in brown, yellow, orange, green and pink paint. For the ornaments, use was made of the new-fangled Parker's Cement. It's a chocolate box of a building, designed to attract attention. It was built to house a shop doubling as a museum, selling minerals and curios, by the local antiquarian and mineralogist John Lavin

(1796–1856). With Devonport in mind, one would not hesitate to ascribe the house to Foulston. But there is a precedent for all of this, and that is the Egyptian Hall of 1811–1812 (demolished 1905) in London, by Peter Frederick Robinson (1776–1858), an architect as versatile as Foulston and a purveyor of every kind of building in every possible style, as well as compiler of a good half dozen pattern books. The Egyptian Hall appears to be the forerunner of them all, also housing a curio collection and intended and used as an exhibition hall, staging many an extravaganza. It resembled all buildings at Devonport, Hertford and Penzance, so the jury is out on the Foulston/Robinson/architect – an unknown conundrum regarding Penzance.

Perhaps Foulston's school was the begetter of another Egyptian-themed building, the **Egyptian House**, 42 Fore Street, Hertford, a shop front, now a restaurant, possibly 1825 and listed Grade II* (Fig 1.5). Its windows were altered later on. The architect is unknown.

Obelisks

A Freemason's Pyramid

Hors de combat, we have an Egyptian motif in the obelisk, an edifice so often used that one might forget its origins. It can be pyramid shaped but sometimes the term 'needle' for a more spiky example applies. Once in a while there is a good story though, and a good design, as with the Knill Monument on top of Worvas Hill, outside St Ives between Halsetown and Carbis Bay. A strange, triangular pyramid with even stranger, but true, stories surrounding it. Every five years there is a great festival in John Knill's honour, with ten virgins ... but more of that later.

John Knill (1733–1811) appears to have been as pleasant as he was easy-going. In William Hone's *Every-day Book* of 1826–1827 he is described as 'of great eminence at St Ives'. The main source, well-researched, is a self-published pamphlet by J[ohn] J[ope] R[ogers] of Penrose, 'Notice of John Knill of Gray's Inn, Helston 1871', and we let him tell most of the story:

> It was in the year in which he ceased to act as Collector [of Customs] at St Ives, 1782, that Knill erected the mausoleum on a neighbouring hill; and, as this act has often been ridiculed as a piece of folly, it is interesting to examine the motives which led to this freak of humour, for such it will continue to be considered as long as the monument lasts, unless a reasonable explanation can be found ... In figure it is a triangular pyramid of granite, 50 feet high, containing within its base a cavity sufficient for a single interment, and rising in courses of hewn stone, diminishing to a point, which is capped with metal and provided with a lightning conductor. An arch constructed in the base gave admission to the cavity, but has always been, from its erection, walled up. A low guard wall of granite was added in 1829, to prevent injury to the foundations by removal of the surrounding stones.

The wording on the sides of the pyramid is 'RESURGAM; I KNOW THAT MY REDEEMER LIVETH'; and together with the Knill arms the motto 'NIL DESPERANDUM' (get it?: Knill – Nil); as well as 'JOHANNES / KNILL. / 1782'.

The designer of the pyramid was none other than fashionable architect John Wood the Younger of Batheaston (1728–1781), 'who furnished [Knill] with the most minutely detailed drawings, which enabled him without difficulty to complete it by the hands of John Dennis, "a joiner of Penzance." The total cost of the monument, including the purchase of the land from Henry, Lord Arundell, for five guineas, was £226 1s. 6d.' Wood was known to Knill, as around the time he also designed almshouses at St Ives, and built Tregenna Castle, St Ives, in the 1770s. After his death, Wood's pattern book *A Series of Plans for Cottages or Habitations of the Labourer,* was published in 1781, including the plans for the almshouses.

John Knill's will of 1809 gives his reason for erecting the pyramid mausoleum:

> During a residence of upwards of 20 years at St Ives, where I was Collector of the Customs, and served all offices within the borough, from constable to mayor, it was my unremitting endeavour to render all possible service

to the town in general, and to every individual inhabitant, and I was so fortunate as to succeed in almost every endeavour I used for that purpose, particularly in respect to the building of their wall or pier [in the late 1760s, by John Smeaton (1724–1792), Knill's fellow Freemason, and builder of the Eddystone lighthouse], and in some other beneficial undertakings; and it was my wish to have further served the place by effecting other public works, which I proposed, and which will, I dare say, in time be carried into execution. It is natural to love those whom you have had opportunities of serving, and I confess I have real affection for St. Ives and its inhabitants, in whose memory I have an ardent desire to continue a little longer than the usual time those do of whom there is no ostensible memorial. To that end, my vanity prompted me to erect a mausoleum, and to institute certain periodical returns of a ceremony which will be found in a deed bearing date 29th May, 1797.

Fig 1.6
The fiddler and the maidens
dancing at the Knill Monument.
[© Gwyn Headley/fotoLibra]

In a letter of 1782 Knill gave his reason for not wanting to be buried in a church. He abhorred the idea of church burial 'and that the churchyard was already too small for the people'. Yet, 'in consequence of difficulties which stood in the way of consecration [of the mausoleum], [he] abandoned that intention, and subsequently, by his will, gave directions for his burial at St Andrew's, Holborn'. Knill also left monies for the maintenance of the mausoleum as well as – and here we come to the crux of the bizarre goings-on – every five years at Worvas Hill, specific amounts to other purposes:

> £5 to accumulate and to be used as follows, at the end of every five years, viz.: £10 for a dinner for the trustees and six guests; £5 equally amongst ten maidens, of ten years old at most, children of seamen, fishermen, or tinners, who dance once round the mausoleum; £1 for the musician; £2 to two widows chosen from the same classes as the children, to accompany them; £1 for white ribbons, &c.; £1 for clerk, and a new account book when needed; the remaining £5 to the married parents, of the like classes, who have brought up the largest family to the age of ten, without aid from the poor rate or from property.

Bachelor Knill, who was a Freemason, being Master of St Ives' Ship Lodge for seven years, venerated Shakespeare, liked a drink or two, and, as will be clear from the preceding, a good deed. The event at the pyramid also included prizes for rowing (presumably a bit further down the hill), racing, and that Cornish favourite, wrestling. The song the maidens sing begins with:

> Quit the bustle of the bay,
> Hasten, virgins, come away;
> Hasten to the mountain's brow &c.

We attended the 2011 ceremony, held in thick cloud, and it proceeded exactly as reported (Fig 1.6). They still take place every five years.

Hermitages

Through history there have been others and there will be others, but the hermit in his ornamental form belongs firmly to the 18th and 19th centuries. The medieval hermit followed a religious calling (although there were some splendid rogues among them, who robbed or even murdered visitors), while the newer hermit followed a profession and was for hire. Modern hermits of the last century seem to have returned to their mystic origins or are just plain odd or mad: misfits and loners who take to the woods and eke out a meagre, vagrant-style existence. We admire them hugely nevertheless – or because of it.

Stephen Duck

Stephen Duck (1705–1756), the Thresher Poet or Thresher Parson (or as Joseph Spence describes him, 'A Poet from the Barn') was tentatively the first of the new breed of ornamental hermit. He was a thresher from Wiltshire and had semi-educated himself, composing not very good rhymes, before (living on a farm near Kew) coming to the notice of Queen Caroline (1683–1737) who made him her pet poet. She had built a sham ruined, classical hermitage in Richmond Park, designed by William Kent (c 1685–1748) in 1730. The *Gentleman's Magazine* of 1733 commented:

> And here is built a clumsy heap,
> Thought beautiful in ruin.
> Three holes there are, thro' which you see,
> Three seats to set your a—e on ...

As far as we know the hermitage lacked a live-in hermit, but a few years later Duck was made keeper of the Queen's Library (a sort of branch library of those at the royal palaces) at the nearby, rather weird Merlin's Cave, also by Kent (1735) and also modelled as a hermitage, but quite different. The Gothick and rustic (three thatched domed tops) building, which contained waxworks among other things, and said library, gave rise to much imitation and even more derision, mainly in the Tory periodical *The Craftsman*. Telling her husband George II of the lampooning, he told Caroline, according to Lord Hervey's *Memoirs*, 'you deserve to be abused for such childish, silly stuff'. The buildings

were demolished some 30 years later. Duck was the poet in residence at Merlin's Cave, in effect an ornamental hermit. Two years earlier there was a precedent: Stephen Duck was in 1733, as a rather lame joke, proclaimed 'Governor of Duck Island', in London's St James's Park, an ancient post that was revived by Queen Caroline for her pet poet. Duck Island was originally a 17th-century duck decoy. Present-day Duck Island sports a rather fetching picturesque **Duck Island Cottage** (built 1840–1841) by J B Watson (1803–1881) for the Royal Ornithological Society (Fig 1.7).

Caroline's well-meaning actions were the ruin of Duck, who came to regard himself as a serious rival to Alexander Pope, and when he was given a living as parson of Byfleet, the poor man, according to Maunder's *Biographical Treasury* of 1845, finally lost his reason and 'in a fit of mental derangement, drowned himself'. Not all ornamental hermits ended their lives in such a disastrous manner, but they appear never really to have succeeded in building a viable career as a hermit.

Richmond's Hermitage and Merlin's Cave seem to have indeed set the fashion for many other hermitages (Richmond Hermitage was, for example, the direct ancestor for the hermitage at Stowe, also by Kent, 1731). They became all the rage, an enthusiasm fuelled by hundreds of plans and designs in the architectural pattern

Fig 1.7

In the heart of London, a stone's throw from 10 Downing Street: Duck Island Cottage.

[© Philip Carr/fotoLibra]

and model books of the second half of the 18th century. Perhaps the best of these pattern books, and our firm favourite, is William Wrighte's (fl. 1767) *Grotesque Architecture. Or Rural Amusement; Consisting of Plans, Elevations, and Sections, for Huts, Retreats, Summer and Winter Hermitages, ... Chinese, Gothic, and Natural Grottos; ... Grotesque and Rustic Seats, ... Many of Which May Be Executed with Flints, Irregular Stones, Rude Branches, and Roots of Trees* (London 1767, 2nd ed 1790). The book's frontispiece says it all: in a wild, rough landscape a patron and his architect are discussing a design, while two labourers are digging foundations, and three hermits (two of them in oriental attire) people the rest of the drawing among a plethora of garden buildings: a summer hermitage, a hut, a sham mosque and a rough-stone eyecatcher arch.

Thomas Wright

Wrighte's near-namesake, Thomas Wright (1711–1786) (Fig 1.8) is better known and he also had pattern books: *Six Original Designs of Arbours* (1755) and *Six Original Designs of Grottos* (1758). They are of a less adventurous, more-polished design than William Wrighte's later efforts. Thomas Wright, son of a carpenter, was born in Byers Green, County Durham, at the intriguingly named Pegg's Poole House. Wright must have been something of a wunderkind, but being a prodigy is not enough – one has to have the patronage, and he was certainly very well connected, taken up by rectors, bishops and lords of the realm alike. He plied his trades as an astronomer, mathematician, instrument maker, antiquarian, architect and garden designer, mostly but not exclusively in northern England. He knew Stukeley, and was, like him, a Freemason. Strangely enough, a biographical account published in the *Gentleman's Magazine* of 1793 mentions that in 1737 he 'spent some days with Mr. [Stephen] Duck, at the Queen's – house at Kew'. Did Wright notice both the Hermitage and Merlin's Cave, and did it give him an idea? His first garden buildings date from the 1740s, and Richmond Park might have set the future folly architect on his course. Eileen Harris, who in 1979 rediscovered Wright for our times, wrote that he

was a descendant, and one of the last, of Shaftesbury, Pope and Kent, and their moral, physical, poetical and pictorial concepts of nature. In plan, his gardens are like Pope's and Kent's – axial but asymmetrical – a mixture similar to the order and disorder of the Universe. To their poetical themes he added his own occult astronomical interests: a 'Talisman' of trees disposed in magical numbers at Badminton; a design for a 'kitchen garden resembling the planetary system with the Temple of ye Sun in ye Centre'; hedges or clumps in a configuration of the arcs of three tangent

circles – a hallmark of many of his designs – providing perpetual openness and closure, light and shade. He fully reinstated around the house the flower beds and rosaries that had disappeared from Bridgemanic gardens. He also enlivened his plantations with flowering shrubs, vines, and roses on pollards. His additions to the garden may be regarded as an expression of his belief in the immensity of Creation, offering moral as well as sensory pleasures.

His follies of the 1740s and 1750s are peppered all over the Gloucester estate of Badminton and are unmistakably in the Wright style. His Ragged Castle, Bath Lodge and Castle Barn have a decidedly pattern-book feel, as has The Root House or Hermit's Cave, but this superb hermitage shows Wright at the height of his powers: thatched and riddled with worm, but still eerily standing, solitary in the deer park. Originally it was in a patch of woodland, giving a different feel.

But then some of the best extant hermitages always have that Wrightian feeling, although some might owe more to William Wrighte (Fig 1.9). **The Root House** at Brocklesby Park, Leicestershire, with a tufa-clad grotto-cum-tunnel vis-à-vis, is in this manner, and dates from the 1780s. The interior has remnants of tree bark cladding and surprisingly much of the furniture survives: a few chairs round a table, all made from tree trunks, and a splendid benchlet in the rustic style. But another hermitage, at **Spetchley Park**, Worcestershire, was apparently taken straight out of *Six Designs of Arbours*, yet only built in the early 1800s. Open fronted and built of bark and boles, knotted roots and chevroned twigs, with pebbles for flooring, it is an arbour all right, not so much a hermitage.

Robert Ferryman

Another hermitage, or rather hut, is certainly in the manner of Wright, but again of much later date. It is Edward Jenner's (1749–1823) hut or **The Temple of Vaccinia** as it was styled, at the back of The Chantry, Jenner's house in the village of Berkeley, Gloucestershire. However, the person of interest here is not Jenner, the father of smallpox vaccination, in whose garden the hut stands, and where he inoculated his first 'victims', but his lesser known friend, the Revd Robert Ferryman (1752–1837), the true begetter of Jenner's hut.

This man deserves a biography. We have managed to reconstruct only partly his life, his occupations and his interests, but he most certainly is a man worth noticing. There is a striking portrait of Ferryman (1797) by Thomas Phillips (1770–1845) at Petworth House, Lord Egremont's estate. Ferryman appears to be as well-connected as was his friend the Freemason Dr Jenner. Ferryman was vicar of Iping and Chithurst in Sussex from 1796 onwards, a position that fell under the patronage of George Wyndham, 3rd Lord Egremont (1751–1837), which partly explains the portrait at Petworth House. Lord Egremont dabbled, among other things, in the sciences and had a laboratory at Petworth House, to which Ferryman and Jenner had access. In the painting Ferryman strikes a romantic pose, sitting on a rock near the stormy sea coast, in informal clothes, and looking quite surprised, gun at the ready, at a seagull that appears directly above his head, like a dove acting as the Holy Ghost. Ferryman was an avid ornithologist and published several studies, and at one point kept a travelling museum. Later on he went at least twice to North America in the guise of missionary to the Canadians, but profited from spending his time observing the birdlife. But there was no end to the man's versatility: Jeremy Bentham (1749–1832), the prison reformer and Utilitarian, refers in one of his books to Ferryman's clever, unpickable 'gaol lock' for Gloucester jail, *c* 1788. Apparently, Ferryman also provided specific patents for a bathing machine and a valve cock (patent: 1793). In 1797 he took out a patent on a machine for blanching, grinding and dressing corn, and in 1802 he published a pamphlet on the matter: *Observations on the Present Mode of Preparing Wheat Flour for Bread*. Things went wrong, however, and after 1800 he got tangled up in debts, and in a court case regarding the claim to the peerage by one of the Berkeley family, he seems to have made himself a nuisance.

But the thing that of course interests us the most is his involvement in Jenner's hut. John Baron in *The Life of Edward Jenner M.D.* (1827) gives the following:

> It was constructed by the Rev. Mr. Ferryman. The knotted and gnarled oak with huge fragments of the roots and branches of other forest trees, arranged with much taste, enabled him to give to an extremely artificial structure the style and character of a natural production ... He could imitate with equal fidelity the abrupt and varied form of a rocky surface ... In the style of ornamental improvement, which within the last half century has done so much to augment the natural beauties of England, Mr. Ferryman was quite unrivalled.

A few years earlier, in 1821, the Gloucester antiquarian Revd Thomas Dudley Fosbroke (1770–1842) described Ferryman as being 'very original and unsurpassing in two particular departments of picturesque gardening, of exceeding difficulty ... viz. exquisite informal primrose tumps and perfect rustic work'. Describing the hut, Fosbroke wrote, 'One might suppose it the residence of a Faun or a Dryad, or an Arcadian Deity. The furniture is a rustic chair, composed of the malleable and elastic stems of ivy, tastefully reticulated'. Jenner himself described the man in 1817, by which time Ferryman appears to have fallen on hard times:

> What a strange jumble of intellect does that unfortunate man possess. How much he has mistaken himself, & put that in front which should have been in the background. He is pre-eminent (in my opinion) as a Landscape Gardener & by pursuing this for the benefit of others, he might have enrich'd himself but he must become an architect & be hanged to him, ruin himself & those who were heedless to employ him.

One of those who employed him was another acquaintance, or rather contact, the theatre-mad Elizabeth Craven, Margravine of Anspach (1750–1828), daughter of Lord Berkeley, for whom in the 1790s he designed the Gothick folly parading as a theatre in the grounds of Brandenburgh House along the Thames in Fulham. The small picturesque faux castle had been destroyed in the 1820s along with the house, but this and the testimonials given above, as well as the superb rustic quality of the Temple of Vaccinia, make one eager to know more about the elusive polymath that is Robert Ferryman.

Hermits

We must confess to being more fascinated by the men who tried to live in these shoddy hermitages, than by the buildings themselves. Researching these hermits for rent is always a difficult task as there are so few true accounts of their lives and because visitors were mostly only interested in whether they struck a convincingly picturesque pose. There are many reports of hermits being advertised for in the newspapers, but on investigation these ads prove mainly unsubstantiated or practical jokes. Ornamental hermits did exist, however, and the claims that most of them had to grow their hair to biblical proportions and were forbidden to clip their nails etc. for the duration of seven years appear to be typical.

The best (and at that still poorly) documented case of the life of an ornamental hermit, which can act as a *pars pro toto* for the whole profession, is that of Carolus, aka Charles Evans (1762–1822), hermit in the employ of George Durant (1776–1844), the squire of Tong in Shropshire. Durant turned out to be not only an inveterate folly builder, but also a dark and menacing character, who domineered the whole village, did as he pleased and fathered innumerable children, both legitimate and bastards. But more of him and his other follies elsewhere.

The hermitage at Tong was probably built in 1815 or 1816, when the nearby Convent Lodge and the madly exotic Convent Wall and Gates were erected. This also tallies with the supposed tenure by Carolus of seven years, who died in 1822. Nothing now remains, but in 1971 'the ruined gable end' was reported to be still standing. Two watercolours survive, at least one of them by a certain Hoones Smith and dated 21 May 1822. They show front and back of the

Fig 1.9
Collective nouns that never caught on: A persistence of hermits. The Hermitage at Hawkstone Park.
[© Len Sparrow/fotoLibra]

hermitage: on the edge of a brook stands an austere stone hut with a crumbled façade. No hermit to be seen. Carolus was by then probably ill, dying four months later. Viator's *A Guide to the View from Brimstree Hill* (Shifnal 1858) gives an extensive description of the hermit, but probably partly mixes him up with a later hermit (see p 27):

> At the extremity of the wood and shrubbery ... is one of the entrance lodges from the road, called the Hermitage; which derives its designation from the circumstance of a miserable, poor, half or quite demented man a few years ago choosing to reside in a deep, dark cave, cut in the rock behind the lodge, who called himself a 'hermit'; dressed in a kind of tunic of coarse cloth, and wearing a long white untrimmed beard reaching down to his chest. This poor wretch had seen better days, having been a gentleman's butler, and had amassed some money; but having expended it all, he afterwards for several years continued to inhabit his dismal cavern; until cold and suffering released him from further troubles. For a considerable period he was deemed by the then owner of the Castle a not unbefitting appendage to the domain; and was permitted to follow his insane desire of wasting away his body and mind in privation and sorrow in this his living grave, with few or none but strangers to notice or compassionate his misery.

A later publication corrects the butler bit: Carolus was said to have been a gentleman in reduced circumstances, so not a gentleman's gentleman. There is a notice in accounts for one shilling 'For Feching [*sic*] the Doctor to the Hurmst. Sept. 1822'. Hurmst may have meant Hermitage or Homestead, as we learn that Carolus had been given accommodation at a house at the back of Tong Castle. This had been necessary because of ill health but possibly also because Durant's sons were incensed at the idea of their father squandering money on an ornamental hermit, so much so that they threatened to shoot Carolus.

However, the hermit was allowed to die peacefully. The Burial Register gives the following: '1822. Sept. 27. Charles Evans, the Hermitage, aged 60, buried'. His death was noted in *The New Monthly Magazine* and two or three other periodicals, always in much the same wording: 'Aged 60. Charles Evans, better known by the name of Carolus the Hermit of Tong, where, in a lonely and romantic cell on the domain of George Durant, esq. he, for the space of seven years, by his manner and conversation, becomingly sustained the character he had chosen'.

William Armfield Hobday (1771–1831), fashionable miniaturist and portrait painter of the day, dashed off Carolus's portrait – in 1823 he exhibited his 'Portrait of Carolus, lately deceased, distinguished as the Hermit of Tong Castle, Shropshire' at the Royal Academy. It was considered his best work, but seems to be lost. There is an account of the portrait in *Arnold's Library of the Fine Arts*, 1831:

> [He] painted a picture, the like of which he never did before nor after; viz. the painting known as the Hermit of Tong, an individual passing under the name of Carolus, living on the estate of Colonel Durant in [Shropshire]. This work is distinguished by a fine subdued brilliancy in the flesh, depth and transparency in the shadows, and great harmony of colouring in the whole. It represented the Hermit at the mouth of his Hermitage, the left elbow resting on a book and hand raised to the temples; the back part of his head

was enveloped in a hood, and the transparency of its shadow on the upper part of the head was particularly clear, rich, and well painted, and the folds of his dark brown habit were broad and easy.

Carolus had a successor, James Guidney (1782–1866), a one-eyed, laid-off soldier, one-time butler, twice married, a hawker and Birmingham original, also known as Jimmy the Rockman (because of his selling rock candy) or Tickman (presumably referring to his doorstepping skills and selling goods). He used to hawk his short, 16-page autobiography (obviously ghosted) 'Some Particulars of the Life and Adventures of James Guidney, A Well Known Character in Birmingham (Written from His Own Account of Himself)', (third, enlarged[!] edition, Birmingham 1862). It contains only a short mention of his sojourn at Tong: on the 11th of June 1825 he went to Tong, 'the seat of J. [*sic*] Durant, Esq., who offered him an hermitage on his estate for a month's residence. He accepted the offer, and left July 11th, and came to Birmingham'.

In 1855 Tong was sold, and the 'Illustrated Particulars ... of the Tong Castle Estate' has it that the hermitage was at the time let to Thomas Dean at ten shillings per annum. The Hermitage by then was inhabited by said Dean who was a wheelwright, and it probably refers not to the original hermitage, but to the house where Carolus spent his last days.

They do things differently in Europe, where hermits are alive and well today. In 2016 there were 50 candidates for the job of hermit at the Hermitage Palfen, 4,600 feet above Saalfelden, Austria. This isn't one of your ten-a-penny bob-a-job 18th-century English fake news hermits, this is the real deal – the Saalfelden hermitage, built into a cliff in 1664, is occupied by one genuine Roman Catholic hermit at a time. For 12 years Brother Raimund von der Thannen lived there, followed by Thomas Flieglmüller, who lasted but one summer, and as we write, the current incumbent is a retired Belgian artillery officer, Stan Vanuytrecht. He already has the requisite white beard.

Gazetteer

County/Authority	Location	Folly
Bristol and Avon	Marshfield	Three Shire Stones
	Nempnett Thrubwell	Nempnett Needle
	Stoke Gifford	Stoke Park Obelisk
Berkshire	Wargrave	Templecombe Druid's Circle
Buckinghamshire	Chalfont St Peter	Obelisk
	Dorney	The Hermitage
	Ellesborough	Obelisk
	Lower Hartwell	Egyptian Spring
Cambridgeshire	Brampton	Brampton Obelisk
	Harston	Wale Obelisk
Cheshire	Alderley Edge	Stone Circle
	Appleton	Obelisk
	Combermere	Obelisk
	Eaton Park	Obelisk
	Farndon	Obelisk
	Frodsham	Frodsham Hill Obelisk
	Knutsford	Obelisk
	Macclesfield	Capesthorne Hall Obelisk
	Nether Alderley	Stanley Obelisk
	Styal	Stone Circle
Cornwall	Boconnoc	Lyttelton Obelisk
	Bodmin	Gilbert Obelisk
	Botus Fleming	Martyn Obelisk
	Cremyll	Cupid Obelisk
	Falmouth	Killigrew Monument
	Fowey	Victoria Obelisk
	Padstow	Victoria Obelisk
	St Ives	Knill Monument
Cumbria	Broughton-in-Furness	Gilpin Obelisk
	Kendal	Castle Howe Obelisk Tolson Hall Obelisk
	Lindale	Iron Obelisk
Derbyshire	Carsington Water	Stones Island
	Oakerthorpe	Horse Obelisk
Devon	Arlington	Arlington Obelisk
	Cheddon Fitzpaine	Hestercombe Witch House
	Great Torrington	Waterloo Monument
	Hatherleigh	Morris Obelisk
	Kenton	Oxton Hermitage
	Killerton	Hermit's Hut or Bear's Hut
	Mamhead	Daymark Obelisk
	Monkleigh	Petticombe Manor Hermitage
Dorset	Encombe	Obelisk
	Milborne St Andrew	Obelisk
	Stalbridge	Thornhill Obelisk

County/Authority	Location	Folly
	Wimborne Minster	Kingston Lacey Obelisks
Durham	Barningham	Grouse Obelisk
	Durham	Salvin Obelisk
	Wynyard Park (Cleveland)	Obelisk
East Sussex	Baldslow	Beauport Park Obelisk
	Brightling	Hermit's Tower Pyramid Mausoleum Obelisk
	Eastbourne	Gothick Hermitage
Essex	Loughton	Warren Obelisk
	Southend	Crow Stone
	Upshire	Boadicea Obelisk
Gloucestershire	Badminton	Hermitage
	Bisley	Wag Obelisk
	Stanway	Stanway Pyramid
Hampshire	Bramdean	West Meon Hut Stone Circle
	Farley Mount	Beware Chalk Pit Pyramid
	Hartley Wintney	West Green Gardener's Obelisk
	Hinton Ampner	Obelisk
	Nether Wallop	Douce Pyramid
Herefordshire	Clifford	Arch and Obelisk
	Downton	Hermitage
	Eastnor	Eastnor Obelisk
	Elton	Elton Hall Hermitage
	Ewyas Harold	Obelisk
Hertfordshire	Barkway	Newsells Obelisk
	Barnet	Hadley Obelisk
	Hertford	Egyptian House
	Tring	Nell Gwynne Obelisk
	Wadesmill	Clarkson Obelisk
Isle of Wight	Appuldurcombe	Obelisk
	Bembridge	Yarland Monument
	Bonchurch	Pyramid
Kent	Bilsington	Obelisk
	Canterbury	Egyptian Temple
	Higham	Higham Obelisk
	Ramsgate	George IV Obelisk
	Riverhead	Obelisk
Lancashire	Dalton	Ashurst's Beacon
	Higher Tatham	Clearbeck House Pyramid
Lincolnshire	Belton	Obelisk
	Stoke Rochford	Obelisk
	Woodhall Spa	Wellington Memorial
Liverpool and Manchester	Dunham Massey (Greater Manchester)	Obelisk
	Liverpool (Merseyside)	Allerton Hall Obelisk
London	E4	Meridian Obelisk

County/Authority	Location	Folly
	E15	Gurney Obelisk
	N22	Band of Mercy Obelisk
	NW4	Shakespeare Obelisk
	SW15	Fireplates Obelisk
	W3	Derwentwater Obelisk
	WC2	Cleopatra's Needle
	Kew	Ruined Arch
	Stanmore	Cassivellaunus Obelisk
Norfolk	Blickling Hall	Blickling Pyramid
	Holkham Hall	The Obelisk
North Yorkshire	Brough	Palmer Obelisk
	Castle Howard	Pyramid Gate Obelisk Hawksmoor Pyramid
	Great Ayton	Cook Obelisk
	Hauxwell	Obelisk
	Richmond	Obelisk
	Ripon	Obelisk
	Swinton	Druid's Temple
	Terrington	The Pyramids
Northumberland	Brinkburn Priory	Manor House Hermitage Tunnel
	Kirkley	Obelisk
	Lanton	Obelisk
	Seaton Delaval (Tyne and Wear)	Obelisk
	Swarland	Nelson Obelisk
Nottinghamshire	Papplewick	Obelisks
Oxfordshire	Holton Park	Earthworks
	Ipsden	Stone Circle
	Stonor Park	Stone Circle
Shropshire	Acton Round	Dog Obelisk Pagoda
	Bridgnorth	Wonderland Pyramid
	Cheswardine	Mini Stonehenge
	Lilleshall	Sutherland Obelisk
	Much Wenlock	Shirlett Obelisk
	Soulton	Long Barrow
	Tong	Egyptian Aviary Egyptian Pigsty
	Weston Rhyn	Quinta Circle
Somerset	Athelney	King Alfred's Monument
	Butleigh	Obelisk
	Ilminster	Obelisk
	Wrangway	Wellington Monument
	Yeovil	The Needle
South Yorkshire	Birdwell	Wentworth Obelisk
	Norton	Obelisk

County/Authority	Location	Folly
	Stainborough	Queen Anne Obelisk
	West Bretton	Pyramid
Staffordshire	Alton Towers	Druid's Sideboard
	Biddulph	Egypt
Suffolk	Brantham	Obelisk
	Great Bealings	Trimurti
	Hadleigh	Taylor Monument
	Helmingham	Obelisk
	Ickworth	Obelisk
Surrey	Cobham	Pains Hill Hermitage
	Virginia Water	Cumberland Obelisk
Warwickshire	Edge Hill	Obelisk
	Stratford-upon-Avon	Obelisk
	Umberslade	Obelisk
West Sussex	Midhurst	Cobden Obelisk
West Yorkshire	Leeds	Temple Mill
	Todmorden	Stoodley Pike
	Wragby	Nostell Pyramid
Wiltshire	Cherhill	Lansdowne Obelisk
Worcestershire	Evesham	Obelisk
	Lickey	Obelisk
	Stourport	Rock Hermitage
	Wolverley	Baxter Memorial

Fig 1.10
The Hermitage at Pains Hill.
[© Nicola Barranger/fotoLibra]

2 | Heaven's Gate: arches, gateways, bridges and lodges

You never get a second chance to make a first impression.

The first glimpse of an estate will colour your viewpoint for ever. This is the opening evidence of the owner's taste, style and attitude, which is why most of our builders took great pains to make the approach and entrance to their properties as impressive as they could. Depending on their characters, they sought to intimidate visitors, to impress, subdue, awe, astonish or amuse.

In a hanger overlooking Highclere in Hampshire, more famous now as Downton Abbey in the television series, stands a great tripartite triumphal arch through which no horseman would ever ride. It is set on Siddown Hill high above the house simply as an eyecatcher, an impressive sight to be seen from the

Fig 2.1

Heaven's Gate, the arch on Siddown Hill overlooking Highclere Castle ('Downton Abbey'). [© Gwyn Headley/ fotoLibra]

distance of the house, and it is called Heaven's Gate (Fig 2.1). There was never a drive through the arch; it was always a sham entrance.

> ... then my state,
> Like to the lark at break of day arising
> From sullen earth, sings hymns at heaven's gate;
>
> William Shakespeare, Sonnet 29

The 2.2-mile arrow-straight drive from Buckingham to Stowe conditions the visitor for intimidation. Already we are on the back foot. This was not Richard Temple's intention. His intention was to have an utterly intimidating arrow-straight drive stretching 52 miles from London to Stowe, but even his hubris and wealth was not quite up to it.

The entrance to the estate prefigures what will be found. A country track may simply lead to a farmhouse. An immaculately tended towering lodge cut in razor-sharp ashlar foretells a precisely ordered and tightly controlled demesne. A roguishly castellated and turreted arch suggests a sense of mischief. But how to read a lodge that looks like the buttresses of a cathedral, without a cathedral inside? There's one at Rendlesham in Suffolk.

Rendlesham

Peter Thelluson was a Swiss banker who became a British citizen in 1761, aged 24. By the time he died in 1797 he was perhaps the richest man in England, but his notoriety stems from his remarkable will, which passed over his children and grandchildren in favour of his as-yet unborn great-grandchildren. Under the terms of the will they stood to inherit over £140 million, so much money in the 19th century that it was deemed a threat to the nation's economy. In the event, incompetent investments and litigation swallowed up much of the capital (this is England, after all), and the eventual beneficiaries only received a fraction of the amount. A law known as the Thelluson Act was passed to prevent

Fig 2.2

Rendlesham Lodge – the world's

smallest cathedral?

[© Gwyn Headley/fotoLibra]

similar bequests, and it is believed that Charles Dickens based the interminable Jarndyce versus Jarndyce lawsuit in *Bleak House* on the case.

Thelluson bought Rendlesham Hall for his son Peter Isaac Thelluson, later Baron Rendlesham, in 1796. Built in a florid Gothick, the house was demolished in 1949, but the lodges survive. One, Ivy Lodge, is a very fine sham ruin – but Woodbridge Lodge is utterly unique (Fig 2.2). It is centred round a hexagonal room with a central chimney supported by three monstrously oversized and pinnacled buttresses, obscuring the rest of the house. There is no indication of what led a hard-headed businessman to buy into this ecclesiastical extremity; even more peculiar is that the name of the architect of this Grade II* fantasy should have been forgotten.

Peter Isaac Thelluson was not a popular man. William Huskisson (later to achieve everlasting fame as the first person to be killed by a steam locomotive) wrote that William Pitt considered him 'an unpleasant and shabby fellow, which he unquestionably is'. He agitated for Pitt to keep to a promise to recommend him for a peerage. Pitt was amenable, but there was a delay while the legal situation was investigated. Then Pitt died suddenly and there was a further delay, which sent Thelluson into a frenzy because he allegedly had 'had all his carriages painted, and plates engraved with coronets'. He eventually achieved his dream in February 1806, becoming Baron Rendlesham, to the mockery of all in power who referred to him as Lord Rendle-SHAM.

Entrancing Entrances

Entrances and exits form statements of approach and departure – this is what you can expect as you enter a great estate. A gate controls and restricts general

Fig 2.3
Grim and imposing – just as the builders of Layer Marney Towers intended. [© Derek Metson/ fotoLibra]

Fig 2.4

Jack The Treacle Eater:
inexplicable name, inexplicable
building. [© Gwyn Headley/
fotoLibra]

access. Lodges, born out of necessity to house the gatekeepers, became vanguards of the main house. Arches always suggest celebration and triumph, while bridges are statements of wealth. Today's gated communities are indicators of insecurity.

The grander the entrance, the greater the expectations. Naturally some of our forefathers got it badly wrong. Take **Layer Marney Tower** in Essex, possibly the grandest gatehouse in the country, a medieval brick skyscraper, four towers with two eight-storey towers flanking a great arched entrance (Fig 2.3). Building started around 1520. Sir Henry Marney, Chancellor of the Duchy of Lancaster, Sheriff of Essex, Lord Privy Seal, was created Baron Marney by Henry VIII in April 1523 aged about 66 and died six weeks later. His son John succeeded him but died without issue two years afterwards, rendering the Marney line extinct, halting construction and leaving the grand house unstarted. The gate towers remain as a monument to the family's towering ambition, thwarted by death.

Layer Marney Tower was seriously damaged in the famous 1884 Colchester earthquake, so much so that *The Builder* reported that 'the outlay needed to restore the towers … would be so large that the chance of the work ever being done appears remote indeed', but they were wrong – subsequent caring owners have restored the towers to more than their former glory.

Buildings such as these also serve as boundary markers, usually being placed on the edge of an estate so they can impress admiring onlookers without troubling the inhabitants of the main house. They count among their ranks some of the most bizarre and fanciful follies in the country, such as Jack The Treacle Eater outside Yeovil and the Needle's Eye at Wentworth Woodhouse.

Jack The Treacle Eater is the favourite folly of many, not least because of its name and its mystery (Fig 2.4). The origin of the name remains speculative – the least unlikely story is that the family who owned Barwick Park, outside Yeovil, had a messenger named Jack who ran up and down to London and trained on treacle – and the mystery remains. Barwick Park has four boundary markers: The Cone, The Fish Tower, The Needle and Jack The Treacle Eater, each a bizarre statement of architecture. In 2016 two portraits came to auction in Asheville, North Carolina, one of a prosperous gentleman named John Newman and the other of his wife Grace. They were painted by Thomas Beach in the 1760s and in the background of Mr Newman's painting is Jack The Treacle Eater (Fig 2.5), and in the background of Mrs Newman's is The Cone. The staid, sensible Newmans, from a wealthy Somerset glove-making family, have thus laid claim to some of the most outlandish follies in England. But instead of the rubbly, random familiarity of today's Jack, the Jack in the portrait is a formal,

straight-shouldered ashlar clad arch. As with the Great Pyramids, the covering has been removed, leaving today's bristling oddity.

In the 1970s these paintings were in the dining room of Little Barwick House, the former dower house to Barwick Park, where the Messiter family, descendants of the Newmans, had moved.

Arches

We will come across Thomas Watson-Wentworth, the 1st Marquess of Rockingham, elsewhere in this book as one of the more committed and enthusiastic folly builders this country has seen. **The Needle's Eye**, on his massive estate at Wentworth Woodhouse in South Yorkshire, is an elongated pyramid 14m high, and pierced by a narrow ogival arch (Fig 2.6). It is a very beautiful building. The story goes that one night the Marquess accepted a flattering wager that he could 'drive a carriage through the eye of a needle'. The sober dawn brought home the monstrosity of the bet and also the impossibility of failure, hence the construction of this elegant wager winner, a narrow arch just wide enough to allow a coach through, called The Needle's Eye. Long attributed to the architect John Carr, it clearly appears in a 1730 engraving when Carr was seven years old.

Near Chesterfield, with its crooked spire is **Renishaw**, home of the tumultuous Sitwell family, and the most courteous No Trespassing sign we have ever encountered: 'Please Do Not Tread On Mr. Sitwell's Snakes'. Osbert Sitwell tells us in his autobiography that it was the then owner Sir Sitwell Sitwell himself who sketched out on a piece of paper the design for the Gothic archway in the park (Fig 2.7). Both its pinnacles and battlements, though, are in a similar style to the house, which was enlarged and gothicised between 1793 and 1808 by Joseph Badger, a local man. Sir Sitwell may very well have sketched the arch, one of the inspirations for the logotype of the Folly Fellowship, but it would appear that Badger put the professional touches to it to keep it in line with the overall style. The arch, with its great painted crest and the Sitwell motto 'NE CEDE MALIS', is curiously placed at the bottom of a dip, just above the river, and evidently was never intended to serve any particular purpose, unless there was formerly a bridge across the river at this point.

By the middle of the 19th century the castellated house itself was considered to be the folly. An owner of the time, Colonel Herbert Hely-Hutchinson, commented 'By whom, or by how many, Renishaw was built, it is a folly'. Later, Sir George Sitwell was let loose on both house and garden, and he started well by stencilling all his white cattle with a blue willow pattern plate design. He brought 4,000 unemployed men over from Scarborough to dig the lake and was forever planning follies on the estate, of which sadly only a few were built. When the family was painted by John Singer Sargent (the spectacular result hangs in the Drawing Room), Sir George tried to have the artist accentuate the irregularities of his daughter Edith's nose. Sargent decided to give a crooked

Fig 2.6
Could a coach and horses be driven through the eye of a needle? Even for a bet?
[© Seth Lilleker/fotoLibra]

nose to Sir George instead. Inside the house, the ballroom and billiard room were both remodelled by Lutyens, who tired of Sir George seeking free advice about the garden. The baronet had strong ideas of his own, having written the authoritative *On the Making of Gardens*, based on his travels around Italy (his other books include *The Introduction of the Peacock into Western Gardens* and *A Short History of the Fork*). One of his many inventions included a small revolver for killing wasps.

The shell of an octagonal aviary lingers on, hopefully described as the Gothic Temple. Dame Edith Sitwell excused herself from visiting it frequently because, according to the head gardener, she claimed to fear 'that her senses would overwhelm her'. Between them, Sir George's children Osbert, Sacheverell and Edith wrote almost 200 books of poetry, palmistry, music, literary criticism, fiction, biography and art, giving expression to their own kind of modernism, an amalgam of cubism, futurism and Dadaism best described as 'Sitwellism'.

Today Renishaw hosts corporate events, and the flags of Japanese car makers fly proudly from the parapets. There is an Arts Museum and Centre in the stable block, and instead of picturesque willow-patterned cattle dotted around the park, the house looks out over crowds of middle-aged white males wearing inappropriate clothing – not a gathering of the Folly Fellowship, but a golf course.

Empty Arches

If you're anything like us, you'll find something deeply satisfying in an arch that doesn't lead anywhere. It reverses logic; it's nonsense; it does not compute. Arches are entrances and the grander the gateway the better. You expect to find a castle at the end at the very least and when there's nothing to be seen, nothing found, a pleasant sense of melancholy and loss sets in, spiced and leavened by a lack of responsibility. It's not your fault there's nothing there. You didn't spoil it.

A quiet satisfaction fills the circulation. Then the wonder begins – Who? Why? Was it a mistake? Has something been taken away? Where is my sense of loss? There are any number of reasons for the survival of arches out of context or place. Some – our favourites – never had any place or purpose from the start; they are simply arches because, one assumes, they are satisfying to make. Some try to make a statement; borrowing from Roman precedent, an arch is a grand way of making a statement, proclaiming a triumph, yet all too often the arch remains when the triumph is long forgotten. Perhaps the commonest reason is the loss of the house. The mansion was demolished years ago and they never got around to tearing down the entrance arch. That always strikes us as strange thinking; if the house is erased, why not the entrance?

Two of our grandest folly arches can be found in Devon and Hertfordshire, one a triumph, the other an entrance. **Boringdon Arch** above Plymouth never led anywhere; like Highclere's Heaven's Gate it was simply intended as a triumphal eyecatcher, to be seen on the hilltop from Saltram House. It was built in 1783 by John Parker from a design by Robert Adam. Parker was MP for Bodmin, then Devon, and was to be titled Baron Boringdon in 1784. As the richest man in the region, a title was all but inevitable – poor people don't get titles – so it is not inconceivable that this was genuinely built as a triumphal arch to commemorate his imminent elevation. The Parker family, originally from the

Fig 2.8
Brookmans Park Folly Arch – a farthing underneath each brick?
[© Adam Bigg/fotoLibra]

Midlands, lived at Boringdon House before moving to Saltram Castle, as it now is, but the arch is nowhere near the house and is now beset by a golf course.

Even the temptation of hard cash has not been enough to get the **Brookmans Park folly arch** in Hertfordshire torn down. Gobions, the related house, was demolished in the 1830s, but the fine, towering archway still stands proud, despite the legend that a farthing was placed beneath each brick. Two tall square battlemented towers are linked by a battlemented curtain wall pierced by a large arch (Fig 2.8). It is a remarkably pleasing building, enhanced by its size, its sheer uselessness and its unlikely survival in what is fast becoming a London suburb. It is attributed to James Gibbs and certainly his signature window surrounds are prominent features. The patron, Sir Jeremy Vanacker Sambrooke (d. 1754), a City of London alderman, was also responsible for the obelisk at Hadley commemorating the actual site of the Battle of Barnet, which has now been moved several times (the obelisk, not the battle). But apart from the folly arch and the obelisk, Sambrooke's posthumous fame is as the subject of a 1743 pamphlet by 'Chevalier' John Taylor, a self-taught eye surgeon, on *The Case of Sir Jeremy Sambrooke, Baronet … Containing a full and exact account of the singular disorder in the eye of this gentleman*, which makes horrific reading as Taylor describes the agonies he inflicted on Sambrooke, who was already blind in one eye. Taylor went on to blind Handel in another botched operation.

Hertfordshire has spelling issues; the Gobions estate was also spelled Gobians and pronounced Gubbins. Little Berkhamsted, not too far away, is also Little Berkhamstead and Little Berkhampstead. The choice is yours.

Just over the Hertfordshire border in Cambridgeshire is the village of Gamlingay, where Sir George Downing (1685–1749), 3rd Baronet, built himself a mansion at Gamlingay Park immediately after his father's death in 1711. All that remains of the vast enterprise are the stumps of two brick gate piers that once supported an oculus named the **Full Moon Gate**. Today it is merely a scrap of a folly, a few scattered bricks, of interest because of its builder and a curious legend that sprang up about it. Downing was a politician, but not as competent as his father and grandfather. George, the 1st Baronet, was born in Dublin, graduated from Cambridge, then went to America and became the second man to graduate from Harvard. He came back to England and donated his name to a well-known, if inaccessible, street in Westminster. His son, also George, built upon his heritage, and George the third spent it all –or at least most of it; when he died, having led 'a most miserable, covetous, and sordid existence', he left estates in trust to his cousin and annuities to his daughter and his mistress. The trustees died before him, the family contested the will and 58 years later the money that remained was used to establish Downing College in Cambridge. It's not even certain that the Full Moon Gate was a gate; it may simply have been decorative. A Victorian visitor to the site, then still a perfect letter 'O', was assured by a local lady that this was all that was left of a grandiose educational project by Sir George who erected the entire alphabet in 20-foot-high brick characters around the village. A lovely idea, but sadly without a shred of truth.

The arches that stand on a grassy knoll hard against a deciduous wood in **Shobdon**, Herefordshire, also lead nowhere (Fig 2.9). In fact, they are not, strictly speaking, arches, as they are the surviving entrances to a demolished Norman church, removed and re-erected here simply as an eyecatcher in 1752. Viscount Bateman (1721–1802), then Lord Lieutenant of the county, was responsible for the destruction of the Norman church, a scandal to our eyes until we discover what he replaced it with: the most beautiful jewel-box of a church imaginable, all Wedgwood blue and white and frothy stucco, a confectioner's wedding-cake of a church. The unverified architect is suspected to have been Richard Bentley (1708–1782), an acolyte of Horace Walpole and a leading light in the Committee of Taste.

Sir Thomas Tresham

What's that thing where you're always starting something but never finishing? The Japanese call someone like that *mikka bouzu*, a three-day monk, one who starts something with enthusiasm then gives up too easily. In building, that's a fair definition of a folly, no matter what style it may be. There are plenty of excuses for not completing a job: laziness, boredom, indifference, distraction, lack of funds; the list is long. A custodial sentence will also do the trick.

Sir Thomas Tresham was the head of an old-established and wealthy Northamptonshire family, very religious, very devout. Unfortunately for him it was the wrong religion at the wrong time and in the wrong place. He was one of the leading recusants of his time, Roman Catholics who refused to recognise the authority of the new Church of England or to attend its services. In his early life he kept his Catholicism under wraps, becoming Sheriff of Northamptonshire when he was 30, and being knighted by Queen Elizabeth two years later. But in 1580 something happened – he was formally received into the Roman Catholic church, he hosted the notorious Jesuit St Edmund Campion at his London house, and so began the remainder of his life, mostly spent either in prison or under house arrest.

During this time in and out of detention Tresham constructed three buildings. He only completed one. He started the Market House in Rothwell in 1578, the Triangular Lodge at Rushton in 1593 and Lyveden New Bield in the middle of nowhere in 1603.

The only one he finished, the **Triangular Lodge** on a narrow country lane (Fig 2.10), could have served as a lodge to his house Rushton Hall, now a luxury hotel, but its original name as the Warryner's Lodge shows that it housed the estate's rabbit keeper. But its practical usage was unimportant. For Tresham this was a testament in stone, an affirmation of his faith and the Trinity. Puns were irresistible to the Elizabethans, whatever their religion, and Tresham delighted that the Tres- beginning his name could be matched with the Trinity. 'TRES TESTIMONIUM DANT' (Three (or Tresham) Bear Witness) is inscribed over the entrance. Everything emphasises the Trinity. Three sides, each 33 feet long, trefoil windows, a triangular chimney, three floors, three gables on each side, inscriptions all 33 letters long – the building is packed with symbols and allusions. This is obsession verging on madness, or folly. It is said, rather mysteriously, that 'certain papers which appeared after his death revealed that his

Fig 2.9
Shobdon Arches, once part of a church. [© Len Sparrow/fotoLibra]

intentions were magical', but equally mysteriously these papers have not since come to light.

Three years after starting the cruciform Market Hall in Rothwell as a gift to his fellow Northamptonshire countrymen, Tresham found himself in Fleet Prison for recusancy. This could explain why he never got around to roofing it. It was finally completed over 300 years later, in 1897.

To our mind the most compelling of Tresham's adventures in stone is **Lyveden New Bield**, pronounced Livden New Beeld (Fig 2.11). If you can get it to yourself at the right time of day (it is now a National Trust property), it is the most magical and mysterious building in England. Lacking the crazed passion of the Triangular Lodge or the municipal conventionality of the Market Hall, this is another expression of Tresham's faith. Ostensibly intended as a summer house – a very large summer house indeed – it is once again a display of piety, this time a celebration of the passion of Christ. We look on our built heritage with affection and familiarity; we expect our abbeys and castles to be ruined, slighted by our ancestors, generals, politicians and iconoclasts. Lyveden New Bield isn't ruined at all. It's simply unfinished, and the difference is immediate and startling. It stands alone in a field, silent but for its circling, screeching kites, invisible from the country lane that passes unknowingly by half a mile away. The sharp cut stone rises from the field, still pure and clean, the windows, which never held glass, stare out over the soft Northamptonshire countryside, the never fitted doorways gape in open expectation. It is an intensely moving experience. What went through Tresham's dying mind as he helplessly, endlessly, built and carved and inscribed? Within two years of starting work he was to meet his Maker.

Numerology fascinated Tresham. If the Triangular Lodge was multiples of three, then Lyveden with its layout in a Greek cross is fives and sevens. The first seven words in the inscription round the top of the bield – 'IESVS MVNDI SALVS † GAVDE MATER VIRGO MARIA' – each have five letters.

Above the ground floor is a frieze of medallions manifesting elements of the Passion of Christ:

- The purse containing the money for which Judas betrayed Christ, and the 30 pieces of silver round the border.
- The lantern, torches, a spear, and a sword.
- The cross, ladder, hammer and nails.
- Christ's garment, and a die, to represent the casting of lots for it.
- The crowing cock to wake Peter, and the scourges with which Pilate flayed Jesus.
- The X within a circle is 'Christus', the P in the middle of a cross is the Chi-rho, a monogram used to symbolize the name of Christ; the wreath round the circle, to which there is neither beginning or end, is emblematic of eternity or 'in Aeternum' – 'Christ a Priest for ever'. The circle is sometimes formed by a serpent with its tail in its mouth.
- The I.H.S. and Cross – 'Jesus Hominem Salvato', and round the border, 'ESTO MIHI' and 'I.H.S.' The sculptures are repeated throughout the whole of the building, with the abbreviations I.H.S. and X.P.S.

There is evidence that the bield was floored, because 50 years later a Major Butler, one of Cromwell's men, removed the timber from the building and built a house at Barwell All Saints from it.

His son Francis inherited his religious fervour, became implicated in the Gunpowder Plot and died imprisoned in the Tower of London in 1605, the same year as his father. He was named by Guy Fawkes, whom he had never met, as a co-conspirator, and although he died of natural causes, he was subsequently beheaded, his estates forfeited and his head put on public display.

Fig 2.11
Sir Thomas Tresham's enigmatic Lyveden New Bield: not ruined, simply unfinished.
[© David Harding/fotoLibra]

Gazetteer

County/Authority	Location	Folly
Bedfordshire	Silsoe	Wrest Park Chinese Bridge
Bristol and Avon	Bath	Pinch's Folly
		Prior Park Palladian Bridge
	Brislington	Arnos Gateway
	Dodington	Bath Lodge
	Henbury	Rustic Lodge
	Orchardleigh	Lodge
	Wick	Gateway
Buckinghamshire	Stowe	Corinthian Arch
		Doric Arch
		Palladian Bridge
	Wotton Underwood	Chinese Bridge
Cambridgeshire	Castor	The Kennels
	Gamlingay Cinques	Full Moon Gate
	Madingley	Sham Bridge
Cheshire	Birkenhead Park	Roman Bridge
		Swiss Bridge
	Liscard	Liscard Battery Gatehouse
	Ness	Burton Manor Gate
	Tilstone Fearnall	Tilstone Hall Folly
Cornwall	Antony	Arch
	Helston	Helston Gateway
	Pentillie Castle	Folly Lodge
	Stratton	Granville Monument
Cumbria	Penrith	Stott Gatehouse
Derbyshire	Eccles Pike	Ruined Arch
	Renishaw	Gothic Arch
Devon	Ashford	Upcott Arch
	Berrynarbor	Watermouth Arch
	Countisbury	Glenthorne Folly
	Filleigh	Castle Hill Follies
	Hartland	Highford Farm
	Lydford	Lydford Arch Dovecote
	Plympton	Boringdon Arch
	Sheepstor	Sheepstor Arches
Dorset	Creech Hill	Creech Grange Arch
	Lulworth Castle	North Lodges
	Wimborne St Giles	Sham Gateway
Durham	Bishop Auckland	Gate House
	Peterlee	Pasmore Pavilion
	Sedgefield	Gothic Ruined Gateway
	Washington (Tyne and Wear)	Penshaw Monument
		Victoria Viaduct
	Witton Castle	Lodges
Essex	Middleton	Arch
	Tolleshunt Major	Gatehouse
Gloucestershire	Amberley	Amberley Eyecatcher

County/Authority	Location	Folly
	Ozleworth	Lodges
Hampshire	Boldre	Arch
	Highclere	Heaven's Gate Dan's Lodge Grotto Cottage
	Houghton	Houghton Lodge Sham Ruin Lodge
	Hythe	Forest Lodge
	Mottisfont	Mottisfont Summerhouse
	Northington	Grange Sham Castle Lodge
	Odiham	King John's Hunting Lodge
	Sherborne St John	Lodges
Herefordshire	Clifford	Arch and Obelisk
	Croft Castle	Croft Castle Gateway
	Shobdon	Shobdon Arches
Hertfordshire	Brookmans Park	Folly Arch
	St Albans	Prospect Road Arch
Kent	Farningham	Sham Bridge
	Goat Lees	Eastwell Park Gatehouse
	Mereworth	Mereworth Arch
	Tenterden	Gatehouse
Lancashire	Ormskirk	Bath Lodge
	Padiham	Arbory Lodge
	Sawley	Eyecatcher Arch
	Wigan	Haigh Hall Plantation Arch
Leicestershire	Loughborough	Garendon Park Arch
	Lowesby	Thimble Hall
Lincolnshire	Ashby Puerorum	Arch
	Belton	Bellwood Lodge
	Branston	Mr Lovely's Bizarre Gates
	Brocklesby	Newsham Lodge Memorial Arch
	Coleby	Roman Gateway
	Fillingham	Gateway Redbourne Hall Gateway
Liverpool and Manchester	Birkenhead (Merseyside)	Chinese Bridge
	Stretford (Greater Manchester)	White City Gates
	Worsley (Greater Manchester)	Chimney Top Fountain
London	E2	Meath Gardens Arch
	E3	Bromley Gateway
	EC4	Temple Bar
	N3	Avenue House Stables
	N22	Mushroom Cottage
	NW3	Kenwood Sham Bridge
Norfolk	Holkham Hall	Triumphal Arch
	Hoveton	Spider's Web Gateway

County/Authority	Location	Folly
	Langley	Chedgrave Gate
	Little Walsingham	Folly Bridge Lodge
North Yorkshire	Aysgarth	Sorrell Sykes Gate
	Castle Howard	Carrmire Gate Pyramid Gate
	Hartforth	Hartforth Hall Archway
	Hunmanby	Hunmanby Arch
	Kirkleatham	Gatehouse Arch
	Leyburn	Middleham Castellated Bridge
	Little Ribston	Arch
	Seaton	Mushroom Cottage
Northamptonshire	Boughton Park	The Spectacles Spare Pair
	Fawsley	Preston Capes Arches
	Holdenby	Holdenby Arches
	Horton	The Arches
Northumberland	Cambo	Wallington Hall Arches
	Twizel	Blake's Folly
Nottinghamshire	Clipstone	Duke's Folly
Oxfordshire	Bucknell	Water Tower Arch
	Mapledurham	Arch
	Middleton Stoney	Lodge
	Oxford	Folly Bridge
	Shirburn	Lodge
Shropshire	Market Drayton	Pell Wall Lodge
	Shrewsbury	Gateway of the Shoemaker's Arbour
	Stanton Lacy	Downton Hall Lodge
Somerset	Bruton	Chequers Towers
	Dunster	Folly Arch
	Yeovil	Jack The Treacle Eater
South Yorkshire	Stainborough	Steeple Lodge
	Wentworth Woodhouse	Needle's Eye
Staffordshire	Admaston	Goat Lodge
	Fazeley	Fazeley Bridge
	Oakamoor	Bolton's Gate Piers
	Shugborough	Triumphal Arch Rococo Railway Bridge
	Tixall	Bottle Lodge
	Willoughbridge	Hunting Lodge
Suffolk	Erwarton Hall	Erwarton Gatehouse
	Euston Hall	Arch
	Redgrave	Folly Lodge
	Rendlesham	Woodbridge Lodge Ivy Lodge
Surrey	Addlestone	Woburn Arches

County/Authority	Location	Folly
	Reigate	Sham Gatehouse
Warwickshire	Arbury	The Round Towers
	Charlecote	Mock Jacobean Gateway
	Combe Abbey	Gateway East Lodge
	Leamington Spa	Obelisks
	Meriden	Cyclists' Obelisk
	Stoneleigh	Tantara Lodge
	Warwick	Spiers Lodge
West Sussex	Patching	Michelgrove Toll House
	Slindon	Nore Folly
West Yorkshire	Aberford	Parlington Park Triumphal Arch
	Batley	Batley Arch
	Otley	Bramhope Monument
	Pool	Avenue des Hirondelles Arch
Wiltshire	Bowden Hill	Gatehouse Lodges
	Compton Chamberlayne	Compton Park Arch
	Devizes	Shane's Castle
	Fonthill Gifford	Arch
	Salisbury	Wyndham House Arch
	Savernake Forest	Lodge
	Tollard Royal	Rushmore Mogul Arch
	Trowbridge	Rood Ashton Lodges
	Wilton	Arch Palladian Bridge
Worcestershire	Wolverley	Lodges

3 | Pavilions of splendour: hovels, cottages, pavilions and palaces

Most follies remain fripperies in the landscape, park or garden. With a little ambition, they can become usable, or even habitable. Some grow to leviathan proportions, others actually attain the status of the main house.

Thomas Grimston

Houses don't have to have four walls. They can have any number from one to infinity, except two. A circular house has one wall. A three-sided building is curiously satisfying. There are few triangular buildings in England that are not follies; indeed, there are very few triangular buildings, largely because a more incommodious use of internal space can scarcely be imagined. Unless you are extremely rich and can afford the dramatic waste of space imposed by the acute angles of the triangle, as in the substantial pile of **Grimston Garth** (Fig 3.1), it is one of the more inefficient architectural schemes. Grimston Garth was named for the family, who lived 20 miles away at Kilnwick, and the old Yorkshire word for an enclosure, from the same root as 'garden'. It was only intended as a summer house, to which the family would move in July, August and September. The main reception rooms of the house are, as might be expected, hexagonal. Since the house was built, the coast has eroded around 300 yards (275m), and the parkland now ends at the cliff edge.

Thomas Grimston, who employed the prolific Yorkshire architect John Carr to build Grimston Garth from 1781 to 1786, was Yorkshire to the core. His family had owned the land since the 12th century. Grimston's correspondence

Fig 3.1
Grimston Garth: a prodigy triangular house with extended wings. [© P+R Boogaart]

and journals display curiosity, bias, pride, wit, prejudice and affection. Deference was not in his nature. At a time when royalty was regarded as semi-deity, he freely commented that George III's legs 'are astonishingly thin, quite like those of a Robin-redbreast in comparison to the superstructure they have to support'. Unlike Lord Hardwicke, whom we shall meet in Chapter 7, he was a fully rounded character, equally interested in ships and snails: 'There are in Yorkshire several species of land Snails that are extremely scarce and even unknown in other parts of England'.

Among his papers was a 'list of vessels belonging to the republic of Algiers' and a 'prescription and instructions for sea bathing as a treatment for John Grimston's headaches'. He kept recipes for preserving strawberries; ink; remedies; milk punch; blacking for shoes; cowslip wine; treatments for disorders in horses; and a prescription for making bronze and cement for repairing china. He wrote a witty letter on the virtues of white and red meat; another remarking on 2,000 Welsh volunteers in Shrewsbury as 'very quiet and very good looking men'. Advice to his friends included 'If you want a young male elephant to turn down into your paddock there is one advertised for that purpose, price 1000 pounds or guineas'. And as for the South: 'The women in the South of England use so much paint ... you might as well kiss a plaistered wall'.

Instead of hanging poachers, like Viscount Cobham, he handed them over to the press gang in Hull.

Arthur Moore

There's an engraving of a building in the British Library that at first glance looks like a monstrous joke, the biggest house ever built. Wentworth Woodhouse, the largest private house in England (and even today still the second largest in the world) is 606ft wide and has only 49 bays. This place has 67 bays, which would argue a width of around 828ft, or one-sixth of a mile. This was **Moore's Folly**. Who or what was behind this behemoth of a building, and what happened to it?

'Make no little plans', thundered the American architect Daniel Burnham and although Arthur Moore MP (d. 1730) of Fetcham Park, Surrey, lived 150 years earlier, he could well have inspired the motto. The son of an Irish gaoler, he somehow became an English politician, getting elected as MP for Great Grimsby in 1695. Thereafter, his climb up the money tree was rapid, becoming comptroller of the army accounts and in 1711 a director of the South Sea Company. Moore wasn't to know what would happen next, but we do, and in 1720 he made the simple error of commissioning work on a new development on 200 acres of prime land at Headley in Surrey, which commanded 'noble views and prospects every way'. His architect John Price was a competent but undistinguished practitioner who must have thought all his Sundays had come at once when he won the commission. The plan showed a mammoth building, easily the largest in the land, looking like the biggest country house imaginable.

The Elevation or West Prospect of
Part of a Design of Buildings already began to be erected on ye Lawne,
Headly, Surry
Design'd by John Price, Architect, 1720

But it wasn't a house. This was to be an urban development of terraced housing in the heart of the English countryside. Eighteen large and luxurious houses – executive homes, we'd call them today – flanked what Colvin described as 'presumably some sort of Assembly Rooms'. The whole ensemble looked like the stateliest of stately homes, even if the architecture was not quite up to the mark. The marketing had started before a brick had been laid: its good water supply and closeness to London were promoted and 'The Higglers come every Day to the Doors with Fish, Fowl, Fruit, Garden Stuff, and other Provisions'. Higgler, eh? There's a word. The man had marketing in his DNA; he was 200 years ahead of his time.

Then the bubble burst.

The South Sea Company imploded in 1720. Many people were badly affected by the fall-out, many more were ruined. Moore had already over-extended himself with his improvements at Fetcham Park, and the development at Headley pushed him over the brink. Building was halted, and he died bankrupt in 1730. The print says 'already began to be erected' – it was said in 1736 that two of the end-of-terrace houses had been built.

There was talk in the 1830s that a couple of houses still standing in Headley might have had some connection to Moore's Folly, but now there's nothing to see. Nothing in the village looks older than 1900. We don't even know where the site was. Nothing beside remains.

Henry Disney Roebuck

In this century of fake news, the endurance of a story that is patently untrue is no longer a thing of wonder. There was a time when editors curated and controlled what you read, when DJs decided what music you would listen to, when conductors interpreted a performance, but now the provenance of a tale is too often overlooked. Even the imprimatur of a BBC or of a *New Yorker* magazine is called into question. When a respected art publisher produced an encyclopaedia in the 1980s listing the little-known Dutch abstract artist Hertz van Rental, it nearly destroyed the company. Today it might produce a dry cackle.

Midford Castle outside Bath, also known as Roebuck's Folly, looks like a formidable round turreted castle when approached face-on up the drive (Fig 3.2). Its playful aspect is only revealed when seen from above, when it unmistakably resolves into the Ace of Clubs. Hence the story that the triangular castle, built by Henry Disney Roebuck (1733–1796) in 1775, was paid for by the turn of a card in a high-stakes game.

Sadly, the story that Roebuck built his house on a fortune won on the tables on the turn of a card – the ace of clubs – is fake news; it has no foundation whatsoever, despite the fact that he built his house in the shape of a trefoil. The story first appeared 50 years after he died. The design, by John Carter, had appeared in *The Builder* in 1775, so the indication is that Roebuck bought the plans off the shelf. Nothing in Roebuck's life suggests he was a gambling man, although gambling was rife among men of his class. When his wife ran off with the footman ten years after the castle was built, he published advertisements denying her credit and put the house up for sale. A later owner, Charles Thomas, added a porch, the stalk to the trefoil, which was what turned it into the ace of clubs.

It was thought that Thomas also built The Priory, a folly in the grounds of a folly, but it had clearly been built by Roebuck, as Benjamin Pugh, to whom Roebuck sold the castle, put an advertisement in the local paper in 1788 describing himself as

> a Gentleman who wishes to live in peace and friendship with all mankind, particularly so with his neighbours and parishioners; – but as very great mischief has been lately done to many parts of the premises, particularly to a building called the Priory, by pulling down and destroying parts of the battlements and ornaments, breaking the fences, and making foot-paths over the fields, robbing the gardens and orchards of the fruit, destroying the hares and rabbits with dogs, guns, nets &c. This is to give general notice, that any and every person who shall be found offending in any of the above particulars, will be prosecuted with the utmost severity of the law.

His Stinkingness

Kent is in Bedfordshire. Most dukes are named after counties with which they have but a passing connection: the Duke of Devonshire lives in Derbyshire, the Duke of Norfolk lives in Sussex, the Duke of Westminster lives in Cheshire, the Duke of Gloucester lives in Northamptonshire, the present Duke of Kent lives in Buckinghamshire, the Duke of Somerset lives in Wiltshire and so on. Why, we cannot say, but the dukes of Bedford and Northumberland deserve plaudits for sticking to their soil.

Lesser peers – earls and viscounts and suchlike – tended to be named after towns, recalling the advice given to a relative when she was eighteen: 'Never sit next to someone who's named after a town', implying that at some stage he'd want to borrow money, or worse.

Henry de Grey, 12th Earl of Kent (1671–1740), was living in Wrest Park in Bedfordshire when he was created Duke of Kent in 1710. He commissioned the remarkable architect Thomas Archer to create the most spectacular and lavish garden pavilion in England, at a cost of £1,806. Grey was nothing if not rich; in fact, he was generally thought of as nothing. He was appointed Lord Chamberlain on the recommendation of the Duchess of Marlborough, to whom it was alleged he had slipped £10,000. Contemporary journalist and politician Arthur Maynwaring drily commented that it was 'a vacancy that was to be fill'd up with something very insignificant'. He lived up to his promise, carrying out his duties lethargically. Everyone commented on how disagreeable the man was. Unfortunately, the poor man also had a body odour problem, leading him to be known as 'His Stinkingness'.

So, the first Duke of Kent, not very bright, not at all nice, incompetent, whinging, smelly and rich (and living in the wrong county) has left us one of the supreme folly buildings in England. Intended as a banqueting house, the English baroque Grade I listed **Archer Pavilion**, as it is generally known, is the cathedral of all garden buildings (Fig 3.3). It was built between 1709 and 1711, with a central circular domed core with three rectangular pedimented wings, creating a triangular outline, a plan based on Borromini's Sant' Ivo della Sapienza, the university church of Rome, with two equilateral triangles intertwined to form a six-pointed star. Most people dismiss follies as buildings of no purpose, but this was a functional, if overly grandiose, place of entertainment. Not only was the majestic central area perfect for a large dining party, there was a substantial kitchen in the basement, along with two privies, and for those who had partied a little too hard there were two bedchambers, with two extra ones for their servants on the upper floor. Given that the de Grey family moved out of Wrest Park in 1917 after the main house had been used as an army hospital and almost burned down the previous year, the preservation of the Archer Pavilion is a cause for celebration. Now cared for by English Heritage, continual restoration is going on as we write, with the building shrouded in scaffolding. 'Bug', the nickname of the odiferous Duke, might be pleased to know that. Then again, perhaps not.

Soap and Water

The Archer Pavilion is huge, a Brobdingnagian garden building, but it is not the largest pavilion in our narrative. That honour is taken by the **Brighton Pavilion** (Fig 3.4), built over 36 years between 1787 and 1823 for the Prince Regent. Four architects worked on successive stages of the building, but the Moorish Hindu confection we see today was the work of his favourite architect, London-born Welshman John Nash. Those who know Nash for Regent Street, All Souls Langham Place and his elegant, formal terraces round Regent's Park will barely recognise his work here. This is an Eastern fantasy.

George IV, better known as the Prince Regent, a role he played for nine years, was the playboy Prince of Wales for the first 50 years of his life. He spent it in envious debauchery, fathering several bastards, drinking and gaming prodigiously. In secret he married a Catholic woman six years his senior – as it was unauthorised by the king, the marriage was invalid – and ran up spectacular debts, despite having an annual parliamentary allowance of £50,000 (£5.5 million today). His father George III agreed to settle his debts on condition he married Princess Caroline of Brunswick. On being introduced to her for the first time by James Harris, Earl of Malmesbury, he 'embraced her, said barely one word, turned round, retired to a distant part of the apartment, and calling me to him, said, "Harris I am not well; pray get me a glass of brandy"'.

This may have been caused by Princess Caroline's aversion to soap and water. Harris had previously had conversations with the princess:

> One on the toilette, on cleanliness ... On these points I endeavoured, as far as was possible for a man, to inculcate the necessity of great and nice attention to every part of dress, as well as to what was hid, as to what was seen. (I knew she wore coarse petticoats, coarse shifts, and thread stockings,

and these never well washed, or changed often enough.) I observed that a long toilette was necessary, and gave her no credit for boasting that hers was a 'short' one.

The marriage was not a success. Princess Caroline gave birth to Princess Charlotte the following year, George's only legitimate child, and then they separated for good, while remaining married. Charlotte died in 1817, before her

Fig 3.4
Brighton Pavilion, a regal
fantasy by the sea. [© Steve Day/
fotoLibra]

father was crowned, while Caroline (who was not invited to his coronation) died in 1821.

All this time George and Nash were pressing ahead with the Royal Pavilion at Brighton. The idea of using an oriental model for the design came from William Porden, an architect who trained under Samuel Pepys Cockerell, who in 1805 had created the 'fantastickal' neo-Mughal country house **Sezincote** in Gloucestershire. Porden had been asked to provide stabling, and he came up with a magnificent glass-domed 'Indo-Saracenic' structure, a circular room 70 feet in diameter and 62 feet tall to hold 44 horses. No longer part of the Brighton Pavilion complex, the structure survives as the Brighton Dome Concert Hall. The prince was evidently much taken with the style, and Nash was instructed to rebuild the Pavilion in a similar style of Regency Exoticism. The minarets caused much comment; the first mosque wasn't to be built in England until the 1880s (by a Jew, as it happens), and there was bafflement as to their purpose. As a Royal Palace, the Pavilion was inherited by Queen Victoria, who did not care to see her subjects blatantly walking around outside and so sold it to the town of Brighton for £50,000.

In World War I the Pavilion was used to house injured Indian troops, because sweetly it was felt they would feel more at home in such surroundings. It has become a major tourist attraction and the visual symbol of Brighton; a much-loved folly, now with a purpose.

What Every Jobless Miner Needs

The New Town of Peterlee was designated in 1948. It was intended to provide housing, leisure and shopping for impoverished south-east Durham, and to provide alternative employment for ex-miners and their wives. Masterplans were drawn up by distinguished architects and rejected; more masterplans were devised by yet more distinguished and higher-paid architects. The design teams were riven by the dissensions and resignations only idealogues can truly enjoy. The region was grindingly poor, unemployment was unfeasibly high, hope was similarly low. So the distinguished fine arts professor and Old Harrovian Victor Pasmore (1908–1998) was commissioned to create something to cheer the locals up. He knew just what they wanted. The benighted population of Peterlee wanted 'an architecture and sculpture of purely abstract form through which to walk, in which to linger and on which to play, a free and anonymous monument which, because of its independence, can lift the activity and psychology of an urban housing community on to a universal plain'. And that's what they got – the Apollo Pavilion, later renamed the **Pasmore Pavilion** (Fig 3.5). It was designed in 1963 to close off the eastern, dammed end of the damned lake, and to provide a pedestrian bridge passable by anyone under 1.5m tall, although it wasn't actually built until 1968. The flat, slab-shaped design echoing 1930s modernism was universally applauded by architectural critics and universally hated by the residents. It originally had murals on its walls, but they faded away, to be restored in 2009. When we first saw it, the stairs had been removed and the pavilion was covered in graffiti, much of it bluntly commenting on the suitability of the structure for its position. It clearly had not been maintained since the day it was built. Since then it has been spruced up and blasted back to its pale

Fig 3.5
Pasmore Pavilion, the fruit of
politicians and artists working
together to fulfil the needs
of jobless miners. [© Dave
Hudspeth/fotoLibra]

concrete at a cost of £336,000, but public opinion remains the same. 'Nobody here wants it', said one local. 'If English Heritage wants to list it, they should take it somewhere else and list it there'. 'It used to be nice when we first moved here but now it's horrid', said another girl. 'They should knock it down'. But it has been listed, Grade II*, and Peterlee's pavilion will be pleasuring the locals for many years to come.

Gazetteer

County/Authority	Location	Folly
Bristol and Avon	Bradford-on-Avon	Budbury Castle
	Bristol	Cook's Folly
	Chew Magna	Chota Castle
	Henbury	Blaise Hamlet
	Kelston	Tower House
	Kingsweston	Brewhouse
	Long Ashton	The Observatory
	Midford	Roebuck's Folly
Berkshire	Basildon	Peacock Pavilion
	Farley Hill	Farley Castle
	Purley	Culloden Pavilion
	Winterbourne	Hop Castle
Buckinghamshire	Cliveden	Cliveden Pagoda
	Gayhurst	Hell Khazi
	Great Missenden	Summerhouse
	Haddenham	Bone House
	Hall Barn	Oak Lodge
	Hedsor	Lord Boston's Folly
	Marlow	Quarry Wood Hall
	Medmenham	Medmenham Abbey
	Stowe	Lake Pavilion Chinese House Gothic Temple
Cheshire	Knutsford	Watts' Follies
	Lyme Park	Lyme Cage
	Wirral	Ness Gardens Summerhouse
Cornwall	Falmouth	Round House
	Newquay	Huer's House
	Penzance	Egyptian House
	Port Isaac	The Birdcage
	Portquin	Doyden Point Tower
	Veryan	Veryan Round Houses
	Zelah	Tinker's Castle
Cumbria	Ambleside	Bridge Cottage
	Conishead	Conishead Priory
	Coniston Water	Rowlandson Ground Summerhouse
	Far Sawrey	The Station
	Grange-over-Sands	Netherwood Summerhouses
	Greystoke	Fort Putnam Bunker's Hill Spire House
	Lower Holker	Cark Hall Summerhouse
	Muncaster	Summerhouse
	Ravenstonedale	The Lane Cottage
	Ullswater	Lyulph's Tower
	West Woodside	Fiddleback Farm

County/Authority	Location	Folly
Derbyshire	Cressbrook	The Gothic
	Swarkestone	Swarkestone Stand
	Two Dales	Sydnope Stand
Devon	Combe Martin	Pack o' Cards
	Devonport	Foulston's Follies
	Exmouth	A La Ronde
	Gidleigh	Prinsep's Folly
	Milton Abbot	Endsleigh Cottage
		Endsleigh Dairy
	Plymouth	Radford Castle
	Widecombe-in-the-Moor	Scobitor Round House
Dorset	Hinton Martell	Cottage Ornée
	Nottington	Spa House
Durham	Durham	The Count's House
	Hamsterley	Summerhouse
	Peterlee	Pasmore Pavilion
	Rowlands Gill (Tyne and Wear)	Gibside Banqueting House
	Sedgefield	Buon Retiro
East Sussex	Barcombe	Shelley's Folly
	Battle	Tower House
	Broad Oak	Braylsham Castle
	Brightling	Observatory
	Brighton	Brighton Pavilion
		Baby Brighton Pavilion
	Framfield	Hamilton Palace
	Hastings	The Clock House
		The Piece of Cheese
		Wingfield's Folly
	Penhurst	Tower House
Essex	Alresford	Fishing Temple
	Canvey Island	Dutch Cottages
	Chingford	Queen Elizabeth's Hunting Lodge
	Clacton-on-Sea	Moot Hall
	Epping	Copped Hall Pavilion
	Great Dunmow	Stone Hall Ornamental Cottage
		Summerhouse
	Little Thurrock	Clock House
	Little Walden	Cinder Hall
	Stansted Mountfitchet	Blyth Inspection Pavilion
Gloucestershire	Alderley	Banqueting House
	Alkerton	Summerhouse
	Amberley	Amberley Eyecatcher
	Chalford	Summerhouse
	Cheltenham	Rock House
	Coleford	Rock Castle
	Drybrook	Euroclydon Hotel

County/Authority	Location	Folly
	Frampton on Severn	Frampton Orangery
	Horton	Owl House
	Lower Swell	Spa Cottage
	Ruardean	Tower House
	Seven Springs	Round House
	Sezincote	Sezincote House
	Siddington	Siddington Round House
	Woodchester	Woodchester Mansion
Hampshire	Avington	Avington Park Pavilion
	Bramdean	Apple House
	Calshot	Luttrell's Tower
	Farringdon	Massey's Folly
	Havant	The Library
	Hawley	Minley Manor Summerhouse
	Hurstbourne	The Bee House
	Lepe	Lepe Tower
	Medstead	Jonathan's Folly
	Odiham	King John's Hunting Lodge
	Sherborne St John	The Vyne Pavilion
	Stratfield Saye	Stratfield Saye Summer House
	Warnford	Dower House Summer House
Herefordshire	Ledbury	Hope End
	Leinthall Earls	The Folly
	Stapleton	The Sulking House
Hertfordshire	Aldenham	Sly's Castle
	Barley	Homestall
	Benington	Summerhouse Tower House
	Bushey	Caldecote Towers
	Patmore Heath	Ness Pavilion
Isle of Wight	East Cowes	Osborne Swiss Chalets
Kent	Fairseat	The Folly
	Riverhead	Shepherd's Watch
	Rochester	Classical Gothick House
	Tenterden	Tower House
	Throwley	New York
Lancashire	Thornton	Hulton's Folly
	Turton	Turton Summerhouse
	Whitewell	Browsholme Spire Farm
Leicestershire	Barsby	Godson's Folly
	Exton Park (Rutland)	Fort Henry
	Ravenstone	Sham Windowed Almshouse
Lincolnshire	Boston	Freemason's Hall
	Brocklesby	Root House
	Eagle	The Jungle

County/Authority	Location	Folly
	Gate Burton	Shatoo
	Harlaxton	Harlaxton Manor
	Saltfleetby St Peter	Round Windowed Houses
	Spalding	Tower House
	Swinstead	Summer House
Liverpool and Manchester	Knowsley (Merseyside)	Summerhouse
	Liverpool (Merseyside)	Abercrombie Square Pavilion
	Liverpool (Merseyside)	Falconer's Folly
	Tottington (Greater Manchester)	Tower Farm
London	NW3	Swiss Cottage
	NW5	Holly Village
	NW8	Crocker's Folly Chas. Addams House
	NW9	Trobridge Houses Trobridge Buck's Lane
	SE3	Pagoda House
	SW3	Izba
	SW12	The Orangery
	SW14	Coach House
	W1	Toolshed Ornée Berkeley Castle
	W4	Chiswick House Garden Buildings
	W6	Grotto Cottage
	W12	Rylett Road Stables Rylett Road West Stables
	WC2	Toolshed Ornée
	Croydon	Water Tower
	Ealing	Southall Water Tower
	Hampton	Huck's Chalet
	Harrow	Tooke's Folly
	Isleworth	Summerhouses
	Sunbury-on-Thames	Arnussi
	Teddington	Cottage Ornée
	Twickenham	The Octagon Strawberry Hill Crane Park Tower
Norfolk	Letton Hall	Summerhouse
	Melton Constable	Bath House
	Potter Heigham	Helter Skelter House
North Yorkshire	Aske Hall	Temple
	Elloughton	The Castle
	Grewelthorpe	Banqueting House
	Grimston	Grimston Garth
	Hillam	Millstone Lodge Summerhouse
	Middleton Tyas	Tempest's Folly
	North Cave (ER)	Castle Farm
	Riccall	Gothic Folly

County/Authority	Location	Folly
	Settle	The Folly
	South Cave	Cave Castle Gatehouse
	South Dalton	Dalton Hall Pavilion
	Studley Royal	The Octagon
	Thirsk	Pattison's Folly
	Thornton Steward	Fort Horn
Northamptonshire	Althorp	The Falconry
	Brigstock	Lyveden New Bield
	Fawsley	Badby Lantern House
	Finedon	Exmill Cottage
	Horton	The Menagerie
	Rothwell	Market House
	Rushton	Triangular Lodge
	Stoke Bruerne	Stoke Park Pavilions
Northumberland	Berwick-upon-Tweed	Wilson's Folly
	Hartburn	Dr Sharp's Folly
	Holystone Grange	Garden House
	Seaton Delaval (Tyne and Wear)	Octagon
	Wark/Warton-on-Tyne	Chipchase Castle Gothick Summerhouse
	Wooler	Ewart Park Tower
Nottinghamshire	Budby	Budby Castle
	Bunny	Bunny Hall Belvedere
	Elston	Middleton's Folly
	Gunthorpe	Gunthorpe Hall
	Linby	Castle Mill
	Wiseton	White Swan Inn
	Woolaton	Woolaton Hall
Oxfordshire	Charlbury	Lodge Farm
	Chipping Norton	Bliss Tweed Mill
	Coleshill	Strattenborough Castle
	Cokethorpe	The Fish House
	Oxford	Cauldwell's Castle
	Woodcote	The Folly
Shropshire	Acton Burnell	Acton Burnell Sham Castle
	Bache	Tower House
	Badger	Temple
	Bridgnorth	Dracup's Cave
	Eyton-on-Severn	Eyton Summerhouse
	Hadnall	Waterloo Windmill
	Hawkstone	The Citadel
	Llanyblodwell	Blodwell Hall Summerhouse
Somerset	Bridgwater	Castle House
	Chilton Polden	Chilton Priory
	Combe Florey	Winter's Folly

County/Authority	Location	Folly
	Dulverton	Pepperpot Castle
	Ilminster	Dillington Lodges
	Keighton Hill	Lodge
	Nether Stowey	Toll House
	Oakhill	Rustic Cottages
South Yorkshire	Barnsley	Cannon Hall Deffer Wood Summerhouse
	Sheffield	Corner House
Staffordshire	Biddulph	Cheshire House
	Brewood	Speedwell Castle
	Clifton Campville	Clifton Hall
	Gailey	Round House
	Ipstones	Chapel House
	Lichfield	Observation Pavilion
	Meretown	The Castle
	Shugborough	Chinese House
	Tixall	Ingestre Pavilion
	Weston-under-Lizard	Pink Cottage
	Wombourne	The Bratch
Suffolk	Elveden	Elveden Hall
	Great Saxham	Grandfather's Tea House
	Ickworth	The Round House
	Lowestoft	Tower House
	Tattingstone	Tattingstone Wonder
	Thorpeness	The House in the Clouds West Bar Tower
	Wattisham	The Castle
	Woolverstone	The Cat House
	Worlingham	Castle Farm
Surrey	Dorking	Stedman's Folly
	Guildford	Moat House
	Lingfield	Starborough Castle
Warwickshire	Arbury	Tea House
	Arlescote	Pavilions
	Edgbaston	George Road Bothy
	Halford	The Folly
	Napton-on-the-Hill	The Folly
West Sussex	Atherington	Bailiffscourt
	Bognor Regis	White Tower
	Colgate	Holmbush Towers
	Cuckfield	Knott's Tower House
	Fisherstreet	Shillinglee Deer Tower
	Petworth	Upperton Monument
	Slaugham	Nymans Pavilion
	Worthing	Castle Goring

County/Authority	Location	Folly
West Yorkshire	Allerton Mauleverer	Temple of Victory
	Rawdon	Spite and Malice Summerhouse
Wiltshire	Bodenham	Longford Castle
	Fonthill Gifford	Remains of Fonthill Abbey
	Stourhead	Rustic Cottage
Worcestershire	Baughton	Tower House
	Croome d'Abitot	Orangery
	Spetchley	Root House

4 | Cloud-capp'd towers: towers, pinnacles and steeples

In popular belief, most follies were built in the 18th century. This is not true, as we shall see, although the epitome of the folly is the tower, Gothick, crumbling, forgotten and raging on a distant hill.

Thomas Gooding

In 1579 Thomas Gooding, a rich mercer from Ipswich, built a fine six-storey red-brick tower on the banks of the River Orwell – and no one knows why. It could be that he wanted to keep an eye on his ships sailing up and down the river. It could be he wanted to impress Queen Elizabeth, who visited Ipswich that year. It could be that he wanted a schoolroom for his beautiful daughter. All we can say with some certainty is that this is the first folly tower in England. It took until this time for private citizens to become wealthy enough to build purely for pleasure before purpose. A folly is a misunderstood building, and this tower is not simply misunderstood, it is a puzzle. Gooding bought the Freston estate in 1553. Why did it take him 26 years to build the tower? On the side of the tower is the mark of a large building that was once attached to it. Why is there no other trace of that building, no foundations, no rubble, no records, no images? East Anglian winters are not notably mild; why is there no fireplace in the tower? Why would he want to look at his trading ships when he had already made his fortune a quarter of a century earlier? All this points towards the tower being a folly, perhaps the first tower folly after the Tower of Babel, but as we say in the Folly Preferences File, a folly tower ideally has a wildly spurious legend attached.

> Had I a daughter I would try
> To give of learning such supply
> As other works should crown
> I'd build a tower six stories there
> With rooms ascending by the stair
> Each one with purpose known

And that is **Freston Tower** (Fig 4.1). The clever and beauteous Ellen de Freston was educated here:

> The lower room, to charity, from 7 to 8 o clock.
> The second, to working tapestry, from 9 to 10.
> The third, to music, from 10 to noon.
> The fourth, to painting, from 12 to 1.
> The fifth, to literature, from 1 to 2.
> The sixth, to astronomy, at even.

And, of course, she ended up on the roof learning the language of love in the arms of her tutor. No matter that there's no historical record of an Ellen de

Freston or even an Ellen Gooding outside the story, it's a satisfying explanation for the tower. The legend was created in 1850 by the Revd Richard Cobbold, and it appeared in his novel *Freston Tower; or, The Early Days of Cardinal Wolsey.* The dark-haired Ellen had two suitors, William Latimer and Thomas Wolsey, five years younger. Latimer glided from tutor to suitor and won her heart, while the broken-hearted Wolsey went into the church and did quite well for himself. It is pure fiction. We think the tower was probably built to catch Queen Elizabeth's eye. All Thomas Gooding lacked for happiness was a title, and this was a way of drawing attention to himself. If that was the case, it didn't work.

Humphry Sturt

The next folly is equally mysterious: **Sturt's Folly**, the mighty Horton Tower (Fig 4.2). No one knows when it was built. East Dorset Council believe it was built by the famous baroque architect Thomas Archer for Humphry Sturt in 1742. Archer died in 1743 aged 75, and his last work recorded in Colvin's *Biographical Dictionary of British Architects* was completed in 1730. Humphry Sturt *père* had died two years earlier aged 53, while Humphry Sturt *fils*, commonly credited with the tower, was 17, not an age when one usually plans to build massive follies. Another source gives 1750 as the construction date; a third 1760. This has long been one of our favourite follies, set in dramatic isolation on Linen Hill, the model of the solitary tower on a windswept hill, big, ugly, misunderstood. Its solitude accentuates its size.

The first mention of the tower was made by the young Edward Gibbon, later author of *Decline and Fall of the Roman Empire,* who wrote in a 1763 letter: 'From this place to Mr. Sturt's, where we saw an artificial piece of water of two hundred acres, and an elegant turret a hundred and forty foot high; but such is the character of the man, that he keeps his place in no order, sells his fish and makes a granary of his turret'. It seems unlikely that Sturt would treat his newly built tower in such a desultory fashion, which points to it having been

built by his father. The first printed mention is as an observatory in 1765, the year Humphry Sturt the younger married Diana Napier, who inherited Crichel House. The Sturts had promptly moved into the grand house and set about making substantial remodelling and improvements, using local builder Thomas Bastard, nephew of John and William Bastard. The Bastards were provincial builder/architects who had worked on the rebuilding of Crichel House after a fire in 1742 for Diana's uncle, Sir William Napier, and it is interesting to note that one of their influences was said to be Thomas Archer.

In 1760 Humphry Sturt the younger was 35, full of confidence and money, the ideal age to think about building something for one's own amusement. His plans for Crichel House involved a 200-acre lake in front of the house, but boringly the village of Moor Crichel was in the way so he demolished it and moved the population to Witchampton, a mile away. As the tower was first mentioned as an observatory, Occam's Razor suggests that that's what it was. Old prints disappointingly show it topped by a domed roof with cupola, with no telescope poking out, but nomenclature was not as important in the 18th century as it is now; by 1789 it was being described as 'Mr Sturt's Obelisk'.

Despite being MP for Dorset for many years and carrying out agricultural improvements on Brownsea Island in Poole harbour, which he owned – he imported vast quantities of manure, planted new crops, and daringly used new-fangled steam power for threshing – Sturt has left little record of his life. The local paper described him as 'a man of inviolable integrity, with many peculiarities, and a good heart. He supports his character as one of the country Members, with great independency and respect, and votes with the Opposition'. His children made more of an impact, in particular his son Charles, who took exception to a fellow midshipman kicking his dog down the hatch on Admiral Digby's ship *Prince George*, and proceeded to beat him up. The midshipman was Prince William, later King William IV. They became friends. Sturt christened one of his daughters Eliza Bizarre, and this leaves us lost for words. Bizarre meant exactly the same in the 18th century as it does today; apart from euphony, why saddle your poor daughter with such a name? The only excuse we can find is that 'bizarre' also referred to a type of variegated carnation. Perhaps she was as pretty as a flower.

Sturt's other reason for building the tower was said to be as a hunting stand, so he could watch the hunt when he was too old and infirm to take part. This ignores the fact that he was young and virile when the tower was built, and is unlikely to have planned that far ahead. The other snag with hunting stands is that when one does become old and infirm, stairs become a big problem.

When we first saw Sturt's Folly it was roofless and ruined, with a scar of ivy on the octagonal drum. It now has a flat zinc roof and the lancet-arched windows in the drum are glazed, because it has discovered a new role as a mobile phone mast.

Beckford/Fonthill

William Beckford (1760–1844) built **Fonthill Abbey**, the greatest folly England has ever seen. Its central tower collapsed in a thunderous cataclasm on the afternoon of 21 December 1825 while its new owner dozed peacefully undisturbed in an adjacent wing. The watercolour by Charles Wild shows the

Fig 4.3
Fonthill Abbey, if the spire had
been built. [Charles Wild]

spectacular grandiosity of the place, more like Salisbury Cathedral than a private home, although sadly the spire shown in the painting was never actually erected (Fig 4.3).

Beckford was a remarkable creature. He was sensationally good-looking, a novelist, collector, pederast, sugar plantation owner, homosexual, folly builder, slave-owner, musician and for a while the richest man in England (Fig 4.4). His notoriety stemmed from an affair that began when he was 19 with the 11-year-old Honourable William Courtenay, or 'Kitty', as he was known, the only son of the Earl of Devon, of Powderham Castle. The passion was mutual and enduring. Seven years later Beckford and his new young wife Lady Margaret were staying at Powderham. Kitty was then 18, and he and Beckford were discovered in flagrante by Kitty's tutor, who heard 'a creaking and bustle, which raised his curiosity, and thro' the keyhole he saw the operation, which it seems he did not interrupt, but informed Lord C., & the whole was blown up'.

Beckford's protestations that he was merely whipping the boy were dismissed. Kitty's outraged uncle Lord Loughborough, the Lord Chief Justice, publicised the incident in the national press, which led to Beckford being ostracised from polite society for the rest of his life.

Today we can accept his homosexuality and almost his pederasty, but his wealth came from Jamaican sugar plantations, which meant he owned slaves, and that now puts him beyond the pale. There are degrees of ancient sins, and every year some hapless prime minister or president is made to apologise for the wickedness of their nation's ancestors. Often some financial compensation is sought. Human memory is long. The Irish still remember the Battle of the Boyne in 1690; the slaughter of 500 Welsh bards by Edward I is still remembered, not by the Welsh but by Hungarians because of a poem they all have to learn in school; Serbians still mark 15 June as Vidovdan, commemorating the battle of Kosovo in 1389. In Kentucky, USA, the McCoy family cemetery is owned by a member of the Hatfield clan, who refuses to let anyone in, in case they might be McCoys. At the moment the spade of slavery trumps the club of paedophilia; who knows when that will change?

If we can still bear to contemplate Beckford, we see that he foretold his future. In 1781 he wrote to Lady Hamilton: 'I fear I shall never be ... good for anything in this world, but composing airs, building towers, forming gardens, collecting old Japan, and writing a journey to China or the moon'.

Fig 4.4
William Beckford: said to have been the most handsome man in England. Hard to tell.
[© Mike Cousins]

Fig 4.5
Ticket to view the Fonthill Abbey sale. [© Amoret Tanner/fotoLibra]

Fig 4.6
All that remains of the astounding
Fonthill Abbey. [© John Cleare/
fotoLibra]

He cannot be blamed for the collapse of the tower at Fonthill, neither can his admittedly slap-dash architect James Wyatt. It is said that in 1825 Beckford was called to the death-bed of George Hayter, Wyatt's contractor, who confessed that he had not laid the relieving arches at the foundations of the tower for which he had been paid, and that it could collapse at any minute. Beckford immediately informed the gunpowder millionaire John Farquhar, to whom he had sold the abbey for £330,000, who seems to have been a man of singular sanguinity because he was untroubled by the news (Fig 4.5). This story might be a little too caring for the Beckford we know through history. After the tower collapsed Farquhar commented that he was glad, because now 'the house would not be too large for me to live in'. Beckford, who had dreamed of building towers for years, seemed fated by them – an earlier version of the tower had collapsed into the octagon in 1800. So not even good at building towers (Fig 4.6).

He redeemed himself, architecturally speaking, at Bath, where he had retired after selling Fonthill, much of his fortune gone with the collapse in the price of sugar. In 1827 his new architect Henry Goodridge built him a fine, fair folly tower on **Lansdown Hill** above the city, one that survives to this day and can be rented for holidays through the Landmark Trust. Beckford was reconciled to the loss of Fonthill because with his new tower came 'the finest prospect in Europe!' What has gone is the mile-and-a-quarter ride he created from his house at 20 Lansdown Crescent to the tower at the top of the hill, a ride he did almost every morning, preceded by a steward on horseback, two grooms with long whips, then five or six dogs, with Beckford and two more grooms to bring up the rear. He may have lost his fortune, but one has to keep up appearances. It took him three years to acquire the necessary land and override any public rights of way.

Powell Powell

Here are five towers from the 19th and 20th centuries, all still in fine condition and all constructed for very different reasons.

John Powell Powell (1769–1849) was the rich nephew of a rich uncle. John Powell-Roberts (1721–1783) bought Quex Park on the Isle of Thanet in Kent in 1777, and left it to his nephew, who liked to build. He knocked down the house he inherited and built a fashionable Regency mansion in its place. Then he built the Gun Tower, a small circular folly tower on an ancient burial mound, but stopped when a ghostly white lady was seen flitting through the trees surrounding the mound, clearly as a result of the desecration of the burial place. This was intended to be a daymark or flag station, as John PP was a keen yachtsman and liked to know when his dinner would be ready.

In 1814 he started work on what became the **Waterloo Tower** (Fig 4.7), a proper full-blown folly tower, red brick, five storeys, castellated, lancet arched windows, octagonal corner towers, sadly not triangular. All well and good, but nothing particularly out of the ordinary, nothing very unusual to see here – until a couple of years after its completion when iron founder William Mackney was employed to add a 'spire' to the building. We put 'spire' in quotation marks because Mackney, working together with Quex's head gardener, produced something quite extraordinary.

Everyone who sees it immediately has the same reaction. Of course, it's the Eiffel Tower, tucked away here in rural Kent, a wedding confection in cast iron plonked on the top of a conventional brick tower. It almost doubles the original height of the tower. It's even more prominent because it is painted a blistering white. In an 1832 print by John Shury it dominates the foreground, relegating the house and the Gun Tower to supporting roles. What makes the heart of every Man of Kent burst with pride is that this predates that cheap French copy by 66 years. It even has a golden cockerel on top, as if to mock the French.

John PP offered to augment the ring of bells at All Saints, Birchington, but when his offer was declined he decided to build his own bell tower. Twelve bells, cast by Thomas Mears of the Whitechapel Bell Foundry, were hung in the Waterloo Tower in April 1819. This doesn't count as a carillon because a carillon is operated by a keyboard; this is a bell tower, traditionally rung with ropes. To celebrate the opening of the belfry that year a peal of Grandsire Cinques was rung in three hours and 39 minutes, followed by a treble bob royal.

There is no record that shows this, but we speculate that the reason that the remarkable cast iron spire was added so soon after the bells were installed was in order to lock and stabilise the tower.

Fig 4.7

The Waterloo Tower at Quex Park. Now where did Gustave Eiffel get his best ideas from?

[© Mike Cousins]

Fig 4.8
St Mary's Church, Faversham –
the actual inspiration for the top
of Waterloo Tower. [© Lisa Valder
Photography]

PENATIBUS BENIGNIS
AMICIS PRAESENTIBUS
SPECULAM QUAM SUSPICIS
(NAVITAE SIT AUXILIO!)
POSUIT
I. P. POWELL ARM:
A.D. MDCCCXIV

(To the kindly gods, and to my friends, J. P. Powell placed a watch tower which you are gazing at (May it help to serve the Navy!))

A misconception about follies is that they are useless buildings. As well as being a splendid bell tower, daymark, belvedere and memorial, the Waterloo Tower was pressed into service by later members of the Powell Cotton family as a mausoleum – five good uses. The Eiffel Tower superstructure is in fact derived from the crowning spire of St Mary's Church in nearby Faversham (Fig 4.8).

A Yorkshire Rumpus

England prides itself on being one of the most tolerant countries in the world. Tolerance is the acceptance of other peoples' manners, opinions and behaviour, and has traditionally been seen as a Christian virtue. One of the most commonly heard words in England is 'Sorry!' Outsiders may think this is an apology, but no – it is usually a polite and slightly distant expression of regret, as 'I'm sorry to hear of your calamitous misfortune' is rendered sympathetically as 'Sorry!'

Do not make the error of confusing English tolerance with weakness, as many have to their cost. It has been tested in recent years, as irritation gives way to offence at the slightest opportunity. Those sensitive souls now known as 'snowflakes' would have had a hard time of it in previous centuries, but they may have found a fellow-traveller in Sir Henry Edwards, MP (1812–1886), who raised new hackles of prickliness. Anything and everything annoyed or upset him.

Living in industrial Halifax in the 1850s, he was perpetually disturbed by factory buzzers and whistles, he was irritated by white cows grazing, he took offence at washing hanging out to dry, he hated seeing smoke coming out of chimneys – he was a member of the Halifax Smoke Abatement Society – and he valued his privacy more than a Montanan American. To live in an industrial town in Victorian England meant you really had to be able to cope with smoke. The traditional English response to such a fragile flower is persiflage, or banter as it's known when accompanied by a clenched fist. From what we know about Sir Henry, he comes across as irritable as a greenfinch; pompous, self-important, irascible, the epitome of the egotistical Victorian industrialist and the perfect balloon for popping. Sir Henry's neighbour, dye works owner John Edward

Wainhouse (1817–1883), could not resist the bait and anointed himself the Archbishop of Banterbury.

One of Sir Henry's many irrelevant boasts was that no one could see into his estate at Pye Nest, surrounded as it was by a mighty wall. But as Chairman of the Skircoat Board of Surveyors, it was Wainhouse who had responsibility for the highways in the district. While carrying out some local road improvements he was seized by an impish need to raise the road level by 18 inches – which meant the general public could now look over Sir Henry's wall.

You can imagine the frothing rage. Delighted by the reaction, Wainhouse stoked the fire by publishing a series of pamphlets, each one calculated to drive Edwards to apoplexy. Titles included *Smoke: Its Vouchers and its Victims – An Account of Corruption in the West Riding Smoke Prevention Association* (Sir Henry had been on the board); *West Riding Law in Halifax, The Only County Family: A Letter* (questioning the Edwards family's right to their coat of arms); *Skircoat Lamps And Justice Lights; The Silver Casket; A Letter To My Friend Toby, A Radical,* all published in 1880, and *What Is A Conservative?* which appeared in 1883. Sir Henry had been Conservative MP for Halifax and later Beverley.

But what really got Sir Henry's goat was **Wainhouse's Chimney** (Fig 4.9). A chimney is a practical building, designed to draw smoke and noxious vapours away from the city and its people, the antithesis of folly. But does it have to be two or three times the height it needs to be? Does it have to have a spiral staircase climbing up 403 steps? Does it have to have two belvederes or viewing platforms at the top? Why make it octagonal when most chimneys are round? And does the top of the chimney really need to be so magnificently crowned with a cascade of arches and buttresses, with columns and balustrades, florid and excessive architectural ornamentation that would not be out of place on St Peter's in Rome (Fig 4.10)? Wainhouse built his chimney over four years from 1871, Edwards watching in open-mouthed horror as it ascended majestically 275 feet into the sky less than half a mile from the walls of his beloved estate. It is a breathtaking sight, and it could all too clearly be seen from Sir Henry's Pye Nest. And anyone in the belvedere could see right into Pye Nest in all its glorious privacy.

To further add insult to this injury, Wainhouse never used the tower as a chimney, as he sold the Washer Lane dyeworks in 1874, keeping the chimney for himself. It was after the sale of the dyeworks that he found another architect to add the crown, cupola and belvederes.

Later that year Sir Henry hosted a flower show in the Pye Nest Fields, and took the opportunity of pointing out to his visitors, by means of a conspicuously posted placard, 'the injury caused to his property by reason of a new chimney [that Wainhouse had] built and which being very near him was too easily seen'.

Fig 4.9

Wainhouse's Chimney. More of a statement than a function.
[© Michael O'Brien/fotoLibra]

It is hard to escape the conclusion that this, the tallest folly in England, was just a very expensive way of irritating a neighbour. Its £14,000 cost equates to £1.5 million today. Wainhouse was hardly the innocent party; he would denigrate Sir Henry at every available opportunity. He commented that 'his memory has never been burdened with the weight of too much expansiveness'. When Edwards was asked to temporarily step down from the magistrate's bench due to a conflict of interest, he wrote a letter of complaint to the Halifax *Courier*, to which Wainhouse responded that 'Sir Henry ought to know that his motives were not impugned. To repeat [that they had been] is not only a mark of ill-temper, but also ill-breeding, and must be reckoned a gratuitous insult'. Strong stuff for Victorians.

A Somerset Spat

Towers engender strong emotions. In Ammerdown Park at Kilmersdon, Somerset, the Eddystone Lighthouse stands far from the pounding of the surf – it is, as the seagull flies, 27 miles inland from the coast. The designer of the **Ammerdown Column** was Joseph Jopling, an architect not noted for his marine work, although the tower does bear a startling resemblance to the Eddystone Lighthouse. It was erected to commemorate Thomas Samuel Joliffe, landowner, MP, lord of the manor and promotor of the Somersetshire Coal Canal. A long inscription testifies to the 'profound and grateful affection' of his bachelor son John who caused the column to be built:

Fig 4.10
Fantastic extravaganza. Note the ladder. [© Michael O'Brien/fotoLibra]

THIS PILLAR IS ERECTED TO COMMEMORATE THE GENIUS, ENERGY AND ACCOMPLISHMENTS OF THOMAS SAMUEL JOLIFFE, LORD OF THE ADJACENT HUNDREDS OF KILMERSDON AND WELLOW, IN EVERY RELATION OF LIFE, IN THE SENATE AND ON THE SEAT OF JUSTICE, IN EXERCISING THE PECULIAR RIGHTS AND DISCHARGING THE VARIOUS DUTIES OF AN EXTENSIVE LANDHOLDER, CONCILIATED THE REGARD AND ESTEEM OF AN AFFLUENT AND INTELLIGENT DISTRICT. TO HIM WHO RECLAIMED THE SURROUNDING LANDS FROM THEIR ORIGINAL AND STERILE CONDITION, WHO CLOTHED THEM WITH FERTILITY AND VERDURE AND EMBELLISHED THEM WITH TASTEFUL AND ORNAMENTAL DECORATIONS, HIS DESCENDANTS, WITH FEELINGS OF PROFOUND AND GRATEFUL AFFECTION, DEDICATE THIS COLUMN.

AMMERDOWN PARK
VI JUNE MDCCCLIII

and in order that the point should not be missed, the same inscription is repeated in full in Latin and in French on the north and east sides. The 150ft column was inaugurated on 6 June 1853 (Fig 4.11).

Coade stone animals guard the four points of the compass on the plinth. The entrance door opens into a cool square room with chamfered corners and marbled walls; the tower extends its foot into this room, so to climb the stone spiral staircase one enters through another doorway to the stair tower, an unusual and pleasing device. The staircase, regularly lit by ten tiny portholes, winds up to a splendid view from the glass lantern at the top. The framework of this ornate lantern has completely disappeared since we first saw the tower.

The Joliffe's neighbour John Turner, whose lands abutted the Ammerdown estate, was on friendly terms with the Joliffes until Thomas's grandson William, later Baron Hylton, inherited the estate. John and William did not see eye to eye, and the Ammerdown column became an obsession with him.

He vowed to outstrip the column with a tower that would dominate the Ammerdown estate. Building started in 1887 and was completed in 1890 (a chair in Hemmington church bears the inscription 'Presented to J. Turner Esq. on completion of the Eiffel Tower 1890'. His square Italianate tower was higher than the Ammerdown column and looked even taller, as it was extremely slender and stepped at the top, where for some reason there was a chair (the one that is now in Hemmington church?).

The tower was designed by a Mr Wilcox of nearby Terry Hill and took three years to build, at a cost of over £4,000. At the top of the stone tower was a wooden construction with a balcony and viewing area. Above that a spire soaring a further 60 feet was added, containing an iron cage halfway up, which was the highest climbable point, accessed by a ladder. The main shaft of the tower contained a spiral oak staircase, with seats provided at intervals for weary climbers. There was a plan to charge an admission fee and provide teas, but it never worked.

It couldn't last, and of course it didn't. True to folly tradition, Mr Turner went bankrupt and his tower was bought by Lord Hylton. We can see the grin on Hylton's face from a century away. It was declared unsafe after being struck by lightning, and in 1910 much of it was taken down, reducing it to a stump. It was finally completely demolished in 1969.

Peculiar People

In 1858 Jesus Christ visited a 30-year-old woman in her bedroom in Ipswich. Six years later He returned at Christmas and told her the Second Coming was at hand. As proof, stigmata appeared on her hands and feet. Mary Ann Girling

Fig 4.11

The Ammerdown Column before the lantern fell off.

[© Gwyn Headley/fotoLibra]

abandoned her husband and two children and went on the road as an itinerant preacher. Itinerant preachers were as welcome in Suffolk farming communities as the Colorado beetle, and she was driven out of the county. No longer at ease with the old dispensation, she found a base in Walworth, south London, soon gained 300 followers and attracted thousands more interested bystanders who came to watch their vigorous style of worship. Initially the Girlingites allied themselves with the Peculiar People of Plumstead, a sect which, after a shrewd name change, is still in existence, but split with them after Mrs Girling revealed that she was actually divine, and that she herself was the Second Coming of Christ. A number of supporters found this too hard to swallow, so Mrs Girling and her reduced band decamped to Hordle in Hampshire, in the New Forest.

Being divine, Mary Girling had written the laws of the New Forest Shakers, as her Children of God sect became known, after their tendency to shake, rattle and roll during their devotions. These laws enforced celibacy, banned commerce and the payment of mortgages. As a result, they were evicted within a year. Just as with prophets unable to foresee the invention of refrigeration, her rules had become as rigid and unyielding as supporters of the American constitution's second amendment. She had to rely on the kindness of the local gentry. At that

Fig 4.12
Even follies have to earn their keep. Peterson's Folly or Sway Tower with telephone antennae.
[© Mike Watson/fotoLibra]

period the New Forest was infested with gypsies, and local landowners found Mrs Girling's group both preferable and a deterrent to travellers, who didn't particularly care to be converted.

Mary Ann Girling was a tall, thin, striking woman and a passionate speaker. When Andrew Peterson, a wealthy retired barrister, for many years leader of the Calcutta Bar and formerly a Judge of the High Court of Calcutta, came to live in nearby Sway, he brought with him his own obsession: the dream of a concrete world. Many may regret that his dream has now come true, but in the 1880s the use of concrete in construction was virtually unknown in Europe. His first encounter with Mrs Girling was not favourable; he was convinced she was a mesmerist (mesmerism was the forerunner of hypnotism, discredited by medical authorities but still popular among the credulous and weak-willed). She made short work of the professional mesmerist he brought down to Hordle in order to expose her, leaving him somewhat at a loss. Too rich and intelligent to join Mrs Girling's sect, he turned to spiritualism, through which he was introduced to Sir Christopher Wren (the Children of God believed that no one ever died), who helped him draft the plans for a tower to be built to prove the merit of concrete as a construction material.

And what a tower (Fig 4.12)! Gaunt, unrendered, coarse and crude, this 218ft, 11-storey tower is the first concrete building in Britain since the Romans built Dover Castle. It erupts like a Victorian rocket out of the flat sandy heathland, its launch gantry the 339-step staircase, perfectly erect, uncluttered by lesser structures crowding around it. The shingle for the concrete was brought from nearby Milford-on-Sea, and the construction work was entirely carried out by local men – another plan to relieve unemployment? Peterson took care only to hire men who were genuinely unemployed, and paid them what he regarded as a living wage, which incensed local employers. His plan for a dazzling beacon at the top of the tower was scuppered by Trinity House, who complained that it would confuse shipping, and his plan for a mausoleum in the basement of the tower was scuppered by his wife. She died three years after the tower was completed and, feeling the chill of the Hampshire winters, Peterson spent much of the rest of his life in Tenerife.

Judge A T T Peterson enjoyed his tower for 20 years, dying in London at the age of 93 in 1906. He partly overrode his wife's wishes, in that at the end he was cremated and his ashes were interred with great ceremony in the basement of the tower. The ashes were enclosed in a polished oak casket, with brass furniture and a brass plate reading: 'This casket contains the ashes of Andrew Thomas Turton Peterson, born 8th Jan 1814; died 29th Nov 1906'. Four local workmen who helped Peterson in the building of the tower, Messrs Gates, Hood, Buckle and Ackland, carried his ashes to the vault, making **Peterson's Folly** the tallest tomb in England.

And Mrs Girling? She died of cancer the year the tower was completed, and as the Children of God weren't supposed to die, the sect broke up and dispersed.

The true saviour in this story is not Mrs Girling or Judge Peterson, but an entrepreneur named Paul Atlas, who bought the tower over 40 years ago and who has dedicated his life to saving it, fearlessly carrying out repairs himself at any height, letting floors out to telecom companies for their aerials, converting several floors into a luxurious hotel, putting it on the market then mysteriously withdrawing it, playing a guessing game with the finest folly in the south of England.

Lord Berners' Folly

The people of Faringdon, now in Oxfordshire but formerly in Berkshire for many centuries, are proud of their eccentric former residents and strive to uphold the tradition. Eccentricity is difficult to sustain in committee, but here they manage reasonably well – the path through the woodland to Faringdon Folly passes over the **Fairly Useless Bridge**, a confection of logs and twigs crossing – well, crossing the forest floor.

The 14th Lord Berners (1883–1950) of Faringdon House was a musician, artist and writer, a small, balding man with a pencil moustache and the mien of a bank clerk. His looks belied his flamboyant character (Fig 4.13). Being gay, apart from it being illegal, did not unduly trouble him. 'I felt it my duty to apply myself to the more manly occupations of hunting and shooting. Not that I was averse to either of them in moderation. But they were always too strenuously practised and they went on far too long'. When a Colonel Stokes, a particularly fatuous friend of his mother's, asked him as a child 'Well young man, what is your aim in life?', Berners retorted, 'Not to have to answer silly questions'. He was tutored for his Eton entrance exam by a Mr Prout, who said that 'the only point he [Prout] had in common with the ancient Greeks was his predilection for athletics, and that games brought him into closer contact with young people'. Berners commented:

> There was perhaps another point he had in common with the ancient Greeks, for I subsequently heard that he succeeded in getting himself into closer contact with young people than was thought desirable by the school authorities. I noticed that he was rather persistent in his demonstrations of affection. He was continually patting my head or stroking my hair. However I suffered this embarrassing friendliness with a good grace. I only wondered if it might not perhaps have something to do with the ceremony I had read of in the Prayer-book called the Laying on of Hands.

But school was not for him – 'No other house at Eton contained so dreary a collection of boys'.

His exceptionally devout maternal grandmother, Lady Bourchier, turned all the pictures to the wall on Sundays and forbade games and toys. Hours not devoted to prayer were reserved for the study of scriptures. As a result, his uncles and aunts grew up worldly and irreligious.

The Berners title was one of those rare titles that could be passed down through the female line. Berners' father was asked about his grandmother, 'Isn't she a peeress in her own right?' and he grumped 'Yes, and she's everything else in her own wrong'. Interestingly the Gender Recognition Act of 2004, which allows transgender people to be fully recognised in their new gender by the law, has one exception. 'The fact that a person's gender has become the acquired gender under this Act (a) does not affect the descent of any peerage or dignity or title of honour, and (b) does not affect the devolution of any property'. So a peer of the realm still has to be cis male or cis female.

Because he was a wealthy man, Berner's work has been dismissed as dilettantism, but he took his music seriously, as did Igor Stravinsky, who valued it highly. Listening to it today one can hear echoes of Alkan and Satie, but introducing humour to music seldom plays well with high-minded critics.

Fig 4.13
Lord Berners with carp.
Alternatively, a lobster is
available. His motto almost reads
'Let the Good Times Roll' in Latin.
[© Gwyn Headley/fotoLibra]

Like anyone worthwhile, he was full of faults, never wanting to be alone with his thoughts. Friends and visitors to Faringdon House (Fig 4.14) included John Betjeman, Patrick Leigh Fermor, Salvador Dalí, H G Wells, Tom Driberg, Elsa Schiaparelli, Cyril Connolly, the Duke of Wellington, Lady Cunard, Osbert Sitwell, Siegfried Sassoon, Evelyn Waugh, Rosamond Lehmann, David Niven, Harold Nicolson, Nancy Mitford, Diana Mosley, Sergei Diaghilev, Stravinsky of course, and many others, a *Who's Who* of society in the 1930s and 1940s. The group described themselves as madly gay, as indeed many of them were.

With his hard-drinking partner Robert Heber-Percy, Berners strewed his estate and village of Faringdon with notices: 'Trespassers Will Be Prosecuted,

Fig 4.14
Lord Berners' bathroom in
Faringdon House, decorated by
Roy Hobdell. [© Gwyn Headley/
fotoLibra]

Dogs Shot, Cats Whipped'; 'Beware of the Agapanthus', dyed his white doves all colours of the rainbow, had a clavichord installed in the back of his Rolls-Royce, adorned his dog with a pearl necklace, and on top of the already named Folly Hill in 1935 he built **Lord Berner's Folly** (Fig 4.15), the last great folly tower in England, employing Gerald Wellesley, the future Duke of Wellington, to design it. Wellesley was an architect and soldier, known by his troops as 'The Iron Duchess', in reference to his sexual preferences, so he mingled well with the Berners set. A notice by the door of the tower read 'Members of the Public committing suicide from this tower do so entirely at their own risk', and right at the very top of the tower, 'No Dogs Allowed'.

Faringdon has embraced these traditions. A stone seat in the market square is inscribed 'A MAN WHO NEVER HAS AN OCCASIONAL FLASH' interrupted by a term of a deep-sea diver (Fig 4.16). It is incomprehensible until you go around the back and discover 'OF SILLINESS • MISTRUST', making a Berners aphorism, which of course reads 'Mistrust a man who never has an occasional flash of silliness'. The diver's helmet references a speech given by Salvador Dalí inside a diving helmet that Berners had procured for him. After delivering the suit, the hire shop telephoned to ask for what purpose the helmet was required, and on being told that it was to be used in a lecture, said they only wished to stipulate that the depth must be limited to 40 fathoms. More examples are scattered throughout the small town. A stepladder leaning against a wall is signed 'Please do not remove this ladder, or steps will be taken'.

Berners was a fascinating, multifaceted character, the subject of several memoirs and biographies. We can only skim his life and interests here. When he was ten he wrote a funeral march for his mother, which apparently she much appreciated. He said that as a child 'I even used to think she [his mother] was beautiful – but as soon as I gained a maturer understanding of the nature of physical beauty, this delusion had ceased'. He amused her by putting a bowler hat over a pet bird and watching the hat scurry across the floor. As a child he loved his four-volume illustrated *Birds of Britain*, and finding the stolidly English birds at Faringdon insufficiently polychromatic, he acquired a flock of white doves and dyed them all colours. The tradition continues to this day: the doves are dyed in early summer, so the sun can dry their feathers. An interesting aside to this is that it shows that either hawks are colour-blind, or colour is an irrelevance: occasionally there would be an explosion of powder-blue or pink feathers as another dyed dove was taken by a raptor.

It was only to be expected that a man of such varied talents and such playfulness should be drawn to folly. This is where we meet our stumbling-block; we feel fairly strongly that a folly is an involuntary building, and ideally the builder has no idea he has built one. The title is an honorific awarded by others, not a deliberate aim. But it is hard to deny that the tower Lord Gerald Wellesley built for Lord Berners in 1935 as a present for his boyfriend Robert Heber-Percy is a folly. Heber-Percy was heard muttering 'I'd have preferred a horse'. He was a queer fish, this Mad Boy, as he was known to everyone. Heber-Percy was handsome, tall, vivacious, lean, active, and very gay, described by Diana Mosley as having 'high spirits, elegant appearance and uninhibited behaviour'. He could converse intelligently on a wide variety of subjects, not all of them interesting. After Berners died and left him Faringdon House, he created his own folly in the grounds, a Staircase To Nowhere, rising in front of the

Fig 4.15
Lord Berners' folly. The recipient, Robert Heber-Percy, muttered 'I'd have preferred a horse.' [© Barry Charles Hitchcox/fotoLibra]

Fig 4.16
What else would you expect to
see in a small inland English
market town? [© Gwyn Headley/
fotoLibra]

orangery then simply petering out. After a while its pointlessness began to irritate him, so to complete it he added a swimming pool at the top of the steps, guarded by two enormous sculptures of winged wyverns, and a little changing room floored with copper pennies.

He gave the folly tower and the surrounding woodland to the town of Faringdon in the 1980s, and they have embraced it wholeheartedly. Long gone were the councillors who caused Lord Berners such vexation in the 1930s. They had point-blank refused him permission to build his folly tower, raising multiple objections. In August 1934 it was reported that 'Faringdon District Council has declined, under the [Town and Country Planning] Act, to sanction the plans for a tower that Lord Berners was proposing to build on his property'. The report went on to comment that 'From the top of the tower, which was to be approximately level with the tree-tops, spectators would have obtained a remarkable view without the tower itself being visible from the surrounding country', which would disappoint the old admiral.

The old admiral? This is, alas, probably apocryphal, but it remains one of the finest folly anecdotes and as such deserves repetition here. At the planning meeting, a furious old salt bellowed that it would totally destroy the view from his house. When counsel for Lord Berners pointed out that the proposed tower could only possibly be seen from Admiral Clifton-Brown's house with a telescope, the sailor retorted that being an admiral, he only ever looked at the view through a telescope. The problem with the story in these days of easy internet access is that the name Vice-Admiral Francis Clifton Brown, CB, CMG, DL, JP (1874–1963) only ever occurs in relation to this tale, with nary a mention of his undoubtedly meritorious and devoted naval service. A long life of loyal service, remembered only for one retort at a planning meeting. Berners' application was refused on the grounds that it was 'likely to cause an eyesore on a noted landmark'.

Berners went over the council's heads to the Minister of Health, and won. He was overjoyed. The tower was inaugurated with a grand firework party held on, suitably, 5 November 1935, attended by Lord Weymouth, Rosamund Lehmann, and many other celebrities of the time. The following year Berners painted it for a Shell advertisement –

TO VISIT BRITAIN'S LANDMARKS
YOU CAN BE SURE OF SHELL

– just as he intended it to look: invisible, but for the belvedere poking above the trees (Fig 4.17). The Tatler commented 'On a clear day six counties can be

TO VISIT BRITAIN'S LANDMARKS

FARINGDON FOLLY   LORD BERNERS

YOU CAN BE SURE OF SHELL

Fig 4.17

Shell advertising poster painted
by Lord Berners, 1936. [Courtesy
of the Motoring Picture Library at
the National Motor Museum. Shell
marks reproduced by permission
of Shell Brands International AG.]

seen from the top of this new Berkshire monument. What exactly Lord Berners intends to use it for is not reported'. 'The great point of it all,' he responded enthusiastically, 'is that it will be completely pointless'.

The tower did not satisfy his craving for the bizarre and surreal. In 1936 he was taking out advertisements offering (fictional) rhinos for sale:

GIVE RHINOCERI THIS CHRISTMAS!

Maybe your wife is lonely ... Perhaps your children are pining for companionship ... What about giving a little rhinoceros this Christmas? Lord Berners advertises to-day that he has one for sale. It is African bred, two months old, as big as a small Shetland pony, answers to the name of Mary, and is tame, companionable and housetrained. Lord Berners also advertised two elephants, but you cannot acquire these for Junior. They have been disposed of.

The House in the Clouds

Twelve years earlier a very different folly tower had been constructed on the Suffolk coast. 'When I was quite a little boy I was a dreamy, imaginative creature, but I got a good deal of this modified by public school life at Rugby,

Fig 4.18
The House in the Clouds. Best
name for a water tank ever.
[© David Ellson/fotoLibra]

where I was much more proud of being in the School Fifteen than in the sixth form. And a good thing too', said Glencairn Stuart Ogilvie, a barrister and would-be thespian and dramatist. He managed to get his play *Hypatia*, starring the renowned Herbert Beerbohm Tree, with music by Hubert Parry ('Jerusalem', 'Dear Lord and Father of Mankind') and with sets by Alma Tadema, the most famous artist of the day, put on in the West End, where it ran for some months until it was succeeded by *A Woman of No Importance*, by Oscar Wilde. Today *A Woman of No Importance* is a staple of AmDram societies; we don't believe *Hypatia* has ever been revived. A contemporary review reads 'All theatre goers feel it incumbent upon them to see "Hypatia" at the Haymarket Theatre …

Excepting for its magnificent and costly mounting, "Hypatia" would certainly be a dull affair.'

If nothing more, it showed that G Stuart Ogilvie was a very well-connected as well as a rich young man. He never lost his love for the dramatic, and 20 years later when he decided to build a holiday village on family land at Thorpeness in Suffolk, he was distressed by the utilitarian functionalism of a water tower that needed to be erected just by a picturesque white clapboarded windmill. So his architect F Forbes Glennie hid the tank inside a conventional suburban house and perched it 60 feet in the air on a black clapboarded stalk. Planning permission wasn't an issue because it was a functional and necessary building – put a cottage on top if you like; it doesn't concern us. But seeing a cottage floating among the treetops is an unnerving experience even today. Ogilvie christened it 'The Gazebo' and had no difficulty finding tenants: a Mr and Mrs Malcolm Mason moved in, and Mrs Mason loved it. She wrote poems for children, and one, inspired by the house, was called 'The House in the Clouds':

> The fairies really own this house – or so the children say –
> In fact, they all of them moved in upon the self-same day ...

When she recited this to Ogilvie one evening he was enchanted, and exclaimed 'The name must be changed to **The House in the Clouds** – and you are my Lady of the Stairs and Starlight!' How she reacted is not recorded, but it did not deter her from her one and only publication, a book of verses titled *The House in the Clouds*, published by J. Saville & Co in 1928. Mains water has arrived, the water tank has been removed and The House in the Clouds is now an unusual holiday let (Fig 4.18).

Gazetteer

County/Authority	Location	Folly
Bristol and Avon	Bristol	Cabot Tower
		Goldney's Tower
		Snuff Tower
	Chewton Keynsham	Wolery
	Compton Greenfield	Hollywood Park Tower
	Cromhall	Priest Wood Tower
	Dodington	Dodington Tower
	Hambrook	Gerizim
	Hawkesbury	Somerset Monument
	Kelston	Tower House
	Lansdown	Beckford's Tower
		Blaine's Folly
	Stoke Gifford	Tower
	Weston-super-Mare	The Tower
	Worle	Worle Observatory
Berkshire	Ashampstead	Blorenge Tower
	Remenham	Remenham Spire
	Sulham	Sulham Tower
Buckinghamshire	Chalfont St Giles	Cook Memorial
	Filgrave	Coronation Clock Tower
	Hughenden	Hughenden Pillar
	Milton Keynes	Clock Tower
		Pagoda
	Stoke Poges	Column
	Stowe	Rostral Column
Cambridgeshire	Norman Cross	Column
Cheshire	Bollington	Clayton's Chimney
	Disley	Woodbank Garden Tower
	Heswall	Barnston Towers
	Knutsford	Gaskell Memorial Tower
	Lyme Park	The Lantern
	Rainow	Rainow Tower
	Sandiway	Round Tower
	Tatton Park	Sheep-Stealers' Tower
	Tabley Inferior	Tabley Tower
	West Kirby	Mariners Column
		Tell's Tower
Cornwall	Botus Fleming	Moditonham Dovecote
	Bude	Tower of the Winds
	Castle Gate	Roger's Tower
	Cotehele	Cotehele Tower
	Fowey	Fowey Hall Folly
	Hessenford	Bake Farm Tower
	Liskeard	Treworgey Clock Tower
	Mawgan in Meneage	Trelowarren Turret
	Penzance	Legrice's Folly

County/Authority	Location	Folly
	Portquin	Doyden Point Tower
	Redruth	Bassett Monument
	St Michael Caerhays	Caerhays Castle Folly
	Trelissick	Trelissick Tower
	Truro	Lander Column
Cumbria	Allithwaite	Kirkhead Tower
	Ambleside	The Tower of Beauty and Friendship
	Appleby	Brampton Tower
	Brough	Fox Tower
	Brougham	Countess's Pillar
	Broughton East	Longlands Tower
	Castle Carrock	Tarn Lodge Belvedere
	Conishead	Priory Tower
	Finsthwaite	Pennington Tower / Finsthwaite Spire
	Greystoke	Spire House
	Kirklinton	Privy Dovecote
	Little Orton	Tempest Tower / Drumburgh House Tower
	Milnthorpe	St Anthony's Tower
	Muncaster	Henry VI Monument
	Penrith	Penrith Beacon / Clock Tower
	Shap Wells	Britannia Pillar
	Stanwix	Stanwix Towers / Toppin Castle
	Ulverston	The Hoad
	Whitehaven	The Candlestick
	Wigton	Highmoor House Tower
	Wray	John Longmire's Folly
Derbyshire	Chatsworth	Hunting Tower
	Codnor	Jessop Memorial
	Crich	Crich Stand
	Hopton	Gell's Tower
	Matlock	Victoria Tower / Millennium Tower
	Osmaston	Chimney
	Stanton Moor	Reform Tower
Devon	Bideford	Wooda Belvedere
	Blackborough	Garnsey's Tower
	Braunton	Mortimer's Folly
	Chagford	Rushford Tower
	Chudleigh	Pitt House Tower
	Colaton Raleigh	China Tower
	Devonport	Foulston's Follies
	Dunchideock	Haldon Belvedere

County/Authority	Location	Folly
	Exeter	Tower
	Hartland	Hartland Belvedere
	Hatherleigh	Pearce Belvedere
	Ilfracombe	Hillsborough Belvedere
	Kingswear	Kingswear Daymark
	Lewtrenchard	Lee Tower
	Lympstone	Mrs Peter's Clock
	Lynmouth	Rhenish Tower
	Lynton	Duty Point Tower
	Offwell	Bishop Copleston's Tower
	Paignton	Little Oldway Tower
	Plymouth	Derriford Tower Leigham Tower Triangular Folly
	Plympton	Two Towers
	Powderham	Powderham Belvedere
	Tawstock	Tawstock Tower
	Teignmouth	Teignmouth Sham Lighthouse
	Water	Tower at Water
	Winkleigh	Court Castle Belvedere
Dorset	Bournemouth	Upper Gardens Water Tower Tuckton Tower
	Durweston	Tower
	Horton	Sturt's Folly
	Kimmeridge Bay	Clavel Tower
	Lillington	Water Tower
	Lulworth Castle	Clare Towers
	Lyme Regis	Observatory Tower
	Melbury Sampford	Prospect Tower
	Morden	Charborough Park Tower
	Moreton	Pillar
	Portesham	Hardy Monument
	Wimborne St Giles	Philosopher's Tower
Durham	Cleadon (Tyne and Wear)	Cleadon Chimney
	Darlington	Clocktower
	Gainford	Edleston House Column
	Hamsterley	Pinnacle
	Hawthorn	Sailor's Hall Tower
	Rowlands Gill (Tyne and Wear)	Column of British Liberty
	Westerton	Westerton Folly
	Witton Castle	Dovecote Tower
East Sussex	Brightling	Dallington Church Spire Sugar Cone
	Brighton	Pepper Pot Sassoon Mausoleum
	Eridge	Saxonbury Tower Grinhams

County/Authority	Location	Folly
	Firle	Firle Tower
	Heathfield	Gibraltar Tower
	Rye	Smuggler's Watchtower
Essex	Brightlingsea	Bateman's Folly
	Colchester	Water Tower
	Colne Engaine	Column
	Epping	Water Tower
	Halstead	Colne Road Water Tower
	Layer Marney	Tower
	Mistley	Tower
	Pentlow	Tower
Gloucestershire	Cambridge	Ryall's Lane Tower
	Fairford	Votive Column
	Gloucester	Addison's Folly
	Ham and Stone	Tower of the Winds
		Park House Tower
	Horton	Widden Hill House Tower
	North Nibley	Tyndale Monument
	Ruardean	Tower House
	Selsley	Stanley Park Column
	Staunton	Staunton Columns
	Stow-on-the-Wold	Enoch's Tower
	Tutshill	Tutshill Tower
	Woodchester	Woodchester Park Tower
Hampshire	Calshot	Luttrell's Tower
	East Tisted	Gardener's Tower
	Exbury	Exbury Tower
	Fritham	Fritham Tower
	Hambledon	Hambledon Tower
	Portchester	Nelson Monument
	Rockbourne	Eyre Coote Column
	Shawford	Bridge Inn Belvedere
	Shawford	Cromwell's Tower
	Stockbridge	Atners Tower
	Sway	Peterson's Folly
Herefordshire	Ewyas Harold	Moor Park Tower
	Hereford	Nelson Column
	Hope under Dinmore	Hampton Court Tower
	Ledbury	Hope End Minaret
	Pembridge	Stone Tower
Hertfordshire	Aldbury	Bridgewater Monument
	Benington	Tower House
	Hatfield	Vineyard Tower
	Hemel Hempstead	Charter Tower
	Little Berkhamsted	Stratton's Observatory

County/Authority	Location	Folly
	Stanstead Abbots	Water Tower
Isle of Wight	Blackgang	Salt Cellar
		Pepper Pot
	Chale	Hoy's Monument
	Ryde	Appley Tower
	Shanklin	Belvedere
Kent	Birchington	Quex Tower
		Gun Tower
	Broadstairs	Crampton Tower
	Canterbury	Dane John
	Crockham Hill	Rusholme Tower
	Doddington	Alexandra Oldfield Monument
	Dunkirk	Dawes Folly
	Farningham	The Folly
	Farthingloe	Samphire Hoe Tower
	Faversham	Belmont Tower
	Gillingham	Will Adams Clock Tower
	Hadlow	May's Folly
	Kingsgate	Hackemdown Tower
	Littlestone-on-Sea	Water Tower
	Pluckley	Madrona Tower
	Speldhurst	Saloman's Tower
	Tenterden	Tower House
	Waldershare	Waldershare Belvedere
	Westerham	Squerries Belvedere
Lancashire	Blacko	Stansfield Tower
	Blackpool	Blackpool Tower
	Capernwray	Gamekeeper's Tower
	Clitheroe	Clitheroe Turret
	Dalton	Ashurst's Beacon
	Darwen	Jubilee Tower
		India Mills Chimney
	Hare Appletree Fell	Jubilee Tower
	Hoghton	Brindle Folly
	Rivington	Rivington Pike
	Silverdale	Lindeth Tower
Leicestershire	Market Bosworth	Bosworth Park Belvedere
Lincolnshire	Aswarby	Column
	Belton	Bellmount Tower
	Boultham	Hartsholme Hall Column
	Caistor	Pelham's Pillar
	Dunston	Dunston Pillar
	Grimsby	Dock Tower
	Holbeach	Black Knight's Tower
	Lincoln	Merryweather's Observatory
	Louth	Vicarage Spire

County/Authority	Location	Folly
	Saltfleetby St Peter	Saltfleetby Folly
	Somerby	Somerby Hall Pillar
Liverpool and Manchester	Clifton (Greater Manchester)	Fletcher's Folly
	Hartshead (Greater Manchester)	Hartshead Pike Tower
	Ince Blundell (Merseyside)	Column
	Knowsley (Merseyside)	White Man's Tower
	Liverpool (Merseyside)	Victoria Tower
		Wapping Dock Hydraulic Tower
	Monton (Greater Manchester)	Austin's Lighthouse
	Ramsbottom (Greater Manchester)	Peel Tower
	Tottington (Greater Manchester)	Tower Farm
	Worsley (Greater Manchester)	Ellesmere Memorial
London	E5	Craven Tower
	E17	Markhouse Road Lighthouse
	N7	Caledonian Market Clocktower
	N17	Bruce Castle Tower
	N21	Quaker's Walk Watertower
	SE1	Oxo Tower
	SE18	Severndroog Castle
	SE19	Prospect Towers
	SE23	Tewkesbury Tower
	SE26	St Antholin's Spire
	SW7	Colcutt Tower
		Albert Memorial
	SW11	Peace Pagoda
	SW15	Barn Elms Tower
	Kew	Pagoda
Norfolk	Brampton	Oxnead Hall Folly
	Briningham	Belle Vue Tower
	Burgh St Peter	Church Tower
	Costessey	Costessey Tower
	Great Yarmouth	Nelson's Column
	Gunton Park	Gunton Tower
	Heydon Hall	Heydon Hall Tower
	Holkham Hall	Leicester Monument
	Hunstanton	Hunstanton Octagon
	Little Ellingham	Clock Tower
	Norwich	Thorpe Tower
		Bracondale Tower
	Westwick	The Obelisk
North Yorkshire	Aysgarth	Sorrell Sykes Pepperpot
		Sorrell Sykes Rocket Ship
	Azerley	Azerley Tower
	Bishopthorpe	Tower
	Castle Howard	Howard Monument
	Cottingham	Thompson's Folly

County/Authority	Location	Folly
	Dallowgill	Greygarth Monument
	Eston Nab (Cleveland)	ICI Beacon
	Harrogate	Harlow Hill Tower
	Hartforth	Tower
	Hazlewood	Hazlewood Castle Tower
	Hilston	Admiral Storr's Tower
	Hornsea	Bettison's Folly
	Hull	Wilberforce Column
	Levisham	Skelton Tower
	Masham Moor	Arnagill Tower
	Oldstead	Mount Snever Observatory
	Richmond	Culloden Tower
	Rowley	Gothic Folly
	Scarborough	Baron Albert's Tower Peaseholm Park Pagoda Tower of Jericho
	Sledmere	Tatton Sykes Memorial Eleanor Cross
	Studley Royal	The Octagon
	Sutton Moor	Lund's Tower Wainman's Pinnacle
	Tadcaster	Grimston Park Tower
	Thornton Steward	Fort Horn
	West Witton	Polly Peacham's Tower Bolton Hall Tower
Northamptonshire	Finedon	Ice Tower Exmill Cottage Wellington Tower
Northumberland	Alnwick	Brizlee Tower The Farmer's Folly, or Tenantry Column
	Bedlington	Market Cross
	Haggerston	Tower
	Lemmington	Column and Façade
	Lilburn	Hurlstone Tower
	Little Bavington	Homilton Tower
	Newcastle-upon-Tyne (Tyne and Wear)	Grey's Monument
	Otterburn	Percy Cross
	Whitton	Sharp's Folly
	Wooler	Ewart Park Tower
Nottinghamshire	Bestwood	Bestwood Pumping Station
	Bunny	Bunny Hall Belvedere
	Nottingham	Arboretum Pagoda
Oxfordshire	Blenheim	Column
	Christmas Common	Christmas Common Tower
	Faringdon	Lord Berners' Folly

County/Authority	Location	Folly
	Stanton St John	Belvedere
	Woolstone	The Tower
Shropshire	Bache	Bache Tower
	Callow Hill	Flounder's Folly
	Ellesmere	Oteley Hall Tower
	Eyton-on-Severn	Eyton Turret
	Hadnall	Waterloo Windmill
	Hawkstone	Hawkstone Obelisk
		Hawkstone White Tower
	Hope Valley	Grain Elevator Tower
	Longner	Tower
	Quatford	Watch Tower
	Selattyn	Tower
	Shrewsbury	Hill Column
		Laura's Tower
Somerset	Broomfield	Frankenstein's Folly
	Bruton	Chequers Towers
	Cheddar	Mystic Tower
	Combe Florey	Winter's Folly
	Cothelstone	Tower
	Curry Rivel	Burton Pynsent Steeple
		Ditcheat Folly
	Dulverton	Tower
	Dunster	Conygar Tower
	East Cranmore	Cranmore Tower
	Elworthy	Willett Tower
	Ilchester	The Bell Tower
	Kilmersdon	Ammerdown Column
	Montacute	Montacute Tower
	Stratton-on-the-Fosse	Clocktower
	West Camel	Parson's Steeple
	Wiveliscombe	Westminster Pinnacle
	Wrangway	Wellington Monument
	Yeovil	The Cone
		The Fish Tower
South Yorkshire	Barnsley	Locke Park Tower
	Bradfield Moors	Boot's Folly
	Hickleton	Bilham Belvedere
	Hoyland Nether	Hoyland Lowe Stand
	Penistone	Hartcliff Tower
	Rotherham	Boston Castle
	Stainborough	Argyll Monument
		Sun Monument
	Wentworth Woodhouse	Hoober Stand
		Keppel's Column
Staffordshire	Adbaston	Look-out Tower
	Alton Towers	Duck Tower

County/Authority	Location	Folly
	Biddulph	Warden's Tower
	Ilam	Necessary Tower
	Kidsgrove	Round Tower
	Sandon	Pitt Column
	Shareshill	Portobello Tower
	Tutbury	Julius's Tower
	Weston-under-Lizard	Knoll Tower
	Wombourne	Bearnett House Tower
Suffolk	Bungay	Tower
	Coddenham	Tower
	Elveden	War Memorial
	Freston	Freston Tower
	Lowestoft	Tower House
	Nacton	Orwell Towers
	Thorpeness	The House in the Clouds
		West Bar Tower
Surrey	Box Hill	The Broadwood Folly
	Caterham	Whitehill Folly
	Chaldon	Water Tower
	Chatley Heath	Semaphore Tower
	Chobham	Bell Tower
	Claremont	Vanbrugh Belvedere
	Claygate	Semaphore Tower
		Ruxley Towers
	Cobham	Foxwarren Watch Tower
	Dorking	Stedman's Folly
	East Horsley	Horsley Towers
	Esher	Wayneflete Tower
	Guildford	Semaphore Tower
		Booker's Folly
	Leith Hill	Hull's Tower
	Merstham	Tower-cum-dovecote
	Nutfield	Redwood Tower
	Sutton	Water Tower
	Virginia Water	Fort Belvedere
	Wisley	Pagoda
	Wonersh	Chinthurst Hill Tower
	Wotton	Broadmoor Tower
Warwickshire	Burton Dassett	The Beacon
	Chesterton	Windmill
	Combe Abbey	Belvedere
	Compton Wynyates	Compton Pike
	Edgbaston	Perrott's Folly
	Edge Hill	Edgehill Tower
	King's Norton	Lifford Hall Watchtower
	Stratford-upon-Avon	Clopton House Tower

County/Authority	Location	Folly
West Sussex	Arundel	Hiorne Tower
	Bognor Regis	White Tower
	Cuckfield	Knott's Tower House
	Fisherstreet	Shillinglee Deer Tower
	Hurstpierpoint	Weeke's Folly
	Lordington	Racton Tower
	Patching	Tower
	Petworth	Upperton Monument Pitshill Belvedere
	Pulborough	Toat Monument
	Steyning	Helter Skelter Water Tower
	Up Park	Vandalian Tower
	Worthing	Tarring Tower
West Yorkshire	Cringles	The Old Tower
	Halifax	Wainhouse's Tower
	Huddersfield	Victoria Tower
	Leeds	Tower Works
	Mirfield	Dumb Steeple
	Steeton	Steeton Tower
Wiltshire	Berwick St John	Ferne Park Tower
	Bowden Hill	Sandridge Tower
	Calne	Maud Heath's Column
	Devizes	Market Cross
	Lacock	Lacock Columns
	Malmesbury	Player's Tower
	Monkton Farleigh	Browne's Folly
	Newton Tony	Jubilee Column
	Savernake Forest	Ailesbury Column
	Stourhead	Alfred's Tower
	Whiteparish	Eyre's Folly, or The Pepperbox
Worcestershire	Abberley	Clock Tower
	Bredon Hill	Bell Castle, or Parson's Folly
	Broadway	Broadway Tower
	Croome d'Abitot	Panorama Tower
	Droitwich	Chateau Impney Tower
	Evesham	Leicester Tower
	Inkberrow	Inkberrow Folly
	Rous Lench	Chaffee's Tower
	Tardebigge	Water Tower
	Tenbury Wells	Pagoda Cadmore Millennium Tower Kyre Park Tower
	Upper Arley	Spite Tower

5 | Rooms with a view: gazebos and eyecatchers

Gazebos

One of the great pleasures in life is sitting in a pavement café watching the world go by. One can stare with impunity, something the English normally find hard to deal with. In Italy and other Mediterranean countries, a regular evening tradition is the *passeggiata*, where young men and women (older people too) promenade in their finery through the streets, to see and be seen. This is so un-English. To stare at people; to be stared at; it's simply rude. But the need is fundamental to human nature, even the English, and the solution soon presented itself – build a special room from which one could see without being seen. Hence the gazebo, an observation room the style and use of which precedes most of the follies in this book. The earliest English gazebos date from the 16th century and were usually placed at the corner of a garden wall overlooking a road.

But what if there isn't anything agreeable to show? Then you have to provide your own entertainment – something to catch your eye.

Let's get the vexed question of the word gazebo out of the way first. There is a very learned article doing the rounds on the web tracing its origins back to a Turkish/Oriental word. But we beg to differ, as to our minds the answer is to be found in the singular travel diaries of that plain-talker and opinionated (rightly so) John Byng, the later 5th Viscount Torrington (1743–1813). A younger son, he had no real chance of succeeding to the family fortunes or to the peerage. He did, however, strike lucky, finally becoming Viscount Torrington – only two weeks before his own demise. Byng had limited means, so he had to refrain from Grand Tours or any stays on the Continent, disguising his relative poverty by claiming to be a true British patriot who would only holiday in England and Wales. His travels were only published from the manuscripts as *The Torrington Diaries* in 1934–1938, but they prove to be a treasure-trove.

Byng made his journeys on horseback, usually accompanied by a manservant. He only had a London town house, no country seat to fall back on, and he regards the mansions he encounters from the viewpoint of whether they would do as his abode. They usually didn't. 'Wait till I get my fortune ... then you'll see something worthwhile', is his comment. He berates the nouveau riche Tong Castle in Shropshire in 1793 for making do without a library. Byng is always his own man, and quite original in intensely disliking Chatsworth. He complains, justly, of the high cost of food, drink and his stay at local inns, and blows his top when one night he is ejected from his bed and room because a guest of higher status than himself arrives. (Wait, just you wait, once I have my title ... !) But he has an educated taste and appears to have been friendly with both Capability Brown and Humphrey Repton, so he knew his stuff. The traditional dispute, leaving the Turks aside, about gazebo is as to whether it derives from gaze-above or gaze-about. Here are some of Byng's usages:

−1781, a visit to Chepstow: 'After a complete shaving, and dressing, and drinking two pint basins of tea, I walk'd thro' the town to a stone gazeabout, half a mile distant; whence is an immense view, down the Severn, to the sea; over the Bristol hills; and to the left, to Thornbury, Berkley Castle, &c. &c.'

−1784, Cymer Abbey: 'It is seated as all religious houses were, in shady retirement, in the calm vale; and near the purling stream; and in my opinion, they were placed better than the modern gazeabouts on the hill top, expos'd to every tempest, and distant from every comfort'.

−1787, Broadway: 'I climb'd by a very pleasant foot-path, to the hill-top where Sir John Cotterell has built the most extraordinary gaze-about house in the world, at the summit of an exceeding steep; without a tree about him, and fronting the west; − there it stands looking to Wales'. (This doesn't concern Broadway Tower, which hadn't been built yet, but according to Pevsner the Fish Inn was 'originally a summer house of Sir John Cotterell's estate. It is a curiously barbaric piece of architecture, with a rusticated Venetian window and a triglyph frieze whose metopes are simply rubble'. Pevsner also quotes Byng.)

−1790, Buckden, 'the Bishop of Lincoln's palace', 'all places of the low, shaded situation, I prefer to the modern hill-top stareabouts'.

So there we have it, the gazebo is a gaze-about. For the curious, some more examples of the word in an earlier use: William and John Halfpenny's pattern book *Rural Architecture in the Chinese Taste* (1752): 'The Elevation of a Chinese Tower or Gazebo'; and in William Wrighte's *Grotesque Architecture* (1767): 'The whole is lighted from the gazebo in the top'. And an even earlier use is recorded, by the rather obscure but interesting author Wetenhall Wilkes (1705/6−1751) in his *An Essay on the Pleasure and Advantages of Female Literature* (1740):

> Unto the painful summit of this height
> A gay Gazebo does our Steps invite.
> From this, when favour'd with a Cloudless Day,
> We fourteen Counties all around survey.

And to the matter in hand, but not without first a further quote from Byng, who in 1789 makes a scurrilous remark, which brings us to the earliest 'stare-abouts'. Staying in Leicester he is advised by the inn-keeper 'to go in the evening to Mrs − − house at Scrapthorpe, not far from this town "dere to see her mount, and her schrubberie, whiche alle de gentlemen like to inspect"' (we were unable to place this obviously ancient reference, but the English adore innuendo). They do visit the house 'where are the gardens we were advised to visit; and so we did, and went to a mount with a summer house at the top, where is a good inland view'.

They came in all sorts: look-out pavilions, belvederes and gazebos on the corners of garden walls and, as mentioned above, on top of a mount usually in the centre of the garden, and their vogue started in the formal gardens of the 16th and 17th centuries. Among the best are the corner pavilions at **Montacute House**, Somerset, *c* 1601: neat mini-houses flanking the garden wall, decked out with all that Elizabethan architecture could provide in the way of finials, fancy battlements, and the essential peek-a-boo glazing, possibly by the Somerset master mason and architect William Arnold (fl. 1595, died 1637?), described by a patron as 'an honest man, a perfectt workman, and my neere neighboure'. The house was built for the lawyer and politician Edward Phelips

Fig 5.1

Kirkby Lonsdale gazebo, For the etymology of 'gazebo', read the text. [© Dave Thompson/ fotoLibra]

Fig 5.2

A gazebo at Hidcote Manor.

[© Mel Longhurst/fotoLibra]

(*c* 1560–1614), who was one of the main people involved in the prosecution of the Gunpowder Plotters.

Coming to the 18th century, the gazebo retained its function and we have many examples of them (nowadays ten remain of what were a few dozen) on the banks of the River Lea in Ware, Hertfordshire. One is tempted to compare them to the Dutch gazebos (or *koepels*) along the River Vecht, but these were in part more complex and extensive buildings. A variation on the theme can be found in Ampthill, Bedfordshire, where in Dunstable Street stands a quaint two-storey brick gazebo on an elongated triangular groundplan, which appears not to have been by choice (triangularity being one of those favourite folly forms of expression), but because of the existing building plot.

The summerhouse, like the grotto, is where women sometimes have their say, often to the dismay of their menfolk. Richard Chamberlaine, second husband to the widow of Thomas Windham of Felbrigg, Norfolk, in 1671 wrote to his stepson William: 'Sir I confess your Mother hath weedled mee into the vanity besides the charge of a needless sumer howse, which (as you well Guess) is more for Quietness sake and peace at home than any Content I can promise myselfe therein, when done'.

Eyecatchers

Eyecatchers were, more so than gazebos, more often wildly diverse affairs, although your common-or-garden 18th-century eyecatcher would consist of a roughstone wall, openings in the wall, Gothick arches and/or finials: something to make an intriguing silhouette against the sky. There is a glut of them, and they are all immensely satisfying to the visitor whose eye they try to catch.

To start with the largest of them all, also the most untypical: **Riber Castle** (Fig 5.3) on Riber Hill, between Matlock and Matlock Bath, Derbyshire. Built for John Smedley (1803–1874) it was called Smedley's Folly because it was well-nigh impossible to get a good water supply going to the top of the hill, and that from the man who owned the now huge hydrotherapy centre in Matlock (1853 and later) and wrote the hugely successful, self-published *Practical Hydropathy* (umpteenth edition 1869), a hefty and entertaining tome. Smedley was one of Matlock's most influential industrialists, involved in cloth manufacture and arguably the first to produce 'long Johns'. His hydro fuelled an already buoyant tourism to the picturesque town. To his workers he was benevolent: working conditions were better than in most mills, and he was a firm believer in Fearn's Family Pills, which were handed out for every ailment, and he provided sickness

Fig 5.3
'Riber Castle possesses the rare distinction of being not only ugly, but perfectly styleless; no building, surely, was ever so lacking in grace'. [© Eric Dodds/fotoLibra]

benefits whenever the medicine failed. As an enthusiastic Free Methodist, he built six chapels.

Apparently inspired by views of the Rhine and of Switzerland, he established Riber Castle on top of the eponymous hill. In 1863 the simulacrum lodge to the house was built and the rest, the castle itself, took till 1868. Its architect is sadly unknown, but the result looks amateurish – possibly designed by Smedley himself. The point of the building is that it is not so much a belvedere, poised as it is on the crag of the hill, but an eyecatcher: it dominates the town, usurping the skyline for miles around. Smedley's original plan had been to build a 70m tower on the hilltop, but he abandoned the idea when he discovered that the telescopes he intended to order wouldn't fit the tower. Smedley was so smitten by his eyecatcher-castle, that he regularly had himself driven into the valley in order to look back upon his illuminated castle.

It is a box of a place, soot-blackened, four towers on the corners of the box, and smaller turrets in between. The castellation is intended purely for the silhouette, and the windows in the three-storey towers are alternately elongated squares or arched or round. The architectural historian John Summerson (1904–1992) went to school there (one of its many later uses – nowadays it is divided into flats), and gave his remembrances in the essay collection *The Unromantic Castle* (1990):

Riber possesses the rare distinction of being not only ugly, but perfectly styleless; no building, surely, was ever so lacking in grace. Hard and hideous in profile, every formal relation a disharmony, every room and every corridor proclaiming that no critical mind had foreseen or determined its dimensions. I cannot recall one ornament, one pleasing arrangement in the entire building. Everything was big and comfortless.

Fig 5.4
Rousham Eyecatcher, a feral
arch alone in the countryside.
[© Jonathan Holt]

Pevsner's *The Buildings of England: Derbyshire* is uncharacteristically sympathetic, even calling it an 'ideal eyecatcher'.

The classic, template eyecatcher is perhaps the one at **Rousham**, Oxfordshire, and if not, it is possibly the earliest anyway, *c* 1740–41. Rousham (Fig 5.4) in its present state was of course the creation of that versatile builder and decorator William Kent (*c* 1685–1748) for his friend General James Dormer (1679–1741). At first Dormer doesn't come across as a man interested in landscape gardens or eyecatchers, being a career soldier, fighting at Blenheim, in Spain, and battling the Jacobites at Preston in 1715. But he was a member of the famous Whig Kit-Kat Club (Walpole: 'generally mentioned as a set of wits, in reality the patriots that saved Britain') and was quite conversant with The Arts, leaving a substantial and fine library that was only dispersed in the 1760s. These gardens had a purpose beyond mere pleasure. They were created for contemplation, as political and philosophical statements. The programme of Rousham's park appears to hover between the symbolism of death and of eroticism, and it is the only one of Kent's gardens that has come down to us in anything like its original scheme.

On top of a hill, across from the park and across the River Cherwell, which provides a natural boundary, stands a large, tripartite arch, buttressed, with blind sidewings as if on second thoughts the architect considered five archways too wasteful. The top is made of rubble, topped by a series of pinnacles. The effect is wholly Gothick, but the building is no such thing – if anything it is faintly vernacular Norman or even vernacular classical. It was intended as a triumphal arch to celebrate the general's victories, but that motive must have been an alibi for providing this very effective eyecatcher: it draws the eye and completes a rural picture that had been started some two years before by adding to the existing low-slung mill-house along the river. The old house received a rough stone front extension in the form of a kind of vestibule with flying buttresses that deliberately make a silhouette, doors only to the side, but the façade itself showing a pretty quatrefoil window above a larger, rectangular one ending in a weak ogee shape. Like the eyecatcher, there are pinnacles. The result: The Temple of the Mill. The whole creates a picturesque ensemble of remnants of a sham ancient past. A contemporary engraving shows the Temple of the Mill with the eyecatcher behind and to the right in a very similar style, reflecting the architecture of the temple, but which does not appear to have been implemented. Miles Hadfield in his *History of British Gardening* was adamant that the garden buildings at Rousham should not be regarded as follies – they were designed as memorials, or symbols. But Rousham's eyecatcher arch is close as one can come to a classic definition of a folly.

Wroxton Abbey near Banbury is nearby in Oxfordshire, and here we have another splendid eyecatcher. Wroxton is Sanderson Miller territory, whose usual haunts were Warwickshire and Oxfordshire. After a campaign of decking out the park with Chinese buildings in the early 1740s, Sanderson Miller (1716–1780), a gentleman architect, had a good try at both the house and Wroxton church, as well as supplying a few garden buildings in the late 1740s. But the authorship of the **Drayton Arch**, our eyecatcher, is disputed (Fig 5.5). Like the Gothic dovecote, it may have been designed by Miller, and stylistically we tend to date it around 1750, but nothing is sure, and of late another date for it has been suggested, as well as another architect. But there it stands, on the edge of a field with the woods as backdrop. This is rudimentary architecture, two shapes like, *excusez le mot*, cardboard toilet rolls standing beside a stepped arch. The rough stone makes this primarily a shape, much less than it is proper architecture. Such a building is akin to the rough-and-ready follies at Barwick Park, but there is a near facsimile of this eyecatcher: The Spectacles near Boughton, Northamptonshire. They are more slender, have some ruined bits on the sides, and are battlemented, which the Drayton Arch is not. Otherwise – the same.

Fig 5.5

The Drayton Arch at Wroxton.

[© Mike Cousins]

The Drayton Arch appears on a sketch of 1781 by the Swiss artist Samuel Hieronymus Grimm (1733–1794), so we have a date *post quem*. According to Michael Cousins, the architect may have been one of the family of nearby builders and architects Hiorne or Hiornes, William (*c* 1712–1776) or his son Francis (1744–1789), both very conversant with the Gothic vocabulary, and Francis, of course, responsible for the splendid Hiorne's Tower at Arundel. Cousins found account entries for building 'The Gateway' in 1771 by a 'Hiorns'. But this may have been a different gate, and as there appears to be no drive, one wonders if this is not an altogether different building that has long since disappeared.

A splendid ruin juts out from the hillside above Doncaster, three storeys, roofless, floorless, collapsed walls, very decayed and extremely dangerous. One glance reveals what a fine and elegant building it once was. It was built for the fine prospect, which encompassed three cathedrals and over 70 parish churches. The prospect remains, and all that we have of **Bilham Belvedere** are its remains (Fig 5.6). It is a very stylish structure, built in 1800 for William Hewett of Bilham Hall, and designed by local architect John Rawstorne (1761–1832). Rawstorne was born in Doncaster, worked in James Wyatt's office, and set up as an architect in Birmingham.

RAWSTORNE
ARCHITECT
BIRMINGHAM
ESTATES
SURVEYED
Pleasure Grounds
Laid Out
&c.

Fig 5.6
Bilham Belvedere had wonderful prospects, except for the patron and the architect. [© Ray Blyth/ fabulousfollies.net]

reads his fashionable business card. He moved back to Doncaster where he won the commission from Hewett to build the Belvedere – and then everything went terribly wrong. Hewett was a country gentleman who shortly afterwards lost his fortune through horse-racing, while Rawstorne also fell upon hard times; his business collapsed and by 1821 he was reduced to beggary. By 1815 Hewett's neighbours the Thelussons had bought Bilham Hall, and demolished it when they built Brodsworth Hall in the 1860s. The Hewett line survived their financial embarrassment; son William became physician to King William IV, and his son,

Fig 5.7
Belchamp Walter Eyecatcher.
Does exactly what it says on the
tin. [© Derek Metson/fotoLibra]

also William, won the Victoria Cross in the Crimea, became a Vice-Admiral and was knighted. After many years of neglect Bilham Belvedere was consolidated in the 1990s on a 'conserve as found' basis, and its future seems slightly more secure.

Belchamp Walter near Sudbury, Essex, completes a triumvirate with similarly derived local place names – Belchamp Otten and Belchamp St Paul – suggesting a rurality and a cosiness that is the stock-in-trade in the more sedate crime series. Some follies are notoriously hard to date, especially when they use vernacular materials – rockwork, flint or any such roughstone – and when they consist more of shapes than style. Such is the difficulty with the eyecatcher at **Belchamp Walter Hall** (Fig 5.7), a rather small but perfectly formed edifice, a jumble of openings, cruciform arrow slits and Gothic arches, made of rubble lined with brick, it was visible from the hall itself (now the view is overgrown), and appeared to date from around 1800. But there are reasons for re-evaluating the possible period of building when one takes a look at the delightful pavilions on each end of a terrace nearer to the house. One of these is now in ruins, but the other one still stands: a square rubble-built turret with large flints, the whole some 5 or 6m high, large rough blocks of stone marking the outlines, and the top sham-ruined. The plump Gothic doorway has the motto 'FORTUNA MEA IN BELLO CAMPO' spelled out in the arch. A wordplay on Belchamp, it means something like 'My fortune lies in a beautiful/fair field', but also (as with the motto of the Lygon family, Earls Beauchamp) 'My fortune lies in the field of battle'. The pavilions appear to have been built in the 1860s or 1870s by the then owner, the Revd John Mayne St Clare Raymond (1814–1893), whose family had owned the place for at least 250 years.

The gazebo-cum-eyecatcher (two for the price of one) aka The Observatory, on **Ratcheugh Crag** (Fig 5.8) near Alnwick Castle, Northumberland, looks like something somewhere somehow has gone awfully wrong, without anyone knowing exactly what. It has a delightfully unfinished look, and not only because it is a sham façade. The original plan for the structure was never executed in full

Fig 5.8
The Ratcheugh Observatory. To see and be seen. [© Jeff Veevers/ fotoLibra]

– the existing building represents only a tiny part of the design, and later on an extra bit was added, making the whole look even more incongruous.

Of course, the Observatory belongs to the ensemble of buildings at Alnwick, the stupendous abode of Hugh Smithson, later Hugh Percy, 1st Duke of Northumberland (1715–1786), who owed much of his position and fortune to his wife Elizabeth Seymour (1716–1776). Horace Walpole did not like the man, nor his wife, whom he accused of being spendthrift and a snob, appearing at the theatre with a significantly larger retinue than the queen, and egging her husband on to larger and larger building projects: 'They live by the etiquette of the old peerage, have Swiss porters, the Countess has her piper – in short they will soon have no estate' (by that time, 1752, they were involved in building projects at Northumberland House, Syon, Stanstead, Alnwick and Wentworth Castle). The Duke nevertheless was said by the Frenchman Louis Dutens (1730–1812) in his *Memoirs of a Traveler, Now in Retirement* of 1806, to have had great talents and more knowledge than is generally found among the nobility '[but] although his expenditure was unexampled in his time, he was not generous, but passed for being so owing to his judicious manner of bestowing favours'. The duke was not only a patron to Dutens, but also to better known names like Canaletto, Robert Adam and Thomas Chippendale.

The Observatory appears to have been built around or before 1784, when the great neo-classical architect Robert Adam (1728–1792) produced a design that elaborated on the by then existing Observatory, into a project for an enormous screen wall with symmetrical towers and pavilions, incorporating the gazebo as '[a]lready executed by the Duke of Northumberland'. John Bell (?–1784), a builder and architect from Durham, working on Alnwick Castle in the 1760s, is credited with the actual implementation of Adam's design so far. The site for the eyecatcher had been chosen by Duchess Betty, as she was called, together with sundry other locations for improvement on the estate. After her death the duke piously noted all her favourite places and had them marked by buildings or landscaped improvements. This was a spot where they used to indulge in a picnic, as the views all round, inland and towards Alnwick as well as the coast, are spectacular. It interacts well with the castle, for it is from the bay window of the dining room that one has the best view of Ratcheugh and the Observatory. The eyecatcher strides along the crest of the hill. Windows all around the gazebo, poised above the long screen wall of pointed arches and battlements earn it the name of Observatory, and the single square room flooded with light from north, south, east and west has views beyond even the expanse of the Percy estates. The southern half-round tower and cottage were added later by the notoriously bad-tempered Hugh Percy, 2nd Duke of Northumberland (1742–1817).

Corsham Court, just plain Corsham House around 1800, had had makeovers around that time by some of the great names in architecture and landscaping: John Nash, Capability Brown and Humphrey Repton among them. Everything was paid for by the great wealth of the Methuen family, who, though of ancient descent, earned their keep as clothiers, a 17th-century forefather being described as 'the greatest cloathier of his day'.

Paul Cobb Methuen (1752–1816), after attending University College, Oxford, immediately set off on a three-year Grand Tour to France and Italy in 1769–1772, and came home to a house that had been altered in the 1760s by Capability Brown, who had also laid out the park with its extensive lake. The house had been filled to the rafters with a collection of continental 16th- and 17th-century pictures. There is a Van Dyck-influenced portrait by Gainsborough, possibly painted after Methuen's marriage in 1775, that shows him as a rather cocky young man, dressed in the finery expected of someone connected to the clothes trade. He seems to have bided his time, for as soon as his father Paul Methuen (1723–1795) died, the son employed Humphrey Repton (1752–1818) to improve the park, and took on John Nash (1752–1835) to gothicise and enlarge the house (the still existing Gothick dairy, adjoined to the house, is a must-see). Paul Cobb Methuen had no taste for politics: succeeding his father as an MP for the rotten borough of Great Bedwyn from 1781 to 1784, he seems to have rarely attended, never spoke and only voted sparingly in Parliament. Notes were made of him by colleagues: 'Is very independent ... A country gentleman'. In short, a man focused on his county (Methuen was High Sheriff for Wiltshire

Fig 5.9
At Corsham Court is England's answer to Ireland's The Jealous Wall. [© Paul Frankland/fotoLibra]

1780–1781), his village, his estate. He also enjoyed composing a poem or two, self-publishing in 1810 *An Epistle from Yarico to Incle, with Other Poems*, rather light verse, somewhat in the vein of Samuel Rogers, the banker poet (1763–1855). The title poem is set in Mexico; for the *couleur locale* Methuen had assiduously taken notes from William Bartram's *Travels* of 1791. His short poem 'Memory and Oblivion' faintly echoes Rogers' celebrated and much longer 'The Pleasures of Memory' (1792). Methuen also paid the Wiltshire author and antiquarian John Britton (1771–1857) for *A Historical Account of Corsham House, in Wiltshire; The Seat of Paul Cobb Methuen, Esq. With a Catalogue of His Celebrated Collection of Pictures* (1806).

So this is the man who had Nash build, around 1797–1798, a rather overwhelming – 60ft high and 100ft long – **sham ruin** (Fig 5.9), a rubble crinkle-crankle wall. It was devised (story 1) in order to screen the four-storey Ethelred House, built around the middle of the 18th century, from view – likely, as Ethelred House's bulk and height were quite obtrusive, or (story 2) to screen the nearby existing stables from view – apparently Methuen wanted to have them down, but Nash demurred and picturesqued them instead. We favour the first, as the top storey of Ethelred House, built by Thomas Broadwood, overlooked Corsham Court and local folk memories describe Methuen as being incandescent with rage.

The sham ruin has an ecclesiastical air. Solidly, massively and very carefully built, with Gothic chimneys perched on the top seemingly as afterthoughts, it is large enough to house small rooms at the base, which probably came in handy as hen houses. Details such as the Gothick window tracery are far more prominent on the north side of the wall, showing it was intended to be seen from the house. Connoisseurs will have their work cut out to sort the medieval spolia (bits from the Methuen's Bradford-on-Avon home The Priory, and/or from Stanley Abbey near Chippenham) and also the quite recent spoils from Capability Brown's Bath House of 1761–1763 in the park, which was altered by Nash and his assistant, Humphrey's son, John Adey Repton (1775–1860) in the 1790s. Parts may have come from various restorations of Corsham Church, and Barbara Jones also noted a sham coat of arms dated 1874. We haven't been able to locate that particular detail.

Gazetteer

Gazebos, belvederes and seats

County/Authority	Location	Folly
Bristol and Avon	Pill	Gazebo
Buckinghamshire	Stoke Poges	Alcove
	Stowe	Pebble Alcove
	Weston Underwood	Cowper's Alcove
Cheshire	Wirral	Ness Seat Wood Park Gazebo
Cornwall	Antony	Clairvoie
	Germoe	St Germoe's Chair
	Mount Edgecumbe	Shell Seat
	Newquay	Huer's House
	Portreath	Gazebo and Summerhouse
Cumbria	Beetham	Ashton House Gazebo
	Brampton	Howard Memorial Shelter
	Hampsfield Fell	The Hospice
	Kirkby Lonsdale	Gazebo
	Newbiggin	Thompson's Folly
	Newby East	Gazebos
Derbyshire	Brampton	Brampton Manor Gazebo
Devon	Clovelly	The Cabin Angels' Wings Gallantry Bower
	Crediton	Shobrooke Seat
Dorset	Castlebridge	Summerhouse
	Piddletrenthide	Gazebo
	Sherborne Castle	Pope's Seat
Durham	Witton Castle	Gazebo
East Sussex	Rye	Smuggler's Watchtower
Essex	Colchester	Minories Summerhouse
	Great Dunmow	Summerhouse
	Saffron Walden	Summerhouse
Gloucestershire	Barnsley	Barnsley Park Alcove
	Chalford	Gazebo
Hampshire	Hawley	Gazebo
	Mottisfont	Fishing Hut
Isle of Wight	Bonchurch	Smuggler's Haven
	East Cowes	Bric-à-Brac
	Kingston	Gazebo
Kent	Tenterden	Gazebos
	Tunbridge Wells	Mount Ephraim Gazebo
Lancashire	Churchtown	Meols Hall Gazebos
	Lee	Lower Lee Gazebo
	Over Kellet	Gothic Convenience
	Turton	Railway Bridge Gazebo
Leicestershire	Swithland	Gazebos

County/Authority	Location	Folly
Lincolnshire	Londonthorpe	Bus Shelter
	Marston	Marston Hall Gazebo
London	E11	Gazebo
	Twickenham	Radnor Gardens Gazebo
Norfolk	Blickling Hall	Blickling Grandstand
	Foulsham	Ivy House Gazebo
	Norwich	Thorpe Lodge Gazebo Colney Hall Pulhamite Conservatory
North Yorkshire	Great Ayton	Roseberry Topping Folly
	Ripon	Gazebos
	Saltburn-by-the-Sea (NY)	Albert Memorial
	Studley Royal	Surprise View Roman Cell
Northamptonshire	Easton Neston	The Gazebo
Northumberland	Alnwick	Ratcheugh Observatory, or The Gazebo
	Belford Hall	Gazebo
	Seaton Delaval (Tyne and Wear)	Starlight Castle
Nottinghamshire	Nuthall	Nuthall Temple
Shropshire	Bishop's Castle	Gazebo
	Bridgnorth	Governor's House Gazebo
	Longden	Longden Gazebo
	Orleton	Orleton Hall Gazebo
Somerset	Brympton	The Alcove
	Cothelstone	Seat
South Yorkshire	Hickelton	Bilham Belvedere
	Wentworth Woodhouse	Bean Seat
Staffordshire	Adbaston	Batchacre Porch
	Consall	Full Moon Seat
	Sandon	Perceval Shrine
Suffolk	Great Saxham	Umbrello
Surrey	Chertsey	Gazebo
	Esher	Traveller's Rest
	Godalming	The Thunder House
Warwickshire	Coventry	Cemetery Gazebo
West Sussex	Goodwood	Carne's Seat
West Yorkshire	Hooton Pagnell	Bilham Belvedere
	Lepton	Black Dick's Temple
	Methley	Clumpcliffe Gazebo
Wiltshire	Castle combe	Bell-Turret Arbour
Worcestershire	Croome d'Abitot	Corinthian Seat

Eyecatchers, colonnades and screens

County/Authority	Location	Folly
Bristol and Avon	Hunstrete	Unfinished Mansion
	Kingsweston	The Loggia
	Newton St Loe	Eyecatcher
	Orchardleight	Boathouse Temple
	Westbury-on-Trym	Eyecatcher
Berkshire	Basildon	Eyecatcher
Buckinghamshire	Aylesbury	Green End House Eyecatcher
	Buckingham	Buckingham Gaol
	Hedsor	Lord Boston's Folly
	North Crawley	Eyecatcher
	Thornton	Eyecatcher
Cheshire	Combermere	Brankelow Folly
	Disley	Wybersley Hall Eyecatcher
	Harthill	Mickerdale Cottage
Cornwall	Botus Fleming	Moditonham Dovecote
Cumbria	Aglionby	Whooff House Folly
	Carlisle	Bunkershill Windows
	Kirklinton	Eyecatcher Columns
	Levens	Levens Hall Eyecatcher Arch
	Sebergham	Fletcher Eyecatcher
Derbyshire	Two Dales	Sydnope Stand
Dorset	Milton Abbas	Milton Abbas Eyecatcher
Durham	Staindrop	Raby Castle Folly
	Whitburn (Tyne and Wear)	Barne's Folly
Essex	Belchamp Walter	Eyecatcher
	Thorndon Hall	Hatch Farm
Gloucestershire	Amberley	Amberley Eyecatcher
Hampshire	Petersfield	Grange Farm Eyecatcher
	Winchester	Abbey House Temple Screen
Hertfordshire	Ayot St Lawrence	Eyecatcher Church
	Stanstead Abbots	Briggens Eyecatcher
Kent	Newington	Temple Cottage Eyecatcher
Lancashire	Elswick	Stable Screen
	Sawley	Eyecatcher Arch
	Whitewell	Browsholme Spire Farm
Lincolnshire	Fillingham	Manor House Eyecatcher
	Louth	Broadbank Folly
	Sleaford	Westgate Walling
	Tealby	Castle Farm
Liverpool and Manchester	Bury (Greater Manchester)	Nabb's Castle
	Manchester (Greater Manchester)	Heaton Park Screen
	Nuttall (Greater Manchester)	Gothic Screen
London	W2	Leinster Gardens Façades
	Barking	Barking Town Square Screen

County/Authority	Location	Folly
	Beckenham	Chinese Garage
North Yorkshire	Bishopthorpe	Church Façade
	Hartforth	Blackhill Folly
	Hedon	James Iveson's Ecclesiastical Collection
	Howsham	Gothic Mill
	North Cave (East Riding)	Castle Farm
	Pateley Bridge	Yorke's Folly
	Sledmere	Castle Farm
Northamptonshire	Brockhall	Ivy House Eyecatcher
Northumberland	Alnwick	Clayport Eyecatchers
	Belsay Hall	Bantam Folly
	Bolton	Jenny's Lantern Crawley Tower Shepherd's Law
	Eglingham	Cockhall Folly
	Lemmington	Column and Façade
	Little Bavington	Homilton Tower
	Simonburn	Eyecatcher Castle
	Swarland	Swarland Old Hall Eyecatcher
Nottinghamshire	Linby	Castle Mill
	Wiseton	White Swann Inn
Oxfordshire	Charlbury	Lodge Farm
	Coleshill	Strattenborough Castle
	Rousham	Rousham Eyecatcher Temple of the Mill
	Whitchurch	The Baulk
	Wroxton	Eyecatcher
Shropshire	Atcham	Attingham Eyecatchers
	Hodnet	Ruinated Eyecatcher Portico
	Shrewsbury	Sundorne Castle Screen
Somerset	Bruton	Chequers Tower
	Burrow Bridge	Burrow Mump Church
	Knowle	Knowle Hall Eyecatcher
	West Camel	Parson's Steeple
	Wiveliscombe	Westminster Pinnacle
South Yorkshire	Barnsley	Cannon Hall
	Bradfield	Castellated Farmhouse
	Brodsworth	Brodsworth Eyecatcher
Staffordshire	Brewood	Speedwell Castle
	Codsall Wood	Chillington Eyecatchers
	Enville	Museum
	Forton	Sutton Monument
	Sandon	Lord Harrowby's Folly
	Somerford	Eyecatcher
	Trentham	Sutherland Monument
Suffolk	Barton Mills	Sham Façade

County/Authority	Location	Folly
	Wattisham	The Castle
Surrey	Gatton	Gatton Town Hall
	Reigate	The Inglis Folly
	Stoke d'Abernon	Wood Farm
	Virginia Water	Leptis Magna Columns
	Walton on the Hill	Folly Façade
	Wisley	Hatchford Gloriette
Warwickshire	Alcester	Oversley Castle
	Arbury	Tower Farm
West Sussex	Staplefield	Tyes Place Portico
Wiltshire	Berwick St John	Ferne Park Tower
	Corsham	Sham Castle Screen
Worcestershire	Baughton	Tower House

6 | No love affair is complete without a grotto*: grottoes, caves and tunnels

The archetypal folly may be the tower, but there is an equally powerful urge to burrow down into the earth, to dig caves and tunnels. A grotto is a decorated sham cave, and here again we encounter passion and fashion. The fashion for grottoes in England sprang from the Grand Tours that wealthy young blades carried out in the 17th century, venturing as far as torrid Italy where delightful shell-lined grottoes with tinkling water and gentle fountains soothed and calmed the overheated brow. To the present day, estate agents rejoice in houses that can boast 'water features'.

There was a snag – three, in fact. Shells from the Mediterranean, Africa and the Orient were always going to be more exotic than those from the cold North Sea. Italian sculptors were generally more humorous, imaginative and skilled than their dour northern counterparts. And, most importantly, the weather. Italy was hot. England was not. For 300 days a year the English grotto was hidden in the mist; instead of providing watery refreshment from the searing heat and sun it more often found itself providing shelter from the shearing wind and rain. There was little need for water features in the English grotto; it was damp and wet right from the start. Dr Johnson was not impressed, famously commenting 'A grotto is a very fine place – for a toad'.

As England's empire expanded from the mid-17th century to far-off coral strands, its ships returned with more exotic and spectacular shells, often used as ballast, as trading then was one-way. Unlike today, in those days we had commodities the rest of the world wanted, and we didn't particularly need anything from them. The fashion became to decorate the dank English grotto with rare and beautiful shells. The results were astonishing: the grottoes at **Pains Hill** (Fig 6.1), **Goodwood House**, **Ascot Place** and elsewhere (see a more comprehensive list below) are transcendentally lovely. The art fell out of fashion in the 19th century and the war-torn 20th century had no time or desire for shell decoration. A few dogged amateurs pursued their craft, plastering the outside of their houses with shells and in one case even encrusting a bus, now regrettably destroyed. If someone created something beautiful, rare and unusual one could usually rely on the local council to step in and demolish it, councils being the single greatest threat to our heritage. Thankfully, towards the end of the 20th century this exquisite craft was revived by such brilliant practitioners as Diana Reynell, Belinda Eade and Blott Kerr-Wilson.

These were follies of fashion. The follies of passion drove right through the grottoes and on into the hillsides and down into the ground. These were the moles, the miners, the tunnellers; blind, obsessive, driven. No decorated caves here: the tunnel was both means and end.

Grottoes

* Victor Hugo, *Les Misérables*

Scott's Grotto at Ware is transitional, both tunnel and grotto, as is to a lesser extent the mysterious grotto at **Margate** (Fig 6.2), mysterious because its

Fig 6.1
Astounding restoration work by
Diana Reynell and Roger Capps
at Pains Hill. [© Gwyn Headley/
fotoLibra]

provenance has been eliminated. It has been a commercial enterprise since its discovery by a schoolmaster in 1835, and it is in the interests of the market to attract paying customers by suggesting lore, legend, superstition and immemorial antiquity. There were claims that Margate Grotto was pre-Roman, even Phoenician, as if cruel, grand sailors from 1000BC had landed on the distant and chilly Kentish foreshore and passed a tranquil, damp summer sticking shells on tunnel walls. We have always felt the Margate Grotto has to have been connected with the nearby Kingsgate follies of Henry Fox, Lord Holland, and as shell decoration was largely a woman's preserve we have to look to his female kin – and we need look no further than his wife. Caroline Fox was the daughter of the Duke of Richmond and Lennox, and the ducal seat of Goodwood has one of the finest grotto rooms in the country, created by the Duchess Sarah in the early 1740s, with the assistance of her daughters – including the eldest, Caroline. Caroline's initials CR can be seen made in shells on the wall. She would have been in her late teens. She met Henry Fox in 1742 and married him (without her parents' consent) in 1744. Fox had a stratospheric rise in politics followed by an even more stratospheric fall when, out of a misplaced sense of loyalty, he betrayed the prime minister, becoming the most reviled politician of his time. As Paymaster General to the Forces, Fox amassed a huge fortune, enough to cover the egregious gambling debts of his sons. In

Fig 6.2

Margate grotto was built by
Phoenicians? More likely by
Lady Holland. [© Philip Carr/
fotoLibra]

1762 Caroline was created Lady Holland, Baroness of Holland, a year before her
disgraced husband Henry became Baron Holland. In his enforced retirement he
found solace in building, showing a passion for the construction of Gothic ruins.
We speculate that this burst of construction could have rekindled Lady Caroline's
shell-based fantasies, and, just two miles away from their house at Kingsgate,
the Margate Grotto is the result, #1 of 52 things to do in Margate, according
to Tripadvisor. We appreciate good shell-work more than most, having seen
more than our fair share of grottoes. Fresh shells have vibrant colours – look at
Vernon Gibberd's polychromatic grotto at Leeds Castle in the same county – but
nearly two centuries of the general public sweating and shuffling through the
winding corridors of Margate Grotto and no doubt smoking all over them in the
past has leached all colour out of the shells. Before the arrival of electricity the
shells were lit by gas lamps, which can't have been any good for them. We have
to confess that the Margate grotto is ... a bit grey. Visitors sometimes express
their disappointment: '£4 EACH to go down a hole in the ground covered in
dirty dust-covered shells!' Magic is not sprinkled on many souls.

There is no such feminine touch about **Scott's Grotto** at Ware, built by
John Scott of Amwell (1731–1783), a now overlooked poet, from the early
1760s (Fig 6.3). Scott was a road-builder by trade as well as being a respected
poet of the time; an unusual combination. His grotto comprises tunnels, tiny

circular rooms with important names (The Committee Room, The Robing Room, The Consultation Room, The Council Chamber, named not by Scott but by a later 19th-century owner) but the intent is clear – to burrow as far into the hill as possible. In the end he managed over 20m in length and 10m in depth, and as it always sounds bigger in feet we'll go for 70ft and 30ft.

Scott, from a strongly Quaker family, had been born in Bermondsey. When he was ten years old his family moved from London to Amwell, now Great Amwell, close to Ware, to escape the smallpox. His father had an obsessive fear of the disease, a fear he passed on to his son, who was frequently kept at home, making it impossible for him to be regularly educated. As a grown man, Scott was too scared to visit London, just 25 miles away, until he was in his thirties, and even then they were anxious, short visits, entered into 'with as much caution as if he had been entering a city ravaged by pestilence'. By then he was recognised and praised as a poet, having had his first poems published in *The Gentleman's Magazine* when he was 17. Ware and Amwell are now dormitory towns for London, and it can be hard to realise today how lovely the surrounding countryside was in the 18th century:

> This delightful retreat, commonly called Langley Bottom, is situated about half a mile from Ware, and the same distance from Amwell. The scene is adapted to contemplation, and possesses such capabilities of improvement that the genius of a Shenstone might easily convert it to a second Leasowes. The transition from this solitude to Widbury Hill is made in a walk of a few minutes, and the prospect from that hill, in a fine evening, is beautiful beyond description.

Isaac Walton, the Compleat Angler, lived here and fished at Amwell Hill and in the Vale of Lea. An echo of the beauty of the place still remains and can be heard today, at the source of the New River at Great Amwell, where the stream is dammed and two bosky islets hold monuments to Sir Hugh Myddelton, the creator of the New River, and verses from Scott's poem 'Amwell'. Despite being

Fig 6.3
Even Dr Johnson admired Scott's
Grotto. [© Jonathan Holt]

pressed by rail and the roads and the garden centre it doesn't feel like suburban Hertfordshire.

The summer of 1757 was exceptionally hot, and Scott wrote a yearning poem:

O ! for some secret shady cool recess !
Some Gothic dome, o'er hung with darksome trees,
Where thick damp walls this raging heat repress,
Where the long aisle invites the lazy breeze !

Although he hadn't yet revisited London, he was aware of Pope's Grotto at Twickenham and may have seen William Shenstone's famous garden at The Leasowes in the Midlands. Closer at hand in Hertfordshire, less than seven miles away, was the Quaker Brassey family's fabulous grotto at Roxford, Hertingfordbury, with *giocchi d'acqua*, demolished in 1786, and he must have been aware of his fellow Quaker William Goldney's grotto in Bristol and William Champion's grot work and giant Neptune in nearby Warmley. As a contributor to *The Gentleman's Magazine* he would have read its articles on shell collecting and grottoes, and also David Garrick's poem on Thomas Wright's grotto at Hampton Court House. The Roxford grotto with its water surprise was a sad loss:

But this the grotto far excels
Which is enriched with choicest shells
And ornaments of different kind
To charm the eye and please the mind
And here a curious fountain plays
Which throws the water different ways
Above, below, on every side
In plenteous streams both far and wide
Were they disposed to lock you in
They soon could wet you to the skin
By curious art and man's device
They'd do it for you in a trice ;
Indeed they never are so rude
Unless a blockhead should intrude.

Scott briefly moved to St Margaret's in 1761 because of an outbreak of smallpox in Ware. In 1764 he wrote to a friend 'I have finished my Shell Temple both the Inner room or Grotto and ye Portico and now begun another cavern or Subterraneous Grot in ye side of the hill behind the former'.

Scott was described as tall, slender, remarkably strong and muscular, and he took much delight in walking. He had a well-cultivated mind and loved gardening, turning his garden at Amwell into an object of such beauty that it became one of the sights of the neighbourhood. His poetic mentor was a bricklayer and self-taught poet, Charles Frogley, and in 1767, when the grotto was complete (and after becoming one of the first people to be inoculated against smallpox) he married Charles's daughter Sarah, who had converted to the Society of Friends but who died in childbirth the following year, their child dying later in August 1768. The word 'FROG' can be seen in one of the niches of the Council Chamber.

Fig 6.4
Shellwork in Scott's Grotto.
[© Mike Cousins]

The grotto has some scattered shell decoration (Fig 6.4), but the main drive is tunnelling. His friend John Turner in Exeter helped him to find fossils and shells. Making the excavations under the hill he marched in first 'like a pioneer' with his pick-axe in his hand, to encourage his rustic assistants. He enjoyed watching his workers at work, earning their pittances for their families.

As a poet he was introduced to the estimable Dr Johnson, whose opinion of grottoes has previously been mentioned, but who had a change of heart on the subject when he visited Scott. Scott's biographer John Hoole brought Sam Johnson to Ware, 'who with pleasantry called the grotto FAIRY HALL, and said with a smile that "none but a poet could have made such a garden"'.

And, of course, the poet in him was inspired by his own grot – this is from Scott's 'The Garden':

> Where, 'midst thick oaks, the subterraneous way
> To the arch'd grot admits a feeble ray ;
> Where glassy pebbles pave the varied floors,
> And rough flint walls are deck'd with shells and ores ;
> And silvery pearls, spread o'er the roofs on high,
> Glimmer like faint stars in a twilight sky ;
> From noon's fierce glare, perhaps he pleased retires,
> Indulging musing which the place inspires.

From 1779 to 1787 the visitors' book for the grotto has over 3,000 names.

As he feared, London would be the death of him – he sickened with 'the putrid fever' and died at Ratcliff, Stepney, in December 1783, aged 54. When Sam Johnson heard the news, he confessed he loved him. The grotto was excellently restored in the 1990s by architect and folly writer James Howley.

Tunnels

It is difficult to overstate the appeal of tunnelling. The costs and time taken are prodigious – Scott spent years on his grotto – far beyond the reach of most individuals, which is why dedicated tunnellers tend to find employment with councils and governments who have the resources and the infrastructure to commission mighty tunnelling projects.

Feisty American billionaire Elon Musk set up the agreeably named Boring Company to tunnel under American and Martian cities using electric sleds on rails (what we used to call 'trains') to transport his electric cars underneath traffic jams, but he is one of a select few today who has the money to indulge his whims. Over 350 years ago at **Albury Park** in Surrey the diarist and garden historian John Evelyn created a somewhat austere grotto room for his patron Charles Howard, later Duke of Norfolk, then impressively trumped it with a straight 500ft (150m) 'crypta', or tunnel through a hill (Fig 6.5) to allow the estate workers, who were quartered in Albury Heath on the south side, to walk through to work. Evelyn was pleased with his work, writing in 1670: 'To Albury, to see how that garden proceeded, which I found exactly done to the design and plot I had made, with the crypta through the mountain in the park, thirty perches in length. Such a Pausillipe is nowhere in England'.

This may require a little clarification: a crypta is a tunnel or subterranean passage; a perch is a length of 5.03m, giving a distance of 150.9m or 495ft, and Pausillipe is now Posillipo, a suburb of Naples, renowned for its 700m tunnel built by Agrippa through the Posillipo hill around 37BC to connect Naples with the Phlegrean Fields. The love of tunnels stretches back beyond antiquity.

At West Wycombe, Buckinghamshire, are the notorious **Hell Fire Caves**, enhanced in the 18th century by Sir Francis Dashwood (Fig 6.6). This is real folly fodder, gloomy, sinister, amateur and threatening, despite the large number

Fig 6.5
The Pausillipe at Albury.
[© Gwyn Headley/fotoLibra]

of visitors going in to see the waxworks and recorded commentaries that sanitise
the caves themselves. The façade is knapped flint, with pointed and broken
arches rising on top of each other like shark's teeth, a jaw open for swallowing
or biting. Inside is a salute to our American cousins: many of the exhibits inside
concern Benjamin Franklin, who once stayed at West Wycombe, and there
is virtually nothing about the lascivious and immeasurably more interesting
British politician John Wilkes, a much more frequent visitor – but our American
cousins know nothing of Wilkes and care less, and they provide much of the
income. Go where the money is.

The Hell Fire Caves were manually dug out from 1748 to 1754 for the usual
excuse – to provide employment for out-of-work labourers – though Sir Francis
wanted a suitably minatory venue for the Knights of St Francis of Wycombe,
as the Hell Fire Club was properly called. The members – men only, preferably
aristocratic, rich certainly – dressed as monks, played with pagan rituals and

orgies, and given today's snowflake attitude to sexual harassment there is no reason to believe that mid-18th-century morals and behaviour would have been as prim and pure as we might have hoped. Human life and human chastity were cheap; rape was common and murder not unknown. The Holy Ghost was singled out for specific blasphemies. Curiously, homosexuality was not mentioned.

Sir Francis Dashwood eagerly promoted his reputation as a hell-raiser. Despite his bodice-ripper name, he was a homely man with a face like a ciabatta. He relished his description as 'politician and rake' and even John Wilkes, himself no slouch in the debauchery department, professed himself astonished and disgusted by what he saw when he visited Sir Francis's seat at Medmenham, where the Hell Fire Club operated while the caves were being prepared. Tantalisingly, we are not told what shocked and awed him. Yet in the rules – this is England, there had to be rules – it says 'Every Member is allowed to introduce a Lady of cheerful lively disposition, to improve the general hilarity'. Wilkes is said to have dressed a baboon as the Devil himself and concealed it in a chest. The chest sprang open and the monkey leapt onto the shoulders of Lord Sandwich, who, rigid with terror, screamed 'Spare me, gracious Devil! spare a wretch who was never sincerely your servant!'

Sir Francis was not exclusively obsessed with caves and tunnels, like two of our builders to come. It is said that the trees in his park were originally planted in patterns of great vulgarity (how?) but that Repton scrubbed it all up when he worked there. What remain are the temples, several of which were designed by Nicholas Revett. Wilkes mentions a 'lewd temple', perhaps demolished by Repton, although he may have meant the Temple of Venus, the entrance of which is indeed extremely naughty if one's mind is set to it. In the anonymous 1786 book *Picturesque Views of the Principal Seats of the Nobility*, the gushing complimentary descriptions came to an abrupt halt at West Wycombe, which was seen as 'an outrage on common decency'. Many of the estate cottages are built in brick and flint, the commonest local building material, and flint is for

Fig 6.6
The commercialised entrance
to the Hell Fire Caves.
[© Alan Terrill]

some reason irresistible to folly builders. The cottages visible from the house usually have some monstrous flint excrescence grafted on, but in the case of St Crispin's Cottage the addition is a beautifully proportioned and well-worked church tower with quatrefoil windows and fretted belfry window, the equal as a sham church eyecatcher of the **Tattingstone Wonder** in Suffolk.

The affairs at Medmenham and West Wycombe were written up by Charles Johnston in his *Chrysal: or, The Adventures of a Guinea,* and Medmenham and its 'gross lewdness and daring impiety' is indeed mentioned, with Wycombe's church described as 'a church, on an eminence near his house, that answered the double purpose of convincing the populace of his regard to religion, and of making a beautiful termination to a vista which he had just cut through a wood in his park'.

The Underground Man

Another duke took tunnel mania to even greater lengths. In 1854 the bachelor William John Cavendish-Scott-Bentinck became the 5th Duke of Portland at the age of 54 and inherited the ancient **Welbeck Abbey** estate in Nottinghamshire. Dukes demonstrated a peculiar affinity to Nottinghamshire – an area of the county is known as the Dukeries because four dukes, Portland, Norfolk, Kingston and Newcastle, had contiguous estates there. As there are fewer than 20 British dukes, this is a remarkable and inexplicable concentration.

Portland was a shy man and decided that by travelling round the estate in tunnels he could avoid the curious stares of his tenants and workers. He was said to have refused the Order of the Garter because it would have entailed presenting himself at Court. He had pet aversions: women, tobacco and anyone dressed as a gentleman. He wouldn't handle coins unless they had been washed.

More legends sprang up, and although modern research has discounted many of them, the error was often a ten-fold exaggeration, like Plato's

Fig 6.7
The Welbeck Underground
Ballroom. [© Gwyn Headley/
fotoLibra]

description of Atlantis. The duke didn't have 1,500 workers to dig his tunnels, each equipped with a donkey and umbrella – but he did have 150 workers digging his tunnels, each equipped with a donkey and umbrella. The tunnels didn't stretch 30 miles, but they did stretch for 3 miles. Most of the tunnels were designed for the servants to get around the estate without troubling the ducal eye, not the other way around. There was talk of an underground ballroom – which actually does exist, not tunnelled out deep underground but as a cut-and-cover pit, with its glass-panelled ceiling at ground level. It is huge, one single room of over 10,000 square feet, measuring 160ft by 64ft, with the largest unsupported ceiling in Europe (Fig 6.7). When Welbeck housed a military sixth-form college, the room was used as a gymnasium.

Like many wealthy men, he became agitated at the thought of public rights of way crossing his estate. He hit upon an elegant solution – he built a tunnel to replace the right of way. With his aversion to the public gaze, he plunged it deep into the earth so that 'it is possible to travel the entire length of its detestable interior without catching the slightest glimpse of the lofty pleasure-dome above it'. He confronted a group walking through his woods: 'Here have I provided for you at enormous expense a clean pathway underground, lighted with gas too, and you will persist in walking above ground!'

One tunnel swoops on an arc towards Worksop station (Fig 6.8), and the speculation was that the duke planned an underground railway to connect with the main line, where his curtained carriage would be hitched to the London train so he could travel in perfect anonymity. In the event, it only reached one and a half miles of the four required.

The tunnels cost Portland upwards of £100,000. At the time of his death in 1879, he was excavating an even larger underground room further to the west, to be known as the Bachelors' Room. Unfinished, it was later adapted as a sunken garden, and now has a black wooden temple, a pergola, fishponds, rose gardens and tennis courts hidden at the distant end. A tunnel, now blocked at either end, although the centre section is still accessible from the sunken garden,

Fig 6.8

Grand entrance to one of the tunnels at Welbeck.

[© Gwyn Headley/fotoLibra]

led 1,020 yards from the ballroom to the great riding school block, built by the Duke of Newcastle in 1623. Walking briskly by torchlight, it took us nine minutes to get from end to end (Fig 6.9). The tunnels were lit by rooflights (now blocked) during the day and gaslights by night. Portland spent a prodigious £113,000 with one foundry for water pipes and gas fitments alone, and at the 1871 census he had a gas and water fitter living with him at the Abbey. The *Dictionary of National Biography* relates a rumour that he even refused to allow the workpeople engaged on the improvements to his estates to show any sign of recognition on meeting him. He retired to a suite, if that's not too grand a word, of five rooms in the Abbey, and every other room in the rambling mansion was equipped with a lavatory pan in the corner. His preferred means of communication with the outside world, including his servants, was through In and Out letterboxes in the door to his antechamber. A trapdoor from his suite led down into his tunnels, so he could suddenly manifest himself anywhere on the estate. The similarity to Howard Hughes is striking.

In 1878 the Nottingham and Midland Counties *Daily Express* announced that the works at Welbeck were 'finished', and that the result would be the dismissal of many hundreds of men. 'On Saturday last upwards of 250 labourers – navvies, chiefly, were dismissed'. The newspaper went on to verify that 'At times the numbers employed about the estate were from 1,500 to 1,600', so perhaps the legends weren't exaggerated after all. And there's more:

> The Duke appears to have got sick of the plan, and he, as it were, ran away from it some ten weeks ago in a fashion as eccentric as any of his many eccentricities. He was placed in his closed traveling carriage one Sunday afternoon, and was driven to Worksop to catch a fast train. On reaching Worksop the carriage was put upon a carriage truck, made fast, placed in the centre of the train, and in it his Grace made the journey up to London, horses being in waiting at King's Cross to take him forward to his town residence.

Fig 6.9
A lesser tunnel entrance at Welbeck. [© Gwyn Headley/ fotoLibra]

A reclusive life is not one for sharing, so it came as no surprise that the duke died unmarried and childless, leaving over £1,500,000. His grandfather, the 3rd Duke, prime minister from 1807 to 1809, had left debts of over £500,000, so William owed a great deal to his scrupulous father.

Portland would be aghast to see what has happened to his estate in the 21st century. It now rings with life, home to a number of thriving artisan businesses, including a brewery, a cookery school, a publisher, a cheesemaker, a bakery, an art gallery and others.

At **High Beach** in Essex's Epping Forest are catacombs that, when discovered, were unquestionably Roman in origin. 'When I was examining the grounds', said a Captain J Cross in 1923,

> I was struck by the striking resemblance of a tower in the corner abutting on the road to the catacombs in Rome. I began excavations, and then discovered there was a lot of water below.
>
> I engaged engineers to pump this up – a task which occupied nine days' and discovered two underground chambers.
>
> These are surrounded by a series of sloping stone passages and a number of stone steps. Both chambers are supported by blocks of solid stone, some of which weigh half a ton.
>
> The ceilings are in mosaic work. Around the top chamber is a beautifully constructed stone balustrade.
>
> In one corner of the catacombs is a stalactite grotto. Alongside a miniature temple is a burial niche, which is capped with a dome of Roman architecture, which could have been built only by a master builder.
>
> Below the two chambers which I explored there is another at a depth of about 18ft. but so far no means of entrance has been discovered. The excavators are clearing the fall of earth from the entrance of a passage which is believed to go underground, connecting up with the cellars of the house, where an entrance to a passage has already been discovered. It is possible that by means of this passage a means of access may also be found to the lower and as yet unexplored regions of the catacombs.
>
> The remarkable thing about this structure is that it is of Roman block stone set in Roman cement, and that, although this has been submerged for so many years, the cement is in a perfect state of preservation.
>
> The mystery is, who built these catacombs, and when? At least a thousand tons of stone were used in building them.
>
> The peculiarity of the building is that all shapes and sizes of stone have been used. Some of the blocks are carved, others plainly indicate that they have formed part of a Corinthian column.

The house used to be Dr Matthew Allen's private lunatic asylum, where poor John Clare, the peasant poet, had been housed, as well as Tennyson before he became Alfred, Lord Tennyson. Allen was an interesting if dubious character, described by Thomas Carlyle as 'a speculative, hopeful, earnest, frothy man'. When Captain Cross arrived, the house had been empty for 40 years, the previous occupant, a Mr Bevers, having vanished without trace. Further research dismissed the Roman theory as the stones appear to have originated from a part demolition of Chelmsford Prison in the 1880s. All indications therefore point to the mysterious Mr Bevers as the responsible mole.

The king of tunnels was Liverpool's **Joseph Williamson** (Fig 6.10). Apprenticed to Thomas Moss Tate, a tobacco merchant, at the age of 11, he married the boss's sister and bought out the business in 1803, aged 34. He purchased a parcel of land on Edge Hill in the east of the city and built a house there for himself and his wife Elizabeth. In 1808 he began to build other houses 'of the strangest description', constructed without the help of plans, 'having rooms without windows, rooms that were all windows and all sorts of cellars and underground tunnelling'. Sadly none of these survives.

Fig 6.10
Joseph Williamson, the Mole of Edge Hill. [Gwyn Headley collection]

The tunnels became an all-consuming passion. After the Napoleonic wars ended, Liverpool suffered mass unemployment. Williamson retired in 1818, immensely wealthy, and created his own safety net for the poor of the area. Men came to him for work. Rather than turn them away, he set them to dig. Many theories as to the reasons why he dug exist: illicit distilleries, smuggling goods, Elizabeth Williamson's supposed adherence to a doomsday cult – he may even have been seeking for coal, because he excavated down at least six levels, from which galleries were driven in all directions. Secrecy was unlikely to be a candidate, as everyone in Liverpool knew what was going on. Williamson himself said that the prime motive in all he did was 'the employment of the poor'. It seems strange to our 21st-century reasoning that he didn't spend his wealth building housing for the poor rather than tunnels, but the concept of a welfare state was then undreamed of.

Elizabeth died in 1822 and work on the tunnels redoubled: 'A series of subterranean passages and huge underground halls [some 40ft high], a positive maze of tortuous catacombs – at depths between ten and fifty feet and stretching for several miles – a labyrinth twisting a serpentine course through solid rock'.

Williamson was well aware of his abilities. Talking to the Unitarian James Martineau, he mused that had he gone into the Church of England he could have been a bishop. Thinking of the endless arched tunnels under their feet, the cleric drily responded, 'At least an ARCH-Bishop?' When Martineau moved into a Williamson property in Mason Street there were already two clergymen living in the street. Williamson commented to him 'What with the Rev. Dr. Hull, and Dr. Raffles, and you, it will be strange if we don't keep the devil out of my street!'

When he died in 1840 his obituary noted that 'Mr. Williamson was a person of very eccentric habits, and well known in his own neighbourhood by a peculiar and, to all persons but himself, seemingly ridiculous propensity of making expensive excavations under the earth. In the pursuit of this propensity he has spent large sums of money – [and] has vaulted and undermined the greater portion of Mason-street, Edge-hill'.

Work stopped the moment he died, as did maintenance. Some tunnels were blocked up, some filled with rubbish, but the network was so extensive that it could not be obliterated, even by Nazi bombs. To this day there is no definitive map of the tunnels, or their extent, but enough of them have been cleared out and cleaned up that a section of Williamson's Tunnels is now a heritage attraction for the city, run by the volunteers of the Joseph Williamson Society. A representative of the society commented that the project will probably never be finished, as more tunnels are being discovered on a regular basis.

A hill like a submarine shelters the village of **Banwell** in Somerset from the south, a long, dank, overgrown ridge diving down to the M5 motorway. In 1780 two local men discovered a very large cave while prospecting for lead; no lead being found, they closed it up again. It was reopened in 1824, and the bones of several prehistoric animals were found, some unidentifiable. George

Henry Law (1761–1845), the Bishop of Bath and Wells, of that sublime scissor-arched cathedral, was a keen palaeontologist, and he soon built a small house, a fashionable cottage orné at Banwell in order to pursue his interest more closely. An assured Christian, he built his own temple at Banwell – a Druid's Temple (Fig 6.11), and sponsored William Beard (1772–1868), a local farmer-turned-fossil collector, to find more fossilised animal bones (Fig 6.12). Up until 1840 Beard collected thousands of specimens, and his collection is now in the Castle Museum, Taunton, Somerset. Bishop Law considered the finds to be proof of Noah's Flood.

A fascination with bones leads naturally to a keener sense of mystery and drama, and Bishop Law built a dramatic garden above his great caves. The site was perfect – a high sunbathed south-facing ridge – but the bishop made his garden on the damp north side with the moss and the slugs. The paths are heavily overgrown with skeletal, light-starved frondy plants that brush wetly

Fig 6.12
William Beard, fossil collector.
[© World History Archive/
fotoLibra]

against your face as you slide on the greasy steps that lead inconsequentially away up the hill. Low stone walls border the paths; unnatural shapes can dimly be made out through the bony overgrowth and suddenly, in classic folly fashion, a tiny alcove appears. It is difficult to imagine it could ever have been intended as a seat as it is perpetually damp.

Directly above is a nicely restored little building covered in tiny pebbles, with three arches facing west, built for meditation and tranquillity. By a trick of the land, the noise of the M5 is particularly intrusive here. The gloomy paths intertwine, climbing and descending the hill randomly. One descends more steeply than the others, becoming steps, and spiralling down into a tunnel, barred by a rotting but still functional wooden door. Is this the entrance to the bone cave? It is very dark and very wet, and a powerful stench of decaying vegetation is everywhere. The slugs are plentiful, huge and juicy. This is the end (Fig 6.13).

People who dig holes and tunnels for a living are called miners. People who bet on their results are called speculators. There is more money in speculating than in mining, and a lot more money can be lost. Whitaker Wright combined both; he speculated as a professional and mined as a dilettante.

Capitalism has many faces, not all of them unacceptable. But left to its own devices, unfettered by the shackles of regulation, it does have a tendency to self-

Fig 6.13

Banwell Bone Cave.

[© Jonathan Holt]

distortion, to wallow in excess. Unconstrained, capitalism becomes cruel, greedy, selfish, intolerant and self-absorbed, and few people demonstrated these failings more vividly than Whitaker Wright.

Born into a modest chapel family in Cheshire or Staffordshire, he went to America in his teens to make his fortune, which he promptly did, becoming a mining millionaire by the age of 30.

Checks and balances in place today are designed to root out corruption, malfeasance and good old-fashioned swindles. Yet as we know, at least 60 per cent of all emails are spam, mostly coming from criminals attempting to steal from you. As Woody Guthrie sang, 'Some will rob you with a six-gun, and some with a fountain pen'. Whitaker Wright came back to England in style aged 43, and in a competition between the Haves and the Have Yachts, he came out top dog.

He spent his money imperially. In 1896 he bought the yacht *White Feather* from the German Emperor, Kaiser Wilhelm II, and in the same year purchased Lea Court, near Witley in Surrey, for £60,000. He then spent an additional £200,000 in building and other improvements on the estate, which was renamed **Witley Park**. These included creating a couple of lakes, moving a few hills, tunnelling deep into at least one of them and creating a crystal underwater ballroom. At least that's what it became in the public imagination: in 1935 *The Yorkshire Post* related that

Fig 6.14
The underwater smoking room at Witley Park. Note the flood mark.
[© Gwyn Headley/fotoLibra]

the house – contains a ballroom, elaborately decorated in chocolate and gold, and copied from the Sistine Chapel in Rome. He also tunnelled a grotto out of a hill, the only approach to which is by water, and within it he placed a plaster Venus floodlit in blue. Beneath the water, which forms an ornamental lake, he constructed an immense ballroom, with a glass ceiling for the observation of fishes, perhaps the most fantastic feat of all.

The 'immense' ballroom actually exists and is just large enough to swing a short cat in, but not big enough for two couples to tango. Whether it was intended to be a ballroom, a billiard room or a smoking room, the fact remains that it is indeed a glass dome, entirely underwater, a remarkable experience (Fig 6.14). The 'grotto out of a hill' still survives, now stripped and bare of plaster Venuses, but providing what must be the most 'fantastickal' approach to a lake ever conceived – a door set in a holly tree, a spiral ramp leading down two storeys into the earth, then into a great cavern with a flooded tunnel leading out onto the lake. All still there and absolutely breathtaking.

Where did all this money come from? There may have been a time when Whitaker Wright worked honestly and with probity, but by the time he came to the attention of the British press it was mainly accounts of accusations and calumnies, of oscillating share prices and suspect claims.

Even in hindsight Wright's ventures appear plausible. His British American Corporation was taking over established mining companies returning dividends of £10,000 a month. The chairman of the board was the Marquis of Dufferin and Ava, former Governor-General of Canada, and his fellow directors included the Lieutenant-Governor of the North-West Territories, the former Governor of the Cape Colony and Hoare the banker. The great and the good surrounded him. His philanthropy was prodigious, as was his wealth.

A bear run in December 1900 exposed the fragility of his enterprises. He had started work on what was to become his greatest tunnelling project and which proved to be his financial downfall. Today we call it the Bakerloo Line.

He was arrested in New York on 15 March 1903 and charged with fraud in connection with the collapse of his London and Globe Finance Corporation Ltd. The NYPD provided a warts-and-all description: 'aged about fifty, height 5′ 9″ or 5′ 10″, stout build, large head, dark hair and moustache, florid complexion, small eyes, receding forehead, small chin with large fat roll beneath, wears gold pince-nez with gold chain attached, speaks with slight American accent. Usually dressed in frock coat suit and silk hat'.

The mention of the accent is interesting. Whether he was born in Staffordshire or Cheshire, Whitaker Wright grew up in Northumberland, and spent over 20 years in America. British commentators remarked on his Geordie burr. One of the best-established ways of gaining confidence is to echo your mark's behaviour and accent, and it's very likely that the chameleonic Wright was all things to all men; Geordie when it mattered, American when it didn't.

At the Old Bailey in January 1904 Wright was found guilty on 24 counts of fraud and sentenced to 7 years in prison. With perfect composure he left the dock to confer with his solicitor prior to being removed to gaol, and collapsed. He had bitten on a capsule of potassium cyanide; death came within 15 minutes. When his body was searched, he was found to have a fully loaded and cocked revolver in his pocket. Searches were less rigorous in those days.

Outside Witley station the trusting and hopeful villagers had erected an arch to welcome their vindicated financier home. They carried his coffin through it.

What links our moles and grottoistes? Wealth, certainly; leisure, passion, focus and perhaps a little obsession.

We all have the kindling within us, but few have the spark to ignite it.

Gazetteer

County/Authority	Location	Folly
Bath, Bristol and Avon	Bath	Vellore House Grotto
		Crowe Hall Grotto
		Sheridan's Grotto
	Bristol	Goldney's Grotto
	East Harptree	Tunnel, Grotto
	Frenchay	Grotto
	Marshfield	Grotto
Berkshire	Reading	Whiteknights Grotto
	Windsor	Windsor Castle Grotto
Buckinghamshire	Ellesborough	Grotto
	Gayhurst	Gayhurst Tunnel
	High Wycombe	Witches' Grotto
	Penn Street	Grotto
	Slough	Grotto Wall
	Thornton	Grotto
	Waddesdon	Grotto
Cambridgeshire	Wisbech	Grotto
Cheshire	Chester	Eaton Hall Grotto
Cornwall	Egloshayle	Pencarrow Grotto
	Fowey	Menabilly Grotto
	Luxulyan	Water Meadow Grotto
	Padstow	Prideaux Place Grotto
	Polperro	Puckey's Shell House
	St Austell	Duporth Grotto
	St Ewe	Grotto
	Whitsand Bay	Lugger's Cave/Sharrow Grot
Derbyshire	Calke Abbey	Grottoes
	Hassop	Hassop Hall Tunnels
	Matlock	Grotto Façade
	Ticknall	Knowle Hill Underground Chambers
Devon	Bicton	Shell House
	Blackawton	Oldstone Shell House
		Grotto
	Exeter	Bishop's Palace Grotto
	Maidencombe	Maidencombe Grotto
	Milton Abbot	Endsleigh Grotto
	Sidmouth	Mr Fish's Grotto
	Stowford	Hayne Grotto
	Tapeley	Tapeley Grotto
	Teigngrace	Stover House Grotto
Dorset	Encombe	Rock Arch Grotto
	Penselwood	Shell House
	Wimborne St Giles	Grotto
Durham	Darlington	Grotto
	Greta Bridge	Rokeby Hall Cave
		Urn and Grotto

County/Authority	Location	Folly
	South Shields (Cleveland)	Marsden Grotto
East Sussex	Ringmer	Wellingham House Grotto
Essex	Hatfield Forest	Hatfield Shell House
	High Beach	Catacombs
Gloucestershire	Barnsley	Grotto
	Chalford	Grove Grotto
	Highnam	Highnam Court Grotto
	Tetbury	Grotto
	Winchcombe	Bleby House Grotto
Hampshire	Boldre	Walhampton Grotto
	Droxford	Studwell Lodge Tunnel
	Houghton	Grotto
	Hursley	Hursley Grottoes
	Warnford	Grotto
Herefordshire	Dinmore	Dinmore Grotto
	Hope under Dinmore	Hampton Court Tunnel
	Leominster	Buckfield Keep Grotto
Hertfordshire	Ware	Scott's Grotto
Isle of Wight	Bonchurch	Grotto
	East Cowes	Shell House
	Shanklin	Grotto
Kent	Eastry	Foord's Folly
	Leeds Castle	Leeds Castle Grotto
	Loose	Boughton Mount Double-Decker Grotto
	Margate	Margate Grotto
	Sheerness	Ship on Shore Grotto
	Throwley	Grotto
	Tonbridge	Cedars Grotto
Leicestershire and Rutland	Belvoir Castle	Grotto
	Burton on the Wolds	Shell Room
	Scraptoft	Grotto
Lincolnshire	Brocklesby	Grotto
	Denton	Grotto
Liverpool and Manchester	Liverpool (Merseyside)	Sefton Park Grottoes Williamson's Tunnels
	St Helens	Victoria Park Grotto
London	E11	Wanstead House Grotto
	N6	Stormont Road Grotto
	NW1	Fountain Grot
	SW1	Shell Houses
	SW15	Grotto
	Hampton	Hampton Court House Grotto Grotto Passage
	Isleworth	Summerhouses
Norfolk	Brettenham	Shadwell Grotto

County/Authority	Location	Folly
	Denton	Denton House Grotto
North Yorkshire	Clapham cum Newby	Ingleborough Grotto
	Grewelthorpe	Fisher's Hall
	Skelton	Skelton Grotto
	Terrington	Shell House
Northumberland	Belford Hall	Grotto
	Hartburn	Grotto
	Horton	Bebside Old Hall Grotto
Nottinghamshire	Nottingham	Alderman Herbert's Tunnels
	Welbeck Abbey	Underground Ballroom Tunnels
Oxfordshire	Abingdon	Grotto
	Henley-on-Thames	Friar Park
	Heythrop	Grotto
	Shiplake	Crowsley Park Grotto
	Tackley	Grotto
Shropshire	Acton Burnell	Acton Burnell Shell House
	Bicton	Grotto
	Bridgnorth	Dracup's Cave
	Hawkstone	Hawkstone Grotto
	Lydbury North	Grotto/Cascade
	Onibury	Stokesay Court Grotto
Somerset	Brockley	Brockley Hall Grotto
	Chantry	Chantry Grottoes
	Cheddar	Holdenhurst Grotto
	Porlock	Ashley Combe Tunnels
	Upton Noble	Canwood Grotto
	West Quantoxhead	St Audrie's Grotto
Staffordshire	Lichfield	19 The Close, Grotto
Suffolk	Claydon	Grotto
Surrey	Addlestone	Worburn Grotto
	Albury	Albury Park Grotto Albury Tunnel
	Cobham	Grotto
	Sutton	Grottoes
	Virginia Water	Grottoes
West Sussex	Clayton	Clayton Tunnel Entrance
	Goodwood	Goodwood Grotto Goodwood Tunnels
West Yorkshire	Knaresborough	Fort Montagu
	Skipton Castle	Grotto Room Waller Beck Grotto
Wiltshire	Amesbury	Grotto
	Bowden Hill	Lodges
	Bowood	Grotto
	Fonthill Gifford	Grotto

County/Authority	Location	Folly
	Marlborough	Marlborough Grotto
	Newton Tony	Wilbury Grottoes
	Stourhead	Grotto
	Wardour Castle	Wardour Castle Grotto
	Wilton	Grotto
Worcestershire	Croome d'Abitot	Grotto
	Tenbury Wells	Kyre Park Grotto Tunnel

7 Mantling ivy: sham ruins and castles

Wentworth Castle

It is not every man, who can build a house, that can execute a ruin. To give the stone it's [*sic*] mouldering appearance – to make the widening chink run naturally through all the joints – to mutilate the ornaments – to peel the facing from the internal structure – to shew how correspondent parts have once united; tho now the chasm runs wide between them – and to scatter heaps of ruin around with negligence and ease; are great efforts of art; much too delicate for the hand of a common workman and what we very rarely see performed.

Besides, after all, that art can bestow, you must put your ruin at last into the hands of nature to adorn, and perfect it. If the mosses, and lychens grow unkindly on your walls – if the streaming weather-stains have produced no variety of tints – if the ivy refuses to mantle over your buttress; or to creep among the ornaments of your Gothic window – if the ash, cannot be brought to hang from the cleft; or long, spiry grass to wave over the shattered battlement – your ruin will be still incomplete – you may as well write over the gate, Built in the year 1772. Deception there can be none.

William Gilpin, *Observations Relative Chiefly to Picturesque Beauty Made in the Year 1772*

Ancestry.com is the 999th most popular web site in the world. People are constantly fascinated by their ancestors, their origins, their antecedents, and they dare to dream of finding a king or a queen bashfully perched in their family tree. We were all indoctrinated throughout childhood with tales of beautiful princesses and handsome princes. Why did we never hear tell of a magical faraway republic?

Three centuries ago your parentage really mattered. Stupendous talent could and did shine through – look at the rise of Thomas Cromwell from butcher's boy to Earl of Essex – but for those of us less prodigiously gifted, our station in life was set. No preferment, no advancement, no well-connected marriage; society was made up of aristocrats and serfs with scarcely a middle class to speak of. Yet some still managed to claw their way up the social ladder, and as commerce began to rival agriculture as a source of wealth, these parvenues – chaps who had to buy their own silver – were still snubbed by society because they couldn't prove their pedigrees.

Being rich or poor wasn't the crime. The crime was not having roots that stretched back three or four hundred years in the county. Hence appeared one of the most bizarre creations of the human mind – the sham castle. It is often claimed (wrongly) that follies have no purpose, but the sham castle had a very specific role: to provide a provenance or an ancestry, however spurious or dubious. When Sir Newlytitled Moneybags acquired his country estate,

the gentry of the county would smile and snigger among themselves, and occasionally they would even deign to accept his entertainment. But as an arriviste he could never be part of Society.

Stainborough

The grandest and earliest of all sham castles was created by that most desperate of pedigree hunters, Thomas Wentworth, 1st Earl of Strafford (1672–1739) at Stainborough in Yorkshire. It is large, spectacularly so; we would guess that this is larger than the majority of genuine castles in England. Wentworth was a social climber. When he finally achieved his much-desired earldom, it was named for a place that doesn't exist – there is no Strafford in Great Britain or Ireland. Even more confusingly, 30 years before he'd been born there was another Thomas Wentworth, also 1st Earl of Strafford, who had been Charles I's most trusted advisor, and who was only distantly related: his grandfather was the first earl's younger brother. When his cousin the 2nd Earl of Strafford died without children, Wentworth succeeded him as the 3rd Baron Raby. However, to his astonishment he did not inherit either the Strafford fortune or Wentworth Woodhouse, one of the largest houses in England, which went to the second earl's nephew, Thomas Watson, his sister's son. This was a mortal blow to Wentworth. His life was a succession of stages to climb, each one a new challenge. In the army he had risen to Lieutenant-General, in court he was a Groom of the Bedchamber, he had been *aide-de-camp* to William III, he became Ambassador to Prussia, and finally in 1711 he was created Viscount Wentworth of Wentworth-Woodhouse (despite Thomas Watson owning Wentworth Woodhouse) and of Stainborough and Earl of Strafford (of the second creation). He then became head of the navy, as First Lord of the Admiralty. As his cousin the earl was childless and he was becoming a Big Cheese, he had great expectations, as they said in those days. He was clearly a talented and useful man, but he felt he had been cheated of his rightful inheritance.

Lord Raby, as he was then known, was tall, handsome, brave and extremely pushy. He had bought Stainborough Hall in 1708, which he greatly enlarged, and provocatively renamed Wentworth Castle. In 1728 he commenced building **Stainborough Castle**. It is a huge folly, driven by noble rage (Fig 7.1). It is the first sham castle in the country, and by far the largest. Alfred's Hall in Cirencester predates it as a sham but not a castle, and has none of its castle-like grandeur. It was placed in an iron-age hill fort on the highest point of the estate, 'like an endorsement from the past', as M J Charlesworth wrote in *The Wentworths: Family and Political Rivalry in the English Landscape Garden*. This perfectly filled the role of the sham castle as supplier of a sham provenance. Strafford named the four towers of the castle after his children, Ann, Harriet, Lucy and William. Completing it in 1730, he placed a plaque reading 'Restored 1730' on the brand new fakery. Son William went on to enjoy the earldom and the life that his father had struggled so hard to achieve, without contributing much to the public good.

Thomas Badeslade engraved a bird's-eye view of Wentworth Castle in 1730 that clearly shows Stainborough Castle standing clean and proud on a hill behind the main house. However, the folly is described as Wentworth Castle, not Stainborough Castle, so the enterprising earl managed to persuade the engraver that he had a more ancient lineage. And just in case anyone mistook which Earl of Strafford Thomas Wentworth had become, the view was captioned

> STAINBOROUGH and WENTWORTH CASTLE in the County of YORK, One of the Seats of the Right Honourable Thomas Earl of Strafford, Viscount Wentworth, of Wentworth Woodhouse and of Stainborough, Baron of Raby, Newmarch and Oversley, and Knight of the most Noble Order of the Garter; who at the Death of Queen Ann, was one of the Lords of the regency appointed by Act of Parliament as First Lord Commissioner of the Admiralty, was Lieut. General Colonel of the Royal Regiment of Dragoons, privy Councellour, Ambassador Extraordinary and Plenipotentiary to the States General as likewise for the Congress at Utrecht.

The folly and the surrounding gardens, known as Wentworth Castle Park, are now owned by Northern College, an adult residential college based in Wentworth Castle. The grounds were run by the Wentworth Castle and Stainborough Park Heritage Trust, who decided to wind down and close the gardens in 2017. However, the National Trust took over the running of the grounds in 2019, and they are open again.

Sanderson Miller

Sanderson Miller (1716–1780) was a Warwickshire squire astute enough to spot a need in the market. Though untitled himself, he came from a comfortable line of Warwickshire gentry, went up to Oxford and moved easily in aristocratic circles. He was wealthy enough to dabble in architecture as a hobby, and on a corner of his Radway Grange estate, which he inherited when he was 21, he had the idea of erecting a **sham castle** on the spot where he assumed that Charles I might have erected his standard before the 1642 battle of Edge Hill in the valley below (Fig 7.2). He began in 1745, completed it in 1747, and within the same year he was putting up a 'ruinated castle' for George Lyttelton at Hagley in Worcestershire. Thus, Sanderson Miller started a national characteristic, one that persists to this day and which was gently mocked 40 years later by Goethe in *Faust*:

> Are Britons here? They go abroad, feel calls
> To trace old battlefields and crumbling walls

The English still love tramping round ruins, and there's something about Gothic architecture that lends itself splendidly to ruination, as Cecil Torr pointed out in his captivating volumes of miscellanea *Small Talk at Wreyland* – 'Gothic is never at its best except in ruins', adding 'Chartres does not equal Tintern'.

Despite his genius at innovation and his remarkable ability to mimic styles of architecture three centuries past, Miller had his demons. One was his loyalty to his workmen, who were not always of the highest standard. The Temple of the Mount at Wroxton in Oxfordshire was begun in May 1750, but his foreman Banister was constantly being 'overtaken in liquor' and it was not completed until the following summer. His master mason, William Hitchcox, was adding an octagon crown to All Saints, Wroxton, but he left off the retaining cramps and the octagon collapsed in a storm, much to the *Schadenfreude* of Horace Walpole

Fig 7.2

Radway Castle: this way madness
lay. [© John Cleare/fotoLibra]

who gleefully commented 'Mr. Miller, unluckily once in his life, happened to
think rather of beauty than the water-tables and so it fell down the first winter'.

Miller's other problem was mental, and as mental health was a taboo subject
in the 18th century, we know very little more. He stopped work in 1760, aged
only 44, and although he lived another 20 years he never worked again. His
friend Charles Talbot wrote to his nephew, Clement Newsham, in late 1759:

> The disorder he has been struggling with at particular periods for several
> years past has at last got the better of him and made him raving mad and he
> is now under confinement at Hogsden [Hoxton] about a mile out of London.
> It is impossible to form any Judgement at present whether he is curable or
> not. He was seized with the frenzy but about a fortnight ago in Warwick
> town where he gave such publick proofs of his being disordered in his
> senses that it was impossible to conceal his misfortune from the world.

Miller was taken to London to see a specialist he had seen the year before
'when he was in a melancholy way. He grew so outrageous the first night that
he alarmed the neighbourhood and it was therefore necessary to put him into a
private madhouse'. The following summer Miller was back at Radway, refusing
to believe he had ever been ill, but the occurrence of further bouts prevented him
from working again.

Philip Yorke

Another prodigiously gifted man of humble birth was Philip Yorke (1690–1764). His father was an attorney in Dover, which in the infinitely subtle nuances of British society placed him on the lower rungs of the legal ladder, below solicitors and barristers. He had the paltry income that befitted such a lowly position, and his son, intelligent, hard-working, ambitious, greedy and clever, was driven to escape the poverty trap. He worked his way up through the legal profession, acquiring powerful and influential supporters along the way until at the age of 47 he was appointed Lord Chancellor, a position he held for 19 years. He has been recognised as one of England's finest lawyers; just, fair, compassionate, unbiased, uncorrupted. Scots might disagree as he banned the right of clansmen to bear arms, highland dress and the wearing of the kilt.

What Yorke lacked was a hinterland: no outside interests, no humour, no conviviality. Later in life, garlanded with honours, these qualities ossified into pomposity, and he noted, perhaps with a pang of regret, that as a youth he had been too busy to be a rake. He was rigidly formal; after he had been made Earl of Hardwicke his eldest son was granted the courtesy title of Viscount Royston, so thereafter he wrote to him as 'My Dear Lord'. At the age of 59 this legal robot decided that what he required at his estate at **Wimpole** in Cambridgeshire was a sham castle. He was pointed toward the expert in the field, Mr Sanderson Miller.

But young Philip Yorke, the former ragamuffin who improbably scampered through the streets of Dover, was now an earl, and it was inconceivable that he should stoop to converse with a commoner such as Sanderson Miller. Commoners were people he sentenced, not dealt with. Sir George Lyttelton of

Hagley Hall, Miller's first sham castle client, was selected as the go-between. Fair play, the Lord Chancellor would have been a busy man. He may have been admired and respected professionally, but his contemporary Lord Waldegrave described him as being 'not quite a gentleman', whereas Sanderson Miller was.

And then there is a hiatus; no one is quite sure why. This pillar of rectitude commissioned his sham castle in 1749, ten years before Miller began to exhibit signs of depression, but nothing was built for over 20 years. The construction was eventually carried out by Cambridge architect James Essex, an expert in Gothic architecture, working with Capability Brown, for Hardwicke's son, the earl having died in the interim. The results were spectacular: Agneta Yorke, his daughter-in-law, wrote to Lady Grey, 'Though I saw them begun and finished, I can scarce persuade myself that they are artificial' (Fig 7.3).

Ralph Allen

A primary school teacher of our acquaintance tells us that in every year's intake there are children who stand out from the crowd through intellect, ability or sheer force of character. Once every decade or so someone truly exceptional comes along. Ralph Allen's family and teachers understood that. He was a publican's son from Cornwall, yet by the age of 11 he was running the St Columb Post Office, at a time when the post office fulfilled the functions of Apple, Amazon, Facebook and Google put together. His talents attracted wider attention, and he was removed to the Exeter Post Office aged 15, then at 17 to Bath where he was rapidly made Deputy Postmaster, with a substantial salary, aged only 19. Such a giddy rise in an age when family counted for more than talent shows that Ralph Allen was a remarkable man.

Settling in Bath for the rest of his life, he amassed a fortune by securing a virtual monopoly on postal services in the area, and later from his acquisition of the Combe Down quarries from which the beautiful building stone of Bath was cut. He was treasurer of the Avon Navigation, a canal from Bath to Bristol that was completed in just three years and allowed him to export his honeyed Bath stone with ease, via a rail link – before railways had been invented. Everything he touched came to success, except perhaps a short and ill-advised foray onto the national political stage. His quarries succeeded for many reasons – the scale of the operations, the innovation, the product. It was a vast undertaking, far bigger than any of the other local diggings, dominating by sheer size. Allen embraced new technology, building a wagonway, the forerunner of the railway, to haul his stone down to the canal he had built. Bath stone was formerly quarried as uneven rubble, but Allen ensured that his stone was cut in clean, crisp blocks.

As well as business acumen, he had a natural ability for friendship, and he counted Pitt the Elder, Alexander Pope and royalty among the regular visitors to his mansion at Prior Park. When Pope died, he employed his gardener John Scott, one of the earliest growers of pineapples in England. The novelist Henry Fielding cast him as the avuncular Squire Allworthy in *Tom Jones*. Only his fellow Bathonian Captain Philip Thicknesse (1719–1792), an eccentric and rather a brute, dubbed Dr Viper because of his venomous pen and tongue, resented Allen, describing Prior Park as 'A noble seat, which sees all Bath, and which was built, probably for all Bath to see'. Modesty was not one of Allen's faults, but blessed with friends and fortune these are the only words we can find said against him.

He was a cheerful and well-tempered man; practical, wealthy, contented, comfortable; not the obsessive, slinking character one expects of a compulsive builder. On his steeply sloping estate at Prior Park he built one of the three major Palladian bridges in England (Stowe and Wilton House are the others), and on Bathwick Hill above the city he built the archetypal eyecatcher folly – **Ralph Allen's Sham Castle**, built by his clerk of works Richard Jones. This is an enchanting folly, neat, two-dimensional, large enough to be interesting, a perfect model castle to be seen from Lilliput Alley where Allen had his Bath town house (Fig 7.4).

Why would such a rational, logical, level-headed man build a folly, and such a sensible folly?

When first built it was referred to as the Castle on the Warren. In between premierships William Pitt the Elder (1708–1778), the gouty politician and family of the *soi-disant* architect Thomas Pitt whom we've met designing the Cyclopic Bridge at Park Place, wrote a letter to Sanderson Miller in 1755 asking for

Fig 7.4

Ralph Allen's Sham Castle:

the first example of billboard

architecture? [© Robert Down/

fotoLibra]

one call upon your Imagination for a considerable Gothick Object which is to stand in a very fine situation on the Hills near Bath. It is for Mr. Allen ... The name of that excellent man will render my desires to you to do your best unnecessary. I shall have a particular pleasure in procuring to him the help of the Great Master of Gothick.

But we have a theory.

There's no doubt that Allen enjoyed building, a necessary precondition for any folly builder, but he was first and foremost a businessman. Bath in the 18th century was a boom town, the most fashionable destination outside London. The John Woods, father and son architects, were building beautiful squares, circuses and crescents, the hot, healing springs were a draw for wealthy invalids and their restless, fun-seeking relatives. Socialite and celebrity Beau Nash was the Master of Ceremonies.

We propose that Ralph Allen's Sham Castle was the first example of billboard architecture, a building designed to attract attention and promote a product or service, in this case Ralph Allen's Bath stone. This is an advertisement high on a hill, the 18th century's Hollywood Sign. Come to Bath, it cries, and you can live the dream.

Allen had kept on his town address, and it is from there that one had a fine view of the eyecatcher on Bathwick Hill. The sham castle is delineated exactly as it stands now on the maps in the manuscript *Survey of the Manours of Bathampton, Claverton and Widcombe belonging to Ralph Allen Esq* of between 1758 and 1761. Common opinion has it that the eyecatcher was built in 1762, after Sanderson Miller's illness had begun, and Allen's Clerk of Works, Richard Jones (1703–after 1772), claimed, after everyone concerned had died, to have both designed and built the sham castle. There's no doubt it owes something, if not everything, to Miller's original design. It presents a case in point about eyecatching, consisting of a castellated frontage, two apparently round towers (in fact only semi-circular) flanking the opening arch, and to the sides are short walls ending in squat, square towers. Everything is castellated and adorned with blind arrow slits and blind windows. The purpose is to provide, for the viewer in Lilliput Lane, the silhouette of a castle-like building. On closer inspection it dupes no one – it is just a wall, with nothing behind it, utterly two dimensional and cardboardy, more eyecatcher than sham castle, and perhaps the most specific in design and purpose. There is a decent plaque commemorating its restoration in 1921, and it seems that ivy never mantled its buttresses. The quality of the workmanship is unmistakable. Two hundred and fifty years later the stone is still razor sharp. This is a masterpiece; an example of how good Ralph Allen's Bath stone could look.

And because he was a kindly, genial fellow, it was also a bit of fun.

The sham castle or half-ruined tower enjoyed a brief flurry of popularity: Mow Cop on the Cheshire/Staffordshire border (Fig 7.5), Old John in Leicester's Bradgate Park, St David's Ruin in Bingley, Ingestre, Hagley, Wimpole, Radway, Wroxton. All were built within a 20-year period and all survive, with the exception of Ingestre, which was demolished in the mid-19th century.

Gazetteer

County/Authority	Location	Folly
Bristol and Avon	Backwell	Larcombe's Folly
	Bath	Ralph Allen's Sham Castle
	Brislington	Black Castle
	Bristol	St Vincent's Priory
		Cook's Folly
	Chew Magna	Chota Castle
	Henbury	Blaise Castle
	Midford	Roebuck's Folly
	Pill	Sham Fort
	Walton-in-Gordano	Walton Castle
Berkshire	Windsor	Sham Ruin Dairy
		Frogmore Sham Ruin
	Winterbourne	Hop Castle
Buckinghamshire	Buckingham	Buckingham Gaol
	Dinton	Dinton Castle
	Fawley Court	Gothic Sham Ruin
	Gerrards Cross	The Keep
Cambridgeshire	Grantchester	Castle Ruin
	Wimpole	Sham Ruin
	Wisbech	Flint House
Cheshire	Bridgemere	Bridgemere Nursery Mow Cop
	Mow Cop	Mow Cop
	Oxton	Folly Castle
	Runcorn	Halton Castle
Cornwall	Mount Edgecumbe	Mount Edgecumbe Sham Ruin
	Redruth	Carn Brea Castle
	Werrington Park	Terrace House
Cumbria	Corby Castle	Vulcan's Forge
	Greystoke	Fort Putnam
Derbyshire	Newton Solney	Hoskin's Folly (Bladon Castle)
	Riber	Riber Castle
Devon	Filham	Sham Sham Ruin
	Kingswear	Mill Bay Cove Castle
	Mamhead	Sham Castle
	Plymouth	Fort Bovisand
		Radford Castle
	Roborough	Maristow Sham Ruin
	Saltram	The Castle
	Shaldon	Sham Castle Kitchen
	Torquay	Sladnor Park Folly
Dorset	Lulworth Castle	Bastion
	Sherborne Castle	The Folly
Durham	Stockton-on-Tees	St Cuthbert's Vicarage Ruins
East Sussex	Eridge	Sham Farm
Gloucestershire	Chipping Campden	Sham Castle
	Cirencester	Alfred's Hall

County/Authority	Location	Folly
	Ozleworth	Robert Parson's Folly
	Stroud	Rodborough Fort
Hampshire	Hursley	The Castle
Herefordshire	Elton	Tortoise Castle
	Goodrich	Coppett Hill Folly
	Weston-under-Penyard	Bollitree Sham Castle
Hertfordshire	Aldenham	Wall Hall Ruined Abbey
	Benington	Benington Lordship Sham Ruin
	Gilston	Sham Porch
	Knebworth	Knebworth Sham Ruin
	South Mimms	Spoils
	Stanstead Abbots	Sham Ruin
	Waltham Cross	Pulhamite Walling
Isle of Wight	East Cowes	Albert Barracks
Kent	Borough Green	Sham Ruin
	Kearsney	Kearnsey Abbey Sham Ruin
	Kingsgate	Arx Ruohim
	Knole	Sham Ruin
	Ospringe	Sham Ruin
	Throwley	Sham Church
Lancashire	Rivington	Liverpool Castle
	Whalley	Baby House Tower
	Wigan	Arley Hall Folly
Leicestershire	Bradgate Park	Old John
	Exton Park (Rutland)	Fort Henry
Lincolnshire	Belton	Sham Ruin
	Cleethorpes	Ross Castle
	East Wykeham	Ruined Church
	Louth	Priory Sham Ruin Brackenborough Hall Sham Ruin
	Skegness	Sham Castle Façade
	Tealby	Castle Farm
Liverpool and Manchester	Stockport	Godley Castellated Pigsty
London	N1	Crumbles Castle
	N3	Avenue House Bothy
	N4	Stoke Newington Pumping Station
	NW9	Trobridge Buck's Lane
	SE26	Sydenham Sham Ruin
	SW19	Sham Castle
	Mitcham	Ruined Sham Ruin
	Woodford Green	Sham Ruin
Norfolk	Crimplesham Hall	Sham Chapel
	Didlington	Kate's Castle
North Yorkshire	Aske Hall	Oliver Duckett Sham Castle
	Bishopthorpe	Bastion

County/Authority	Location	Folly
	Constable Burton	Akebar Caravan Park
	Crayke	Crayke Castle
	East Witton	Tilsey Folly
	Grewelthorpe	Mowbray Castle
	Kirkleatham	Bastions Fortresses
	Leyburn	Sham Castle
Northumberland	Cambo	Rothley Castle Codger's Fort
	Capheaton Hall	Sham Chapel
	Ford	Castle Gates
	Kielder	Kielder Castle
	Twizel	Twizel Castle
Nottinghamshire	Budby	Budby Castle
	Newstead	Small Sham Fort Sham Fort
Oxfordshire	Abingdon	Sham Ruin
	Highmoor	Sham Castle
Shropshire	Acton Burnell	Acton Burnell Sham Castle
	Bridgnorth	Fort Pendleton
	Hawkstone	Hawkstone Citadel Hawkstone Red Castle
	Ironbridge	Severn Wharf Building
	Quatford	Quatford Castle
	Wroxeter	Sham Ruin
Somerset	Banwell	Banwell Castle
	Bridgwater	Castle House
	Burrow Bridge	Burrow Mump Church
	Crowcombe	Crowcombe Sham Ruin
	Dulverton	Pepperpot Castle
South Yorkshire	Stainborough	Stainborough Castle Steeple Lodge
Staffordshire	Consall	Pompeii
	Ecton	Sham Castle
	Longdon	Hanch Hall Cathedral
	Meretown	The Castle
	Mucklestone	Oakley Folly
	Seighford	Sham Church
	Shugborough	The Ruins
	Stafford	Stafford Castle
Suffolk	Claydon	Ruins
	Euston Hall	Sham Church
	Eye	Sham Castle
	Great Saxham	Umbrello
	Hadleigh	Sham Ruin
Surrey	Cobham	Sham Abbey

County/Authority	Location	Folly
	Esher	Leahurst Sham Castle
	Godalming	Little Fort
	Guildford	Moat House
	Peper Harow	Sham Ruin
	Viginia Water	Sham Ruins
Warwickshire	Alcester	Oversley Castle
	Solihull	Sir Anthony's Keep
West Sussex	Hickstead	Hickstead Sham Castle
	Worthing	Castle Goring
West Yorkshire	Roundhay	Sham Castle
Wiltshire	Corsham	Sham Castle Screen
	Devizes	Devizes Castle
Worcestershire	Belbroughton	Castle Bourne
	Clent	Sham Ruin
	Croome d'Abitot	Dunstall Castle
	Hagley	Ruinated Castle

Fig 7.5
Mow Cop. [© David Siddons/
fotoLibra]

8 The genius of the place: folly groups and gardens

Even the least spiritual among us has felt that catch in the throat, that momentary disequilibrium when the landscape appears to shift and we're gazing with wild surmise at another world, one virtually the same but indefinably different. Then in a flash it's gone, and we're back to banal normality again.

For centuries men and women have been trying to capture and preserve that difference. Today the word 'genius' is applied to people. In the 18th century it was applied to places as well – *genius loci* was the genius of the place, the special attributes that marked a site out as being out of the ordinary. And out of the genius of the 18th century, England produced the magi to achieve this magic – William Kent, Capability Brown, Humphrey Repton and others.

Selecting the right place to build is beyond art, it is metaphysical, and one of the troubles with living in the 21st century is that most of the best places have already been taken. There's something about old houses that simply feels right, as if they were born of the soil. Local building materials have something to do with it; a house built from local stone will always be more at home than any brick-faced breeze-blocked implant. There are practical considerations as well. There needed to be a regular water supply from a river or a well; today we just tap into the mains. Light and shelter were important; now we draw the curtains and turn up the heating. The Bible advised us not to build our houses upon sand but forgot to mention flood plains, so politicians and developers eagerly pressed ahead, with the inevitable soggy consequences. Great views are always a plus, though few of us have the time or funds to order the landscape to our wishes as our forebears did, knowing they were working for succeeding generations. Plant a cedar of Lebanon today and it's a certainty that you won't live to see it at its full glory in the landscape.

Two thousand years ago Vitruvius got it right, excepting perhaps the infectious breath of venomous animals:

> In the Situation of a Country-House, Respect should be had to the Region of the Air, to the Climate, and to the Conveniency of the Place ; that the Place should be easily accessible, fertile, plenteous in itself, and adjoining to Rivers and Ports, capable of serving it with all the Commodities of the Neighbouring Parts : That above all it should be healthful, not situate in a low and marshy ground, because of the Corruption caused by the infectious breath of venomous Animals which breed there, and occasion many noxious Humours and Distempers : That, on the other hand, the Situation be not too high and mountainous, lest it be subject to Fogs and Storms of Wind, which destroy and tear up all before them : and lastly, that the House be not turn'd to the South, or West, because heat weakens the Body, and Cold strengthens it. To seat a Country-House well, it should be considered, in the first place, what Exposition is most wholesome, and let the House be turn'd that way.

Landscape is such an everyday English word that it is mildly surprising it only entered into the language in the 17th century. Now we have landscape architecture, landscape photography, landscape design, landscaping; it has even come to mean oblong, as in landscape versus portrait images. It came from a Dutch word, *landschap*, borrowed by artists as a technical term for a picture representing natural inland scenery as opposed to a seascape. Towards the end of the 17th century, poets, writers and gardeners began a quiet rebellion against the existing ordered formality of gardens and verse:

> Tir'd of the scene parterres and fountains yield,
> He finds at last he better likes a field.

The first celebrity gardener was William Kent, who followed the irregular paths of gardeners such as Stephen Switzer (1682–1745) and Charles Bridgeman (d. 1738) and the pioneering Philip Southcote at Woburn Farm, Chertsey, the first *ferme ornée*, a phrase unknown in France. Within a couple of decades the *jardin anglais* swept Europe as England's first real cultural export. *Le style anglais* become a byword for elegance and sophistication and has never really lost that early glitter. What is seldom mentioned is that the naturalistic style of landscape gardening was much cheaper to implement than formal parterres, box hedges and borders, and cost is always a consideration, although then, as now, there was money in gardening: in 1728 Bridgeman was appointed to the Royal Gardens on a salary of £2,220 a year.

John and William Aislabie/Studley Royal and Hackfall

Gardening and corruption make strange bedfellows. Corruption is decried by everyone and practised by everyone who has the opportunity. It goes without saying that all third-world countries are corrupt – although technically Switzerland, Sweden and Ireland are third-world countries – and a politician who fights an election on an anti-corruption platform is often fighting to conceal corruption rather than expose it.

But we have nothing today remotely like the corruption that was practised in England in the 18th century. Have you ever wondered why you never see the descendants of former prime ministers sleeping under bridges? Even though MPs weren't paid a salary until 1911, politicians who achieved power ruthlessly shook down the economy to benefit themselves, their families and to a lesser extent their constituencies. If you're sitting under an apple tree, why not eat a few apples? There's plenty to go round.

Few exemplified this greed and plunder better than John Aislabie, a Yorkshireman through and through (Fig 8.1). How do we judge him from our moral high ground nearly three centuries distant? As an unprincipled villain and rogue (which he was, and perhaps it ran in the blood – his father was killed in a duel after his antagonist had called him 'the scum of the county') or as the creator of one of the most beautiful corners of one of the most beautiful counties in England? For that he was too.

The talented Aislabie rose to become Chancellor of the Exchequer. In this position, the most senior financial policy-making appointment in the land, he vigorously promoted the South Sea Company's bid to take over the national debt in exchange for government bonds, against Robert Walpole's backing for

Fig 8.1

Hero or villain? John Aislabie.

[Gwyn Headley collection]

the Bank of England. Aislabie won. There was no greater folly in the 18th century than the South Sea Company. The South Sea Bubble burst in 1720 and Aislabie was discovered to have acquired stock valued at £77,000, which he had sold for nearly double that sum. His guilt was 'so apparent and so heinous that nobody had the courage to stand up in his favour'. He was found guilty by the House of Commons of the 'most notorious, dangerous and infamous corruption', expelled from the House and sent to the Tower of London. Speaker Arthur Onslow described Aislabie as a 'dark, cunning' man, 'suspected and low in all men's opinion'. He was as unpopular as a heron but luckier than Secretary of State Earl Stanhope, also severely compromised, who spoke with such vehemence defending himself against corruption charges during a debate in the Lords that he burst a blood vessel and died.

But rich men often muddle through somehow, and within a month Aislabie was released from the Tower to go and cultivate his garden at Studley Royal, in North Yorkshire. Somehow he was allowed to retain his money and estates, and had enough spare cash left over in 1724 to endow a dowry of £13,000 on his daughter. Then this dark, cunning crook produced a work of sublime beauty that still has the power to take our breath away today, long before Kent, Bridgeman, Brown and Repton came to wreak their magic. One of the companies anonymously promoted in the South Sea Bubble was 'for improving of gardens' – who can say if there was a connection?

He had the natural advantage of the land, an escarpment overlooking a bend in the river Skell, and he had no need of a sham ruin as Thomas Cromwell had seen to that for him when he removed the roof of Fountains Abbey a couple of centuries earlier. In 1986 the abbey and park were designated a World Heritage Site by UNESCO as a masterpiece of human creative genius.

Studley Royal is a garden for showing off, all done in the best possible taste. No foolish eccentricities here; it's refined classicism all the way. We are led past temples and octagons, a fishing house, a banqueting house, Anne Boleyn's Seat (the poor queen is unlikely to have visited), along a path bordered on the right by a thick, impenetrable hedge – at least, that was the intention; when we were last there it was disappointingly transparent – which breaks suddenly at the **Surprise View** to reveal Fountains Abbey in all its glory (Fig 8.2). When it works, it works spectacularly. His son William, also MP for Ripon, continued and improved his work.

Genius or crook? Both, in Aislabie's case. When the singer Aretha Franklin died, obituaries noted that as a person she was truculent, mean-spirited, small-minded, extremely insecure and jealous of anyone else's success, but who will remember her all-too-human flaws when she left us that voice? Among the many enraptured visitors today to Studley Royal there will be a few whose ancestors were reduced to beggary as a result of John Aislabie's machinations. But they are long forgotten, and the beauty he created lives on.

After John Aislabie died in 1742 young William came into his own. He developed Mackershaw, a side-valley and part of Studley Royal, into an area 'partaking more of nature and less of art', but art took shape in 'the Roman pill-box', dedicated to the three Horatii, and at Chinese Wood a pagoda and pavilion (there are bills in 1744/45 for 'ye Cheineys Building ... in South scarr'). But William was also concerned with tastefully augmenting the supply of garden buildings in Studley itself, gothicising at least one temple and adding Anne Boleyn's Seat. It has been argued more than once that part of Studley represents a 'political landscape'. It must have been, for there we also have the remains of a Column to Liberty and a Quebec Monument. William left an unpublished text entitled *Essay upon some Particulars of the Ancient and Modern Government, Conventions and Parliament of England*. Nearer the end of his life he succeeded in buying the ruins of Fountains Abbey, thus crowning the glory that is Studley.

But it was only at **Hackfall** that William felt he had a completely free hand. Its appearance was dictated by the lay of the land: the wooded and rocky valley of the river Ure, at most times a docile piece of water but after the rains becoming a foaming white monster of a river. We were there in the early 1980s when an army helicopter following the course of the river was looking for a drowned soldier who had fallen into it during exercises. And on other days there were startling gun shots fired by hunters (we hoped), or there'd be sudden patches of quicksand to contend with. All in all, Hackfall was not only a sublime garden in appearance. Aislabie developed his park during the 1740s–1760s, and

Fig 8.2
The Surprise View at Studley
Royal. [© Erik Strodl/fotoLibra]

punctuated the existing landscape with garden buildings that were in keeping with the rough-and-ready genius of the place. Hackfall, near the small village of Grewelthorpe, became one of the first and perhaps the most truly 'romantick' sublime gardens in Great Britain. With its hanging woods, wild river, rivulets, miniature cataracts and rocky cliffs, only Hawkstone and perhaps Piercefield in Wales are contenders for the title.

The garden has been taken on by The Woodland Trust and other organisations, and our initial fears that they may take the spirit out of the garden have been proved wrong: they restored several buildings and cleared some of the overgrowth, but Hackfall mostly remains as it was.

Most of the follies are examples of minimum effort, maximum effect. Near the entrance is the rather dull stone and tufa seat known as Kent's Seat (a hero of Aislabie's), facing the Alumn Cascade, which still trickles feebly down the mossy stone. A little further on is **Fisher's Hall**, perhaps referring to fishing, but possibly to Aislabie's head gardener for Studley, William Fisher, who died in 1743 (Fig 8.3). A delightful little edifice, 'a small Octagon Room, built of petrifactions' so the *Tourist's Companion* of 1822 tells us, Fisher's Hall has lost its rustic roofing, but the inside walls still carry the remains of shells and pieces of glass. Above the door is a tablet inscribed 'W.A./1750'. It seems to owe something to a design in the pattern book *Architectural Remembrancer* by Robert Morris (1702?–1754), but that was only published in 1751. Yet his kinsman, the architect Roger Morris (1695–1749), had worked at Studley; the two appear to have been close and did indeed on occasions collaborate.

To the north is the Fountain Plain, the only spot at Hackfall where there was a formal layout, with a 'Fountain throwing Water to a great height'. That has now been reinstated, as is the nearby Grotto, which is more of a Seat, recently rebuilt and a little too fresh for our tastes. The nearby Rustic Temple, a simple enough building in the cyclopean vein, has had its gap-toothed castellations restored. In one of the interior walls is a niche for a statuette. Still further to the north lie the remains of what was once called the Sand Bed Hut, and a small obelisk, broken in two and probably dating from Victorian times when Lord Ripon owned Hackfall.

The two largest and more intricate follies are each on the edge of the cliffs that form the natural boundary of the estate. **Mowbray Castle**, which towers high above the Ure to the south, is visible from the other side of the garden. The view towards Mowbray Castle was painted by Turner in 1816. The castle is a sham ruined open tower, meant to be seen from both sides. Gothick, with cruciform arrow slits and pointed entrances and windows, it also has sham features on the inside. Its name refers to the local De Mowbrays, fierce medieval knights, and the romance was augmented by the fact that almost all of them died violent deaths.

Above the Fountain Plain stands **Mowbray Point** Banqueting House, with a ruined Servant's Hall nearby (Fig 8.4). Here the family had their meals, as Hackfall has no residence, although they may have had small meals at Fisher's Hall, which has the remains of a small kitchen close by. Mowbray Point, now restored by the Landmark Trust, with its splendid view, has two distinct façades, one turned towards the fields and showing an Elysian Greek front (or back), the other facing the great expanse of land beyond Hackfall itself (Fig 8.5). This façade represents a sham Roman ruin: three arches of crumbling sandstone, looking like a minor edition of the Baths of Caracalla, as well as the Baths of

Fig 8.3
Fisher's Hall, Hackfall.
[© Karen Lynch]

Diocletian, both in Rome, and perhaps inspired by the engravings of sham Roman ruins in Batty Langley's *New Principles of Gardening*, which Aislabie seems to have used also for the design of the Fountain Plain. Langley (1696–1751) was a Freemason who called his four sons Hiram, Euclid, Vitruvius and Archimedes. Despite their august first names, they do not seem to have made

Fig 8.4
Mowbray Point Ruin before restoration by the Landmark Trust. [© Gwyn Headley/ fotoLibra]

Fig 8.5
... and after. [© Paul Brooker]

an impression in later life. There is one other contender for the design though: Robert Adam produced a design for a very similar building, mixed up with the papers for Kedleston Hall but never produced there. Adam worked on projects for two London houses of Aislabie's. Who said architectural history was easy?

Sharawaggi

Sir William Temple (1628–1699) was dashingly handsome, with a mane of rich dark brown curls (Fig 8.6). He was multilingual, well-travelled, sophisticated, Cambridge-educated, musical and good-humoured. Of course, he had a fatal flaw – he was vain (and also worryingly fond of fruit. He once gorged on so many peaches in Brussels that he felt unable to take a boat to Antwerp, for fear of asphyxiating his fellow passengers). As British Ambassador to the Netherlands he was astoundingly adept at negotiations, signing off a treaty with France in less than five days. Where is his like today?

In 1692 he published an essay that introduced the word 'sharawadgi' (or sharawaggi) to the English language.

> What I have said of the best forms of gardens is meant only of such as are in some sort regular; for there may be other forms wholly irregular that may, for aught I know, have more beauty than any of the others. But they must owe it to some extraordinary dispositions of nature in the seat, or some great race of fancy or judgement in the contrivance which may reduce many disagreeing parts into some figure which shall yet upon the whole be very agreeable. Something of this I have seen in some places but heard more of it from others who have lived much among the Chinese, a people whose way of thinking seems to lie as wide of ours in Europe as their country does.

Among us, the beauty of building and planting is placed chiefly in some certain proportions, symmetries, or uniformities; our walks and our trees ranged so as to answer one another, and at exact distances. The Chinese scorn this way of planting and say a boy who can count to a hundred may plant walks of trees in straight lines and over against one another, and to what length and extent he pleases. But their greatest reach of imagination is employed in contriving figures, where the beauty shall be great and strike the eye, but without any order or disposition of parts that shall be commonly or easily observed. And though we have hardly any notion of this sort of beauty, yet they have a particular word to express it; and, where they find it hit their eye at first sight, they say the Sharawadgi is fine or is admirable or any such expression of esteem. And whoever observes the work upon the best Indian gowns or the painting upon their best screens or porcelain will find their beauty is all of this kind [that is] without order. But I should hardly advise any of these attempts in the figure of gardens among us; they are adventures of too hard achievement for any common hands; and though there may be more honour if they succeed well, yet there is more dishonour if they fail, and it is twenty to one they will; whereas, in regular figures, it is hard to make any great and remarkable faults.

Fig 8.6

The peachy Sir William Temple.

[© World History Archive/ fotoLibra]

Essentially sharawaggi is using a lack of symmetry to achieve beauty, the thesis of all English landscape gardens since Kent. There's no such word in Chinese – scholars agree it cannot belong to that language – but the Japanese have a word that sounds like 'soroete', which means 'all together in harmony'. Just as it's hard for a Japanese to distinguish between an Austrian and a Dane, so Temple may have confused the Chinese with the Japanese. And just as feng shui guides the interior layout of a house, so sharawaggi influences the surrounding external landscape.

Had Temple looked across the border to Wales he may have encountered the ancient word *cynefin*, meaning the habitat, the landscape and all that is in it; the Welsh version of sharawaggi. The pitifully few grand country houses built in Wales all had parks carefully shaped by *cynefin*.

Kent/Stowe

Everyone with the mildest interest in landscape has heard of Capability Brown, but the man who really started it all in England was William Kent (1685–1748). The most famous compliment paid to him was by Horace Walpole, who said 'He leapt the fence and saw that all nature was a garden'. Born William Cant in Yorkshire, he showed remarkable artistic gifts from an early age. Charming, talented, cheerful by nature, extremely talkative but by no means well educated, his home town of Bridlington would not detain him long and by the age of 25 he was in Rome under the patronage of a group of Yorkshire businessmen.

The Grand Tour, which wealthy young men undertook as a kind of 18th-century gap year, was designed to increase their awareness and appreciation of classical art and architecture. What is now barely remembered is how perilous these expeditions could be. Protestants had to keep very quiet about their religion. Robbers, footpads, pirates, thugs and bandits roamed at will. Small wars broke out at random. Disease, sickness and injuries were ever-present dangers. Wolves, bears and other wild animals were common and aggressive. There was no European Union or Schengen agreement; the traveller had to pass through a plethora of statelets and petty kingdoms to reach Rome, each demanding passports and identification and fees. The richer the traveller, the more insulated he was from these dangers, but Kent, from a humbler background, was perpetually short of money. Within the English community in Rome, he lived in relative safety, and even won a medal from the Pope for his drawing ability.

For ten years Kent studied in Italy, and when he returned to England, referring to himself jocosely as Signor Guigliemo Kentino, he was commissioned by Lord Burlington to paint ceilings at Burlington House. By now he was 35 and there was, as yet, no hint of the future revolutionary garden designer. He spent ten further years working for his good friend Burlington.

But then in 1730 he came to Stowe.

Richard Temple of Stowe (1675–1749) was a military man to the core. Born Richard Grenville, he was not related to the previously mentioned Sir William Temple. He joined the army aged nine and within a year was court martialled for disobeying orders, the naughty little fellow. This was merely a hiccup; by the age of 30 he was a major-general. He distinguished himself by his military skill and bravery in the War of the Spanish Succession in Flanders.

He was obliged to take up paid employment to pay off the debts his family had built up over the years. As we saw with John Aislabie, dabbling in politics was a sure way at the time to amass a fair-sized fortune, and he obtained several sinecures such as Constable of Windsor Castle and Plenipotentiary to the Imperial Court at Vienna. He also felt obliged to live like a duke, or certainly to spend like one. If he was eclipsed in profligacy by his son and grandson, who finally succeeded in bankrupting the family with old masters and young mistresses, he did the best he could. Before long he fell out of favour in the political world and took gardening leave – perhaps the greatest gardening leave ever taken.

From 1713 he embarked on a tumult of building and gardening. His grand house at Stowe, Buckinghamshire, was enlarged and extended; the finest gardeners in England, including Charles Bridgeman, Kent and later Capability Brown were employed to design and build the new estate; he was even credited with inventing the ha-ha, a sort of sunken fence. By running the grass right up to a ditch bounded by a retaining wall, the line of sight from the garden into the surrounding countryside flowed seamlessly, without a visible wall to break the transition. This was the infinity pool of the 18th century, a master stroke that other landowners rushed to copy. Temple certainly introduced it to England. His garden foreman John Lee has also been mentioned in its creation, while Walpole credited Bridgeman. Its first mention was in 1712, in A-J Dézallier d'Argenville's

EARL TEMPLE.

Fig 8.7
Richard Temple, a fine gardener
and murderer. [© Malcolm
Warrington/fotoLibra]

Theory & Practice of Gardening, translated by J James: 'The End of this Terrass is terminated by an Opening, which the French call a Claire-voïe, or an Ah, Ah, with a dry Ditch at the foot of it'. A claire-voïe today is an opening in a garden wall closed by only a grille, while the French for a ha-ha is *un saut-de-loup*, a wolf's leap, a trifling obstacle, which they lugubriously anticipated a wolf would inevitably cross in a single bound.

The invention of the ha-ha charmed and delighted the civilised world. Sadly, its end is now in sight, because most ha-has were deployed in the gardens of country houses, which in the 21st century have resorted to holding wedding receptions to defray running costs. Weddings in England inevitably come with very drunken guests, the sort of people who never would have been invited to the house in former times, who fall into the ha-ha and break their bones. When they sober up they sue the venue. So ha-has now have to be fenced off, destroying the very reason for their existence.

The gardens at Stowe rapidly became famous, and in 1717 Temple opened the New Inn just outside the grounds to accommodate the growing number of visitors. He held £32,000 of South Sea Company stock, which must have hit him hard when the bubble burst in 1720. He acquired the title Baron Cobham – and this superlative garden creator was a cruel, vindictive and domineering man. Two peasants were captured poaching on his 55,000 acre estate. He promised their wives they would be released the following Tuesday. On the appointed day a cart rolled up with two coffins, and a message to the widows: 'Lord Cobham says to remind you that he kept his word' (Fig 8.7).

Kent arrived after Cobham had been working on his gardens for 17 years. The five years he gave to Stowe were inspirational, influential creativity. He planted dead trees purely for the effect. He created the Vale and built at least seven new buildings. In Hertfordshire Sir Jeremy Sambrooke's 'pleasure ground' at Gobions was much admired as 'a sensible Resemblance in Miniature of Stow', wrote George Bickham the Younger in his *Beauties of Stow* (1750). All that remains is the Folly Arch at Brookmans Park.

By the age of 42 Cobham had been elevated to a viscountcy. This abhorrent creature (by our standards) created something of great beauty and importance. How do we judge men like him and Aislabie? By the standards of our time, or theirs? His sins and crimes are unknown to most present-day visitors entranced by the sylvan loveliness of the Stowe estate and the splendour of its architecture. Cobham framed his politics in stone, strewing the grounds with monuments, towers, temples, bridges, arches – what we call today follies – but which here are genuinely misunderstood buildings. These gardens had a purpose. They were created for contemplation, as political and philosophical statements. It is interesting that most landscape gardens seem to have been created by Whigs. Perhaps it was the Tories who first derided them as follies. An 18th-century visitor would have caught the allusions instantly: the Temple of Ancient Virtue,

Fig 8.8

The landscape gardens at Stowe.

[© Peter Vallence/fotoLibra]

intact and glowing with classical beauty, was juxtaposed with the sham ruins of the Temple of Modern Virtue with a headless torso representing Prime Minister Walpole, a dig even our distant ribs can feel (Fig 8.8).

Kent died at the age of 63, succumbing to 'high feeding and an inactive life'.

Stourhead

The other great English folly garden is **Stourhead** (Fig 8.9). It has for a long time been considered the quintessential English park/garden. But present-day Stourhead is a falsification, by omission, or rather by destruction. The cleansing of this glorious park had already started shortly after its creator Henry Hoare (1705–1785) left for the Elysian Fields. His grandson, Sir Richard Colt Hoare (1758–1838), did most of the damage, but see below. Henry's father 'Henry the Good' (1677–1725), managed the family-led bank of C. Hoare and Co., and consolidated its standing, originating from a goldsmithing business and a horse dealership. 'Our' Henry was, according to the bank's official history in a burst of humility, known as 'The Magnificent'.

Magnificent or not, Henry II led the bank, and despite being an MP for a spell, appears not to have been overly interested in politics. '[T]all and comely in his person, elegant in his manners and address and well versed in polite literature', is how his grandson Richard described him. From his correspondence and his other writings Henry certainly appears to have been a cultured man. His first interest was in art: paintings and sculpture; his second gardening. His collection of Italian paintings is often said to have been fundamental in the creation of the Stourhead garden. But canvas is one thing, mud and greenery are a totally different medium. He had made his European travels, was, as noted, well versed in literature, and he had already started the landscaping of Stourhead before acquiring his first Claude. And that is exactly what makes Stourhead a work of genius: it is emphatically not a painting, but better. Stourhead was a hard taskmaster. Hoare kept adding to it, finicking and fine-tuning till he thought he got it just right. The trouble was that by the 1760s he had turned over a new leaf regarding the decorations for the garden. Till now they had been either pristinely classical or rustic: well-designed temples that stood out in the overall picture, a splendid grotto (almost the *raison d'être* for the garden) and a few bridges, as well as that tremendous sheet of water in front of it. But now he introduced the Gothick, the Chinese and the Turkish. And it was over this that there was a posthumous Style War with his grandson, Richard Colt Hoare.

Henry Hoare senior had acquired Stourhead around 1719, torn down the old house and built the Palladian mansion that was finished by 1724, awaiting Henry's death a year later. Henry II spent his first 15 years of ownership adding to the house's collection of paintings. The garden was only devised when his mother, Jane Benson, died in 1741. The artificial lake still forms the centre of the garden, and the surrounding temples, those of Ceres (later dedicated to Flora), Hercules and Apollo, together with the extensive grotto and the bridge, look as if they were designed in one splendid throw. They weren't. 1744, 1754 and 1765 are the respective dates for the temples (Fig 8.10). The elaborate grotto, constructed from brick covered with tufa, where Ariadne sleeps and the River God presides, dates from 1748, and was apparently built by the mason William Privett (?–1772?), who came from the quarrying hamlet of Chilmark

Fig 8.9

Stourhead; one of the glories of

English landscape architecture.

[© Paul Groom/fotoLibra]

Fig 8.10

The 1765 Temple of Apollo at Stourhead. [© Stephen Owen/ fotoLibra]

near Tisbury, and was involved in the practical building work for more than one edifice at Stourhead. The bridge dates from 1762.

Most of the buildings at Stourhead were, however, designed by the same architect, Henry Flitcroft (1697–1769), who though a confirmed Palladian, was also the originator of such follies as the rather weird and triangular Hoober Stand at Wentworth Woodhouse and the three-sided Shrub's Hill Tower, aka Belvedere Tower, at Virginia Water. This same decidedly follyesque shape was applied to Flitcroft's posthumously built **Alfred's Tower** of 1765, but only completed in 1772 (Fig 8.11). Alfred's Tower, all 160 feet of it, was built from brick, is virtually windowless, and manages to look a bit dour, but is the only true folly here. There is a statue of King Alfred (849–889) in a recess in the entrance wall. In 1944 a warplane crashed into the tower, ironically a Canadian-built Noorduyn Norseman – ironic because Alfred so valiantly fought the Norsemen or Vikings.

The tower bears witness to a change in Henry's tastes during the 1760s, changing from classic to Gothic and exotic. He also had two removal follies erected: St Peter's Pump, a late medieval (1474) conduit from Bristol, on top of a small grotto (1768), as well as Bristol High Cross (1373), which had been taken down in the early 18th century and was given to Henry by the Dean of Bristol in 1764/65. It is sited most fortuitously overlooking the gardens. He also had a greenhouse erected (in or before 1762) in what Walpole noted as 'false Gothic', later removed. Still standing is The Convent, a Gothick capriccio from around 1765, a mock religious concoction that used to have pictures of nuns along its inner walls. The outside is made rustic with irregular stones, and Gothic windows, while three rather weird spires top the irregular roofings. The architect is not known. In 1771 Hoare writes that he is building 'a Hermitage ... It is to be lined inside & out with old Gouty nobbly oakes, the Bark on ... I believe I shall put it in to be myself The Hermit'.

It was taken down by grandson Richard Colt Hoare, who mightily disapproved of the second phase of building at Stourhead. He also removed Henry's Chinese Alcove, the Chinese Bridge, and the Turkish Tent and much more. Sir Richard deserves attention in his own right, being a noted antiquarian and an avid Grand Tourist with a matching taste for publishing his travel accounts. By the early 1800s his interests in the Continent had turned to a deep and abiding interest in British topography and antiquity, publishing seminal archaeological works on Wiltshire (*Ancient History of North and South Wiltshire* in two volumes, 1812/1819), Wales and Ireland, although he kept publishing on his Italian travels. He acquired Glastonbury Tor and restored its church tower, and many barrows were excavated by Colt Hoare or by means of his finances.

An anecdote concerning the notoriously tetchy William Beckford sheds

some light on Colt Hoare's character. Joseph Farrington notes in his *Diaries* for 16 October 1806, that Jeffry Wyatt (1766–1840) had gone over to Fonthill to see the ongoing work of his uncle James. He was told by Beckford that Hoare had visited and was later censured by the county gentlemen for consorting with England's least-loved son. An over-anxious Hoare then explained himself to his fellow Wiltshire dignitaries by saying the 'meeting with Mr. Beckford was accidental & to Him unexpected'. Beckford came to know of it and remarked 'how He [Wyatt] could be such a d----d fool as to allow Sir Richard to see the Abbey'. Nevertheless, Beckford stated that Hoare 'while looking over the Abbey made some good observations but He afterwards sd. "Sir Richard had no taste"'.

Richard's dislike of rococo frivolity (a portrait shows him as a rather prissy man) wasn't extended to the late-in-life preference his grandfather displayed regarding the Gothick. Colt Hoare did destroy the Gothic greenhouse, but by 1806 built a mock-medieval structure of his own: the **Gothic Cottage** (1806) by that specialist for all things Gothic, John Carter (1748–1817) (Fig 8.12). Carter, earning from three different people the epithets of 'nervous, irascible, and eccentric', 'that well-known compound of nature' and 'a harmless inoffensive drudge', had when young published a tale about a female who had scorned him, complete with an

Fig 8.12
The Gothic Cottage at Stourhead:
eyecatching and picturesque.
[© Peter Vines/fotoLibra]

engraving of the lady in the nude, the eighteenth century predecessor of revenge porn. Later in life, according to Colvin, he was accompanied on his trips by a female servant 'dressed in boy's clothes'. How it came about that someone like Colt Hoare sought the advice of odd-ball Carter can only be explained by the taste for the medieval they both had in common, and their fervent attachment to the true Gothic and the pleasures of antiquarianism.

The Gothic Cottage, really the last of the Stourhead ensemble to be built, is nice and picturesque, but lacks the gung-ho atmosphere of The Convent. Possibly an extension of an earlier, simpler building, it sports a bay window with an ornamental seat, a hipped straw roof, and a porch. Carter, according to a letter, saw it as a project for self-assembly: 'It is possible to do the porch in town under my eye, and then sent down by the waggon, the seat also and what other parts you may wish done in this way'. And there we have Stourhead: a perfect picture, but cleansed of many of its more eccentric buildings.

Charles Hamilton/Pains Hill

Permit us our mild obsession with how rich these folly builders were, but when you come across a man who was the ninth son among 14 children, who never did a day's paid work in his life, and who rented land to create a park that pulls in awed visitors over 250 years later, the scale of inherited wealth in those days becomes apparent. The Hon Charles Hamilton (1704–1786) was the last child of the 6th Earl of Abercorn. While his father was still alive he went on two extended Grand Tours of Italy. Although he served as MP for both Strabane and Truro, this was at a time when MPs were not paid. He was in the Prince of Wales's household, as well as having the sinecure of the Receiver-General of His Majesty's Revenues in Minorca when the British still owned it, but he was perpetually short of cash. When he was 33 he bought 300 acres of poor-quality land running down to the river Mole at Cobham, Surrey, for £8,000, borrowing

£5,000 from his Oxford and Westminster schoolfriends Henry Fox (later Lord Holland) and Henry Hoare, the banker who created Stourhead, and over the next 46 years he created a garden that lives to this day, despite the vicissitudes of neglect, lack of money, road builders and public indifference. Seeing the excellence of the work he was creating, Fox commissioned him to design his garden at Holland House in London.

Pains Hill's current splendour is down to the campaigning zeal of the Painshill Trust, founded in 1981. When we first visited the site in the 1970s, then under confused and multiple ownership, the ruined abbey was buried under elder and saplings, the grotto had virtually been destroyed and many of the buildings now standing new and proud had been completely erased. The M25 hadn't been built and the A3 was in the process of being widened, revealing the Gothic Tower, which had previously been hidden in overgrown woodland. By the 1980s the Turkish Tent and the Hermitage had disappeared, and only traces of The Temple

Fig 8.13
Charles Hamilton's sublime
landscape at Pains Hill. [© Gwyn
Headley/fotoLibra]

of Bacchus remained. The temple, designed by Robert Adam and much praised in its day, housed marbles collected by Hamilton including a 7ft-high statue of Bacchus, smuggled out of Italy for £1,200. In 1797 Christie's auctioned the contents of Pains Hill, including the marbles in the temple, but none of them has been heard of since. The statue could have been bought by William Beckford, and destroyed when Fonthill collapsed in 1824. The portico of the temple was moved to the east front of Pains Hill House in 1925, and it was still standing in 1948. Since then buildings have been replaced and restored: the Turkish Tent (Henry Hoare had a replica built at Stourhead) has been recreated, thanks to the discovery of architect Henry Keene's original drawings (Fig 8.13).

Fifty years on and the road problem won't go away – the park is threatened anew by a land grab to widen and enlarge the A3 and the M25 roundabout. Pains Hill Park is a Grade I listed Historic Landscape, but this affords scant protection from Highways England. Highwaymen are still alive and thriving in Surrey.

Somewhat surprisingly, Horace Walpole was not overly impressed:

> Went again to see Mr Charles Hamilton's at Pains Hill near Cobham, to see the Gothic building and the Roman ruin. The former is taken from Batty Langley's book (which does not contain a single design of true or good Gothic) and is made worse by pendent ornaments in the arches, and by being closed on two sides at the bottom, with cheeks that have no relation to Gothic. The whole is an unmeaning edifice. In all Gothic designs, they should have been made to imitate something that was of that time, a part of a church, a castle, a convent, or a mansion. The Goths never built summer houses or temples in a garden. This at Mr Hamilton's stands on the brow of a hill; there an imitation of a fort or a watch tower would have been proper.

Hamilton was married three times. All we know of his first wife, 'Mrs Hamilton', is that she gave him two daughters (when daughters didn't count) and is thought to have died after the birth of the second girl. He spent the next few decades absorbed by Pains Hill, even planting a vineyard there. In 1755 he was selling his wine for £60 a barrel, 'superior to any Champaign I had ever tasted. I have sold it to wine merchants for fifty guineas a hogshead and one wine merchant, to whom I sold five hundred pounds worth at one time, assured me he had sold some of the best of it from 7s.6d. to 10s.6d. a bottle'. John Parnell, a young visitor who made meticulous notes, commented in 1763 that 'a fine vineyard is planted, large enough to produce twelve hogsheads a year'. The Pains Hill gifte shoppe now offers Painshill Sparking Rosé at £25 a bottle. We have yet to sample it.

John Parnell also noticed the start of work on the grotto, constructed by Josiah Lane between 1763 and 1767 for £40 per annum. The grotto, the largest in England, survived in reasonable condition until World War II, when soldiers billeted at Pains Hill stripped the lead off the roof, allegedly to pay for a VE party. When Osvald Sirén, author of *China and Gardens of Europe*, visited in spring 1946, the grotto was still fairly intact, but by the following year it had collapsed. Fortunately, it has now been stunningly restored by Diana Reynell and Roger Capps.

Later in life Hamilton married again, aged 68, and fathered another daughter. A year later he had to give up Pains Hill to repay his debts to Henry

Fox and Henry Hoare. His father had left him £3,000, but for some reason his brother, the 7th Earl, withheld £1,000 of it. The 8th Earl settled up in 1778. His last marriage, at the age of 70, lasted until his death in Bath in 1786. After his death, Pains Hill, his most beloved child, was visited and admired by two US Presidents, John Adams and Thomas Jefferson.

In 1998 Pains Hill was awarded the Europa Nostra Medal for the 'exemplary restoration from a state of extreme neglect of a most important 18th century landscape park and its extraordinary buildings'.

James Mellor/Pilgrim's Progress Garden

Fig 8.14
The Celestial City in the Pilgrim's Progress garden. [© Gwyn Headley/fotoLibra]

Passion of a different kind drove the construction of the Pilgrim's Progress garden at Rainow in Cheshire: religious fervour. James Mellor founded the Hough Hole cotton mill, and after his death it was run for a while by his son James Jr, before he become a farmer. James Jr retired from farming to pursue his real interests, which were religion, John Bunyan's *Pilgrim's Progress*, and the works of Emmanuel Swedenborg. Mellor spent his time in spiritual contemplation, guided by the works of Swedenborg, in preaching and in the creation of the garden.

With the money made from the mill James Jr could indulge his passion. His garden at Hough Hole House was designed for the visitor to follow the journey to the Celestial City made by Christian in Bunyan's *Pilgrim's Progress*. Here is Doubting Castle and the Slough of Despond, Mounts Gerizim and Sinai, the Valley of the Shadow of Death and Vanity Fair, all packed together in little more than an acre, rather like walking through a virtual Victorian aquatint. A marshy lawn becomes the Slough of Despond; a small hole in the overflow of the pond the Cave of the Holy Sepulchre; the dreaded Apollyon, a gigantic and fearsome demon with fish's scales, the jaws of a lion, feet of a bear, a second mouth on his belly, and dragon's wings is represented by a small carved figure of a dolphin; the house itself is Vanity Fair; the Howling House is a little summer house in which Mellor built an aeolian harp that whistled eerily in the wind to simulate the howls of souls in torment and with a fireplace on which he threw sulphur to conjure up the burning pits of hell; and, finally, passing Mellor's own tomb in the garden, we arrive at the Celestial City:

With all
thy getting
get
understanding
1844

reads the inscription on a plaque above the doorway. The Celestial City is a luminous and peaceful first-floor chapel room reached by a tiny spiral staircase at the end of the garden. In front is a sundial, inscribed 'MIND YOUR OWN PEACE JEMMY JEMMY' (Fig 8.14).

Jemmy was Mellor's father, who evidently did not share his son's Swedenborgian enthusiasms. He also added Uncle Tom's Cabin, which does not feature in Pilgrim's Progress, and seeded the garden with inscriptions and exhortations he urgently carved in stone himself.

The garden was always open to the public and became a major local attraction. People came in charabancs from Manchester; some came from abroad. On the Easter weekend over 500 visitors could be expected. The gardens fell fallow when Hough Hole House was sold, but were restored and re-opened in the late 20th century.

When the humanitarian hostage Terry Waite, who was born in nearby Bollington, was being shown round the garden by the present owner's young daughter, he commented that the pit into which Christian cast his sins seemed a trifle small (it contains the stop-cock for the pond). 'Ah yes', retorted the girl smartly, 'but Christian was burdened with very few sins'.

How wonderful is this? It's pretty amazing; there is nothing else like this in the country. But you do need a good guide, and a very, very vivid imagination. Otherwise all you'll see is a garden pond, a summerhouse and a converted barn. Be careful not to trip over the mighty and fearsome Apollyon, the size of a mantlepiece ornament.

Gazetteer

County/Authority	Location	Folly
Bristol and Avon	Badminton	Folly Group
	Banwell	Folly Group
	Bath	Prior Park Follies
	Bradford-on-Avon	Belcombe Court Garden Buildings
	Stoke Gifford	Stoke Park Folly Group
Bedfordshire	Old Warden	Swiss Garden Group
	Silsoe	Wrest Park Garden Buildings
Berkshire	Bray	Monkey Island
Buckinghamshire	Hall Barn	Garden Buildings
	Ibstone	Wormsley Follies
	Lower Hartwell	Garden Buildings
	Stowe	Folly Group
	West Wycombe	Crowstepped Garden Wall
	Wotton Underwood	Garden Buildings
Cambridgeshire	Abbot's Ripton	Garden Buildings
	Castor	Garden Buildings
	Hemingford Grey	Garden Buildings
Cheshire	Adlington	Adlington Hall Group
	Birkenhead	Birkenhead Park Folly Group
	Chester	Eaton Hall Group
	Rainow	Pilgrim's Progress Garden
Cornwall	Mount Edgecumbe	Garden Buildings
Cumbria	Corby Castle	Folly Group
	Derwent Island	Pocklington's Follies
	Wreay	Garden Buildings
Devon	Cheddon Fitzpaine	Hestercombe Folly Group
	Filleigh	Castle Hill Follies
Dorset	Durweston	Folly Farm
Durham	Sedgefield	Hardwick Hall Folly Group
East Sussex	Brighton	The Rockery
	Groombridge	Groombridge Place Gardens
Essex	Audley End	Garden Buildings
	Harlow	Gibberd Garden
Gloucestershire	Batsford	Japanese Garden
	Cheltenham	Caduceus Garden
	Cirencester	Garden Buildings
	Painswick	Painswick House Rococo Garden
	Prestbury	Remains of Grotto Tea Gardens
	Stinchcombe	Stancombe Park Follies
Hampshire	Hartley Wintney	Folly Group
	Havant	Leigh Park Folly Group
Herefordshire	Ross-on-Wye	Kyrle's Follies
	Stapleton	Bryan's Ground Garden
Hertfordshire	Cottered	Japanese Garden
	Ware	Japanese Garden

County/Authority	Location	Folly
Kent	Chiddingstone	Garden Buildings
	Cobham	Garden Buildings
	Greenhithe	Ingress Abbey Follies
	Kingsgate	Lord Holland's Follies
	St Margaret's at Cliffe	Garden Buildings
Lancashire	Rivington	Roynton Gardens
Leicestershire	Long Whatton	Whatton House Gardens
Liverpool and Manchester	Worsley (Greater Manchester)	Worsley New Hall Ice House
London	SW16	Park Hill Garden Buildings
	W3	Gunnersbury Park Follies
	Hampton	Ice House Fernery
	Kew	Kew Gardens Follies
Norfolk	Corpusty	Last Follies
	Felmingham	Folly garden
	Norwich	Plantation Gardens
	Saxthorpe	Mannington Hall Removals
North Yorkshire	Aysgarth	Folly Rock Garden
	Castle Howard	Folly Group
	Grewelthorpe	Hackfall Follies
	Harrogate	Harlow Carr Gardens
	Helmsley	Duncombe Park Temples
	Studley Royal	Folly Group
	Tupgill	The Forbidden Corner
	Wetherby	Bramham Park Folly Group
Northamptonshire	Boughton Park	Folly Group
	Castle Ashby	Garden Buildings
	Finedon	Folly Group
Northumberland	Alnwick	Folly Group
	Belsay Hall	Romantic Gardens
	Stannington	Blagdon Hall Folly Group
Oxfordshire	Henley-on-Thames	Friar Park
	Rotherfield Greys	Greys Court Garden Buildings
	Rousham	Folly Group
Shropshire	Hawkstone	Folly Group
	Hope Valley	Terrill Garden
	Tong	Durant's Follies
Somerset	Cheddon Fitzpaine	Hestercombe Mausoleum Witch House
	Goathurst	Hallswell Follies
	Yeovil	Barwick Park Follies
South Yorkshire	Stainborough	Folly Group
	Wentworth Woodhouse	Folly Group
Staffordshire	Alton Towers	Folly Group
	Biddulph	Biddulph Grange Gardens Japanese Garden

County/Authority	Location	Folly
	Enville	Folly Group
	Shugborough	Folly Group
Suffolk	Cavenham	Folly Garden
	Sternfield	Garden Buildings
Surrey	Cobham	Painshill Park Folly Group
	Godalming	Busbridge Folly Group
	Guildford	Clandon Park Follies Merrow Grange
	Wotton	Wotton House Follies
Warwickshire	Farnborough	Garden Buildings
West Sussex	Arundel	Bridge Statue Garden Collector Earl's Garden
	Goodwood	Folly Group
	Parham	Parham Garden Buildings
	Stansted	The Garden in Mind
	Worthing	Home House Rock Garden
West Yorkshire	Bramham Park	Gothick Temple Bretton
	Oakworth	Oakworth Park
Wiltshire	Bowden Hill	Folly Group
	Bowood	Folly Group
	Bradford-on-Avon	Belcombe Court Garden Buildings
	Calne	Bremhill Follies
	Fonthill Gifford	Folly Group
	Melksham	Seend Manor Garden
	Stourhead	Folly Group
	Tollard Royal	Larmer Tree Theatre
	Wilton	Folly Group
Worcestershire	Croome d'Abitot	Folly Group
	Hagley	Folly Group
	Kidderminster	Stone House Folly Group

9 | Animal crackers: aviaries, deerfolds, dairies, dovecotes, pig palaces etc.

If there's one thing the English like better than themselves, it's their animals – roast, fried, boiled, braised, or even as pets and companions. Mind you, try to take a dog into an English restaurant and you won't get through the door, whereas in France it's likely there'll be a litter of Bernese mountain dogs blocking the door. A surprising amount of grotesque architecture has been expended on keeping, raising, sheltering, feeding or simply observing animals. Pigs, doves, deer, cats, tortoises, dogs, owls, horses, bears, fish – buildings have been designed for all these creatures, or to commemorate them. About the only companion animal we haven't yet discovered a building for is the ferret. However, the English do not go for zoomorphic architecture, leaving that to Greeks and Americans.

Robin Hood's Bay/John Warren Barry

We may joke about eating them, but a large number of these buildings were designed for exactly that purpose. In former days, chickens were an expensive luxury, but doves and pigeons were tasty and plentiful, hence the profusion of dovecotes, more popular in the north and in Scotland than in southern England, and apparently far more effective when heavily castellated. Deerfolds kept a ready supply of venison to hand. And pigsties – every Wodehouse fan will know the magnetic attraction a pig can hold for a certain type of Englishman. Some might even go so far as to build them a palace, which is what we find at Robin Hood's Bay in North Yorkshire. Hidden among the narrow vertiginous lanes

Fig 9.1
Fyling Hall Pigsty: pigs always appreciate a temple sty.
[© Alan Terrill]

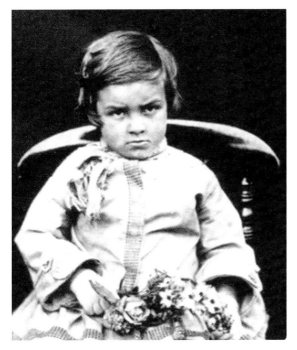

Fig 9.2
J W Barry, not best pleased at
having his photograph taken by
Lewis Carroll. [Gwyn Headley
collection]

is a palatial pigsty screened by a classical temple façade, said to have been built over two years from 1888 for John Warren Barry JP (1851–1920) of **Fyling Hall**, who was undoubtedly an inspiration and precursor for Wodehouse's Lord Emsworth. The Barry family fortune came from shipbuilding in Whitby, and the income was sufficient for the squire to pursue his own interests without the tiresome chore of having to work for a living. It took three men two years to build the pigsty because of the squire's constant dithering. Undecided whether to go for Doric or Tuscan columns, he added Ionic and eventually settled on a combination of all three. They look crude and amateurish, albeit colourful (Fig 9.1).

Here two empresses of Fyling (large whites, for the porcophiles among us) luxuriously wallowed in glorious mud, admiring the tremendous view to the south, until loss of interest or death led to its inevitable dereliction and decay. Three years after Barry died childless, his house became a girls' school, and no doubt the pigsty was surplus to requirements.

Locals say that Squire Barry, who as a child was photographed (wearing a foul grimace) by Lewis Carroll, commissioned the building and improved the grounds in an attempt to lure his estranged wife back from France (Fig 9.2). This is unlikely, as he never married. The pigsty is extraordinarily adventurous for a man so formal that he insisted that his staff remove their hats whenever they met him. He became passionate about Corsica, where wild boars snuffle among the woods. His first visit lasted five months, studying coastal trees. This enthused him so much he went back and lived there for nearly three years from September 1882 to February 1885, this time recording the social mores as well as the flora and fauna. Leaving his men to get on with the pigsty, he published *Studies in Corsica, Sylvan and Social* in 1893.

In 1990 the pigsty was cleverly restored and converted into a holiday cottage by the Landmark Trust, replacing four of the six squat wooden pillars of the façade. During its restoration the date October 1906 was found on what appeared to be an original roof timber, and as the sty didn't appear on the Ordnance Survey map until 1914 this argues the given date of 1888 was too early. The trapezoid windows at the back of the building lend it a distinctly Egyptian air.

Brookbank House/Joseph Hibbert

Another splendid pigsty, the **Godley Castellated Pigsty**, lies half-forgotten on the outskirts of Manchester. Buried in the large back garden of Brookbank House, a nursery in the once prosperous district of Godley, is this extraordinary edifice, which at first sight resembles a miniature castle, a huge toy fort for a very spoilt child. The spoilt children here appear to have been pigs, because this

Fig 9.3

Another palace for pigs, this time in Manchester. [Gwyn Headley collection]

was constructed as a palatial pigsty (Fig 9.3). The Godley Pigsty came to public attention when a previous owner applied for planning permission to demolish it and build a housing estate. A Folly Fellowship member managed to get it spot listed because she had its twin at the bottom of her garden. It is a four-square sham castle with machicolations, a round tower and a bartizan turret, a lead coat of arms with the date 1767. Historic England sniffed and dated it to the mid-19th century. The most likely perpetrator is Joseph Hibbert, the sixth of 14 children of Randal Hibbert, a Unitarian born in 1769. The Hibbert family were leaders in the cotton industry in Hyde, influential in public life.

Revd James Gifford/Samuel Russell Collett

The Revd James Gifford of Wootton in Lincolnshire felt his pigs deserved special treatment as well, so he provided a suitably ecclesiastical setting for the porkers with a Gothic wall to screen them from curious passers-by.

The ultimate example of animal architecture is also to be found in Lincolnshire – **The Jungle** in the village of Eagle, by Samuel Russell Collett. Built in 1820, it was a conventional farmhouse with a wildly unconventional façade. It is a crinkle-crankle wall of burnt bricks, piled on top of each other with no thought for courses, punctuated at random with Gothick windows (Fig 9.4). There's a squarish turret with arrow slits at the south end, and a half-round turret to the north. The door and window frames are formed from bent oak branches, making rough ogee arches. A hobbity central oval door looks as if it should lead into a tree trunk. Pevsner described it as 'an ancestor of Gaudí, if ever there was one'.

What prompted Collett to create this fantasy? Originally from Worcester, he married into the Curteis family who clearly were richer than he was. Although he had sold an estate in Herefordshire for £10,500 in 1808, shortly afterwards he was agitating for money from them to assist his purchase of the Swinthorpe estate, bordering Eagle. And then this is what he did with their money. Although he sought respectability, becoming a magistrate and then a Conservative candidate, 12 years after The Jungle was built there was still a £2,000 mortgage outstanding on his Swinthorpe estate. He was much exercised by the Malt and Beer Tax in the late 1820s and was a determined correspondent to the local paper.

A few years later the Lincolnshire *Chronicle* described him, standing for election, as 'the candid, open-hearted and generous Mr. Collett, whose urbanity and frankness have deservedly gained him the esteem of all. Mr Collett is growing in favour from his honest, upright conduct and his gentlemanly and good-tempered manners'. We can't help feeling that some money may have changed hands here.

He did indeed keep a menagerie at The Jungle, including buffalo, deer, golden pheasants and even several kangaroos. Nothing but the frontage remains; the house behind Collet's fantastickal burnt-brick façade is now a conventional house dating from 1976 and the current owners have done their best to play down this fabulous frontage, screening it from the road with ugly, vigorous Leyland Cypress and planting trees right up to the façade.

A menagerie was a place where animals of several kinds were kept for curiosity, what we now call a zoo. They were for personal pleasure, and seldom open to the public. Several were scattered around the country – a small menagerie of flamingos, wallabies and a llama could be found at Highmoor House in Wigton, Cumbria; Hawkstone in Shropshire had a Gothick menagerie, now ruined; Mrs Child's menagerie at Osterley Park was famous in its day; the aviary-cum-menagerie at Castle Ashby, Northamptonshire, has been

Fig 9.5
The Pyramidal Hen House or
Egyptian Aviary at Tong, with
Wayne Anthony of Vauxhall
Farm and Iain Gray of the Folly
Fellowship. [© Gwyn Headley/
fotoLibra]

converted into a house; while Horton in the same county has the once delectable Menagerie by Thomas Wright housing storks and raccoons, derelict not so many years ago, then sensitively and delicately restored by Gervase Jackson-Stops, who added a new grotto – which has now been eviscerated by its new owners.

At Stowe in Buckinghamshire the 1780 menagerie is now the school shop, while Wentworth Woodhouse had a menagerie from 1738 in Menagerie Wood. Also in Yorkshire, the menagerie at Nostell Priory became the keeper's cottage.

Tong/George Durant

Perhaps our favourite piece of animal architecture is a hen house in Tong, on the Staffordshire/Shropshire border. George Durant, of whom much more elsewhere, was certainly blessed with the edifice complex, which did not extend to earlier buildings on his lands. An almshouse, which since 1410 had housed up to 13 poor people, was ruthlessly torn down, leaving only a picturesque eyecatcher wall. Yet he had time to build a pyramidal fowl house at Vauxhall Farm, once covered with inscriptions – 'EGYPTIAN AVIARY 1842'; 'LIVE AND LET LIVE'; 'SCRAT BEFORE YOU PECK'; 'TRIAL BY JURY'; 'TRANSPORTATION'; 'TEACH YOUR GRANNY'; 'CAN YOU SMELL'; 'GIVE EVERY DOG HIS DUE'; 'HONESTY IS THE BEST POLICY'; 'BETTER COME OUT OF THE WAY, LOVE' – all of which have weathered away from the friable red brick and can no longer be deciphered. Whoever inscribed these homilies knew their chickens: familiar and affectionate exasperation can clearly be heard in 'BETTER COME OUT OF THE WAY, LOVE'. The only inscription that can still be discerned is the dedication at the top – 'AB OVO', From The Egg, below a pyramidal capstone pierced by an egg-shaped hole (Fig 9.5). He created a very similar pyramidal pigsty and a cowshed like the chancel of a church in neighbouring Bishop's Wood, inscribed 'TO PLEASE THE PIGS' and 'RANDZ DE VACHE', which is an alpenhorn melody played by Swiss herdsmen taking their cattle to and from pasture. A soothing lullaby, no doubt.

Another animal pyramid is a tomb, magnificently exposed on a mound on the windswept Farley Down in Hampshire:

UNDERNEATH LIES BURIED
A HORSE
THE PROPERTY OF
PAULET ST. JOHN ESQ
THAT IN THE MONTH
OF SEPTEMBER 1733 LEAPED
INTO A CHALK PIT TWENTYFIVE
FEET DEEP A FOXHUNTING
WITH HIS MASTER ON HIS BACK
AND IN OCTOBER 1734 HE WON THE
HUNTERS PLATE ON WORTHY DOWNS.
AND WAS RODE BY HIS OWNER
AND ENTERED IN THE NAME OF
'BEWARE CHALK PIT'

and there really is nothing more that need be said (Fig 9.6).

Many of the buildings in this chapter are pens, houses or shelters of exceptional magnificence for creatures who probably didn't care either way. A few are memorials to individual animals: at Rousham in Oxfordshire, 'TO RINGWOOD, AN OTTER-HOUND OF REMARKABLE SAGACITY', and on an obelisk at Nether Lypiatt in Gloucestershire:

MY NAME IS WAG, WHO ROLLED THE GREEN
THE OLDEST HORSE WAS EVER SEEN
MY AGE IT NUMBERED FORTY-TWO
I SERVED MY MASTER WELL AND TRUE

There is a monument to a now anonymous cat at Shugborough in Staffordshire, and even a modern tribute to Ivy The Camel, built roughly in the shape of a camel by artist Gerald Scarfe at Milland in Sussex (for the

reason, see below). These all testify to the hold our animal companions can have over us.

We have a wolery (for owls), tortoiseries (for tortoises), several dairies and aviaries, kennels, a salmon coop (crenellated, obviously in case of trout attack), lots of dovecotes, deerfolds, pigsties, menageries and bear pits. Cats do seem poorly served, but then it is famously difficult to herd them, and the cat's independence clashes with the folly builder's generally totalitarian persuasion. The Cat Monument at Shugborough is one of the very few, said to commemorate the ship's cat that sailed round the world with Admiral Anson on the Centurion, and successive Lords Lichfield have believed the cat is buried in the urn. On visiting Shugborough, Joseph Banks commented on the first Persian cat he had seen, a breed kept by Thomas Anson over many years.

At Netherby in Cumbria the **Coop House** – a coop is a wicker basket for catching fish – has been converted into a holiday let by the Landmark Trust, whose devotees share a partiality for animal architecture. It consists of two small battlemented towers joined by a castellated screen wall, a fine fortification for fish. William Gilpin visited Netherby in 1772 and wrote in his *Observations, relative chiefly to picturesque beauty*: 'At this place salmon coops are placed; where all the fish, which enter the Esk, are taken'. The Coop House was built on a terrace where an elaborate series of fish pens could be created by fixing hurdles into a stone pavement, now earthed over. Next to these and below a weir was a fish ladder, all this to feed off the salmon for which the Esk was famous. The squarson of Netherby Hall, the Revd Dr Robert Graham, built it *c* 1772, perhaps as an ornamental belvedere to watch the salmon leaping. The Graham family had a mixed reputation. As they were Border lords no one was entirely sure whether they were English or Scottish, so they raided both sides with impunity. But a consequence of Dr Graham's ingenious and effective farming system was a calamitous drop in the number of salmon to be taken upstream, and several Scottish borderers wanted to know the reason why. When they discovered the cause, a party of around 300 of them came down to Netherby Hall to discuss the matter with the reverend doctor. Despite being a man of the cloth, Dr Graham retained his family's antique enthusiasm for a scrap and raised and armed over 400 of his tenants to receive the Scottish delegation. The coop remained, although the weir was destroyed by a build-up of ice in the 1780s and the Coop House then fell into disuse. It was later used as a dwelling for the river bailiff and afterwards as a shepherd's cottage.

Tortoises (the standard southern European *Testudo graeca*) can survive and thrive in chilly England as far north as Cumbria, hibernating deep in fermenting grass cuttings for six months then eating frantically to make up for it through the brief English summer. These little tanks have an extremely loyal following among those with whom they share their lives, and what better for such an armoured animal than to have its very own castle, as a lucky tribe of tortoises do in **Elton Hall** in Herefordshire, where head gardener Anthony Brooks has built a red brick chelodian castle with two turrets, a sturdy central wooden door and, of course, a flag (Fig 9.7). Brooks cares for the other animals as well: he has created an ogee-arched chicken run that looks suspiciously like the Museum at Enville in Staffordshire.

As we mentioned earlier, dovecotes appear to be more effective when castellated, and the same applies to the much rarer deerfolds. If you come across a large brick structure, an open unroofed rectangle taking up a couple of acres, then you've probably discovered a deerfold. Our two favourites are in Derbyshire and Durham. The earliest date for the deerfold at **Sudbury** is 1723, but that makes little sense as the owner of Sudbury Hall, Henry Vernon, died in 1719 when his son George Vernon (1709–1780) was just ten, and it is unlikely that

Fig 9.7

This is a Tortoiserie, a castle for tortoises. Every tortoise deserves one. [© Alan Terrill]

the young heir would have been commissioning deerfolds at the age of 14. It first appears on a map of 1751, so some date between the two would fit. This is a sham castle for deer, with turrets, castellations and a mighty gatehouse, added in the early 19th century. The Vernons were part of the Norman French invasion, and held property all over the country, including Tong, Hodnet, Nacton, Clontarf and Haddon Hall. George added the surname Venables by royal licence in 1728, became MP for Lichfield, then Derby, until in 1762 he was created Lord Vernon, Baron of Kinderton, in the County of Chester. His life has not troubled any biographers, and it seems that the strangest thing he did was to create this massive deer castle, now listed Grade II* and looked after by the National Trust. It can clearly be seen on the north side of the A50 (Fig 9.8).

Bishop Auckland in Durham has an even finer deer castle, and this time the protection may not all have been show, as border raids were not unusual, even in the civilised 18th century. But the protection is wildly elaborate, an arcaded and pinnacled enclosure with massive battlements and a gatehouse so huge it would scare off any border reiver (Fig 9.9). At a time when bishops had rather more say in the disposal of their income than they do today, it was built in 1757 for Richard Trevor, Bishop of Durham (1707–1771), who clearly had a taste for venison. Horace Walpole waspishly called him 'fat-bellied' and referred to him as 'St Durham' for his obvious piety. He spent the summers in Durham and wintered at Glynde Place, his estate in Sussex, dying in London of gangrene after serving as Bishop of Durham for nearly 20 years.

When the present writers' first book on follies was published in 1986 the BBC bought the television rights. Producer Edward Mirzoeff had a regular documentary series on BBC2 titled *40 Minutes* in which he was allowed virtually a free hand to fill in any way he liked, and as he was a brilliant man with eclectic tastes, the programmes were always surprising, quirky and interesting. It's a great shame we don't have brave programming like that today, but we are in thrall to ratings, and idiosyncratic or characterful features might offend or lose viewers. Mirzoeff chose cartoonist Gerald Scarfe to host the programme, which

Fig 9.9
A palace for the Bishop required
a palace for his deer.
[© Karen Lynch]

he did largely from the back of a camel named Ivy, loping by some of Britain's finest follies with the participation of his wife Jane Asher, together with John Bird, Julian Glover, Terry Jones, Ian McKellen, Bob Geldof and others. The programme ended with Scarfe building his own folly in Sussex, constructed in the rudimentary form of a camel in honour of his camelid folly fellow Ivy (Fig 9.10). The Ivy Folly is thus named after a camel, rather than the pernicious plant that envelops it. Could today's BBC be seen to fund the building of a folly with licence payers' money? Too risky by far.

Fig 9.10
The Ivy Folly.
[© Angela Hampton/fotoLibra]

Gazetteer

County/Authority	Location	Folly
Bristol and Avon	Chewton Keynsham	Wolery
Buckinghamshire	Burnham	Brookend Dairy
	Dropmore	Aviary
	Waddesdon	Aviary
Cambridgeshire	Castor	The Kennels
Cumbria	Kirklinton	Privy Dovecote
	Netherby	Fortified Salmon Coop
Cheshire	Chester	Eaton Parrot House
Derbyshire	Sudbury	Deerfold
Dorset	Piddletrenthide	Dovecote
Durham	Bishop Auckland	Deer House
	Burn Hall	Cow House
	Coatham Mundeville	Hallgarth Deer House
	Shildon	Pigeon Palace
Essex	Fingringhoe	Bear Pit
Gloucestershire	Nether Lypiatt	Wag Obelisk
Herefordshire	Elton	Chicken Run
	Hereford	Urn
Hertfordshire	Driver's End	Node Dairy
	King's Langley	Ovaltine Dairy
Kent	Knole	Birdhouse
	Mereworth	Aviary
	Woodchurch	Tortoiserie
Leicestershire	Belvoir Castle	Dairy
Liverpool and Manchester	Dunham Massey (Greater Manchester)	Deer Shelter
	Stockport	Godley Castellated Pigsty
Lincolnshire	Eagle	The Jungle
	Wootton	Gothic Pigsty
London	SE26	Dinosaurs
North Yorkshire	Robin Hood's Bay	Fyling Hall Pigsty
	Scampston	Deerhouse
	Swinton	Classical Dovecote
Northamptonshire	Horton	The Menagerie
Northumberland	Cambo	Griffin Heads
	Haugh Head	Dovecote
	Nunwick	Kennels
Nottinghamshire	Newstead Abbey	Boatswain's Grace
Shropshire	Hawkstone	Hawkstone Menagerie
	Munslow	Millichope Dovecote
	Tong	Egyptian Aviary Egyptian Pigsty
	Worfield	Dovecote
South Yorkshire	Sheffield	Botanical Gardens Bear Pit
	Wentworth Woodhouse	Bear Pit
Staffordshire	Brocton	Octagonal Dovecote

County/Authority	Location	Folly
	Shugborough	Cat's Monument
Suffolk	Stoke-by-Nayland	Fishing Temple
Surrey	Epsom	Amato Tomb
Warwickshire	Idlicote	Dovecote
West Sussex	Milland	Ivy Folly
West Yorkshire	Leeds	Bear Pit
Worcestershire	Hagley	The Dairy
	Wolverley	The Aviary

10 | We too: women and follies

Until the Married Women's Property Act in 1870, a wife's property was assumed by her husband. She had no legal control over it. In most cases this didn't matter, as wives generally have control of their husbands, who are the ones to discover that it's they who have to love, honour and obey. We may find this a shockingly tardy law, but then incest was not seen as a crime until 1908. And not until 1926 were women allowed to hold property on the same terms as men. As society looked upon marriage with favour, this meant there were lots of rich men and very few independently wealthy women. Widows, of course, proved the exception, and a series of tactical marriages meant that women like Lady Anne Clifford and Bess of Hardwick found themselves in control of vast fortunes.

Bess of Hardwick

Elizabeth Talbot, Countess of Shrewsbury (1527–1608), is better known as Bess of Hardwick. Although she came from a good family she grew up in some distress. Her father died when she was a year old, and his property was seized. Then her stepfather spent time in debtor's prison. She married young Robert Barlow, apparently for love, but he died within a year, 'before they were bedded together, they both being so very young' according to the Duchess of Newcastle (Fig 10.1).

At the age of 20 she married Sir William Cavendish and began her climb to wealth and influence. Of their eight children, two were created dukes – Devonshire and Newcastle. They bought Chatsworth, held jointly in Bess and Sir William's names, as was all their property. When we asked the previous Duke of Devonshire why his title was Devonshire when his family had been rooted in Derbyshire for 700 years, he harrumphed that it had merely been a slip of a scribe's pen. After Sir William's death in 1557 Bess married Sir William St Loe, much richer than Cavendish, who died eight years later leaving his estate to her. Then she married her fourth husband, the Earl of Shrewsbury, one of the richest men in England. This was a turbulent marriage, with much fighting over property ownership, which was finally resolved when Shrewsbury died in 1590 and Bess acquired one-third of his estates.

She was now the wealthiest woman in England, and what she liked doing best – after accumulating cash and titles – was building. She had already carried out extensive works at Chatsworth, and now she turned her attention to Hardwick Hall, although it didn't detain her long as she soon devised plans for a new and far more

Fig 10.1

Bess of Hardwick, the richest woman in England.

[Gwyn Headley collection]

magnificent seat a couple of hundred yards away: Hardwick New Hall, which was completed in 1599.

The house still looks remarkable today, virtually presenting a glass frontage to the visitor. The famous contemporary couplet still rings true: 'Hardwick Hall, more glass than wall'. She was testing, with her architect Robert Smythson, the limits of technology. At the time glass was an extremely expensive material; this is obvious ostentation.

This wasn't the only heavily fenestrated building that Bess built. Her only true folly was the often forgotten **Hunting Tower** at Chatsworth. Because it precedes the surge of 18th-century follies, because it had a purpose, however improbable, perhaps because it was built by a woman, it has been omitted from many folly compilations. Yet on other counts it ticks all the boxes. It's a freestanding belvedere, it's hard to find, its function is obsolete, it cost a fortune to build – although Bess had several fortunes. Its date of 1582 places it firmly outside the popular mass of folly towers. Yet that is what it is. It is a lookout tower, a hunting stand, built for pleasure before purpose, and that is a definition that has been used before now to describe a folly. Robert Smythson is credited as the architect, which makes it more likely that Bess would have employed him at Hardwick. The concept of the hunting stand was that people who were too frail to follow the hunt on horseback could watch it at their leisure from a goodly height. This ignores the possibility that they may have been intimidated by the hundred or so narrow winding steps they needed to climb to the viewing gallery (Fig 10.2).

Fig 10.2
Not quite more glass than wall, but in the same spirit.
[© Raymond Boswell/fotoLibra]

Lady Anne Clifford

Lady Anne Clifford (1590–1676) was Countess of Pembroke, Dorset and
Montgomery through her marriages. In her youth she was petite and attractive,
with a fine figure and beautiful brown eyes (Fig 10.3). Raddled by smallpox
at 34, widowed twice by the age of 59, she found consolation in building, and
she had acquired the fortunes to enable her to do so. Abrasive and litigious, she
had been tempered through battle with her husbands, both of whom had been
spendthrift and unfaithful. They died leaving her a rich woman, with estates
throughout most of England – in Kent, Sussex, Essex, Wiltshire, Westmorland
(now Cumbria) and Yorkshire.

Fig 10.4
Lady Anne's Pillar in memory of
her mother. [© Paul Brooker]

186

And so she set about building and restoration. Lady Anne was a shrewd woman who suffered no fools and lived frugally, and the idea of folly would have been anathema to her. She renovated her four castles in Westmorland and two in Yorkshire, restored at least eight churches, built almshouses and erected the nearest thing to a folly we can credit her with, the **Countess Pillar** (Fig 10.4), a Grade II* listed column on a bank above the A66:

> ERECTED ANNO 1656 BY YE HON'BLE ANNE COUNTESS
> DOWAGER OF PEMBROKE AND DAUGHTER AND SOLE HEIRE
> OF YE RT HONO'BLE GEORGE EARL OF CUMBERLAND AND
> FOR A MEMORIAL OF HER LAST PARTING IN THIS PLACE WITH
> HER GOOD AND PIOUS MOTHER YE RT HONO'BLE MARGARET
> COUNTESS DOWAGER OF CUMBERLAND YE 3RD OF APRIL 1616.
> IN MEMORY WHEREOF SHE ALSO LEFT AN ANNUITY OF FOUR
> POUNDS TO BE DISTRIBUTED TO YE POOR WITHIN THIS PARISH
> OF BROUGHAM EVERY 2ND DAY OF APRIL FOR EVER UPON YE
> STONE TABLE HERE HARD BY.

This was a statement of pride in her ancestry and wealth, a common trait among women builders of the time. In fact, 'Look who I am, look what I've got' is a call that echoes down the ages – the chanteuse Mariah Carey is a splendid modern-day example, albeit without the charitable annuities and cobwebbed ancestry.

Mary Sidney Herbert/Houghton House

Although the number of women builders is just a small fraction of the men, they created some important houses. An interesting feature shared by almost all houses commissioned by women at this time was that they had a centrally placed hall buried in the middle of the house, like a womb. **Houghton House** at Houghton Conquest, Bedfordshire, built by the widowed Mary Sidney Herbert, Countess of Pembroke (1561–1621, died of smallpox), was a typical example. John Aubrey described it as 'a curious house – built according to the description of Basilius's house in the first book of [Sir Philip Sidney's] Arcadia'. That would make it well worth seeing, as Basilius's house was star-shaped and built of yellow stone, which proves that Aubrey never saw it, as Houghton House was disappointingly red brick and conventional. Mary Sidney Herbert was Sir Philip Sidney's sister and very, very close friend, so close that Aubrey speculated that 'the first Philip Earl of Pembroke was begot by him'. The house has been a ruin since the 1790s, deliberately destroyed for whatever reason by the 5th Duke of Bedford, and recorded in detail with sorrow and regret by the Hon John Byng at the time. There are strong indications that Byng was one of the earliest possessors of a conservation mentality, going so far as to propose a creative reuse:

> But for thee—poor Houghton House—I must lament: herein were labourers employed to levell—thy strong built walls: —Down go the floors: Crash fall the rafters—; the overseer—sent by his Grace the Duke of Bedford to oversee this havock, (at which let me suppose the last noble repairer—and inhabitant, the Marquis of T[avistock] to gaze with grief and astonishment)

came forth to wonder at my overseeing—but he felt the delight of a butcher at killing a sheep.

(Byng) So I see you are hard at work here?

(Overseer) Yes Sir it is hard work for it is so strongly built; the materials were to have been sent to Bedford, but that I believe is given up now.

(B) Did you find anything curious?

(O) Some coins Sir—and much painting upon the wall when we ripp'd off the wainscot.

(B) That of course you attempted to preserve? And before that attempt the D of B had accurate drawings taken from them?

(O) No. They were beaten to pieces.

(B) I remember a room wainscotted with cedar, what became of that?

(O) Thrown amongst the other rubbish.

(B) I see that his Grace is felling all the old timber as well upon the hill; as in the wood below.

(O) Yes, his Grace is making a fine fall—; and this avenue, — Sir, a mile in length—and which contains one thousand trees—will come down in the autumn.

F. grinn'd anger, and contempt.[*]

Now why all this havock, and ruin? Only a job for the artful, performed by cunning stinginess. Shall I live to see all the noble old mansions of the Kingdom pull'd down, or deserted!! Why not have lent this to any relations, or friends who would inhabit it? Why not let it for a school! Why not permit the Emigrés to reside therein: putting up some useful furniture for them? Or why not establish some manufactory?

But such wanton desolation! Such unnecessary levelling! But the D[uke] is a leveller: Perhaps it may come to him and he, in his turn, may be levell'd. There is a quantity of fine and curious stone work about the building, LR's with crowns, and other emblems.

Over 200 years later conservationists still echo the same sad cry.

Ashley House in Ashley Park, Surrey, was built by Lady Jane Berkeley in 1602–5, then altered over the years until it was demolished in 1925. Weston Park, Staffordshire, was built for Elizabeth Wilbraham (1632–1705) and Stapleford Park, Leicestershire, for Abigail Sherard (c 1600–c 1657). These were all commissioned by women, and all had a centrally placed hall.

Jane and Mary Parminter/A La Ronde

In the late 18th century the Parminter cousins Jane and Mary created **A La Ronde** outside Exmouth in Devon (Fig 10.5). It is the only 16-sided house in England, perhaps the world, although there is a 16-sided church in Vermont, USA. It was inspired by the eight-sided church of San Vitale in Ravenna, which the cousins had visited in the 1780s. Of course, the house has a centrally placed octagonal hall, but the real wonder is hidden above – a narrow, confined gallery, skirted by a very low baluster, decorated mainly with shells, but also trinkets, pottery shards, seaweed, sand, lichen, mica, stones, bones, paint, glass, mirrors and feathers, impossibly fragile and never intended for men's eyes, or feet (Fig 10.6). Sensibly, access is now forbidden as it is not only flimsy, but frankly

[*] F. was Byng's son Frederick.

dangerous. One false step and the knee-height baluster will tip you 35 feet over to the stone-flagged floor below (Fig 10.7). The National Trust provide a video walk-through of the shell gallery, where you can examine it in far more detail than if you were actually there, blundering through the delicate shellwork as we did.

It is perfectly possible for sisters or cousins or brothers to live together without accusations of homosexuality or lesbianism, but prurient minds will always create innuendos. In the case of the Parminters, Mary was orphaned at the age of 12, when she went to live with Jane, who was 29. Jane is therefore the more likely to have been the instigator of their adventures, and she was credited by the family as the designer if not the architect of A La Ronde. Higher up the hill from the house the cousins created a quirky chapel, named **Point In View** (Fig 10.8). They shared two – two what? It may be unkind to call them obsessions, but they were two passionately held convictions. One was for the sustenance of unmarried women, and the other was for the conversion of the Jews, a mission embraced by middle-class Christians for centuries.

Fig 10.5
The 16-sided A La Ronde.
[© Gwyn Headley/fotoLibra]

Fig 10.6
The shell gallery at A La Ronde.
Access is now forbidden as it is
so fragile. [© Gwyn Headley/
fotoLibra]

Fig 10.7
A detail of the Shell Gallery.
[© Gwyn Headley/fotoLibra]

And you should, if you please, refuse
Till the conversion of the Jews.

An unmarried Jewess converting to Christianity would be enough to make them faint with joy and anticipation, and to that end they built an almshouse at Point In View to be run by an unmarried woman who had converted from Judaism. Build it and they shall come. This became an obsession: in their wills they stipulated that the oaks on the A La Ronde estate were only to be cut down in the event that boats were needed for returning converted Jews to Palestine.

Point In View is crude compared to the house, which makes us feel that the Parminters' cousin John Lowder, a trainee architect from Bath who was 19 when A La Ronde was built, could have assisted cousin Jane with the details. Against this suggestion is the cousins' fervent enthusiasm for unmarried women, and indeed women in general, which is sometimes allied with a distaste for or even dislike of men. Mary lived by herself for 38 years after Jane died, and her will specified that A La Ronde should only ever be owned and occupied by women, naming six unmarried relatives who would inherit in sequence and who would have to relinquish the property should they marry or die. In 1880 the sequence finally ran out, and A La Ronde was bought by a man.

Sarah Losh

A few women were brave enough to defy contemporary society and remain single. Sarah Losh (1786–1853) of Wreay in Cumberland, now in Cumbria, was one of the most remarkable women in 19th-century England, astonishingly overlooked perhaps because she lived in an obscure part of the country and did not mingle in high society – or else she was modest. Whatever the reason, she was outrageously talented. She is always mentioned among women folly builders because there are so few of them, though to our minds none of her buildings qualify as true follies. Whimsical, yes, because living needs and architectural styles change over time, and to build a replica of a 2,000-year-old

Pompeiian cottage for your local schoolteacher to live in is capricious to say the least, just as it is to build an Anglican church bereft of Christian symbolism.

Losh was brainy and beautiful. She mastered Latin and Greek at an early age and was fluent in French and Italian. In the evenings she liked to read to family and friends, and one day a visitor picked up the book she had been reading from and found it was in Latin. Sarah had been translating it into English as she read.

Fig 10.9
St Mary's, Wreay. An Anglican church without Christian symbolism. [© Karen Kelly/fotoLibra]

Fig 10.10
The apse of St Mary's, Wreay.
[© Karen Kelly/fotoLibra]

What drew her to architecture? A curious and lively mind, a dexterity with drawing and modelling, a desire to improve her habitat, and the wealth to carry it out. She conceived and built the church of **St Mary in Wreay**, idiosyncratic and unique in England, incorporating ideas and motifs from 2,000 years in the past and a hundred years in the future (Fig 10.9). It is a remarkable structure, not simply because it is possibly the only Christian church in the country that does not display a cross. Instead it is populated by tortoises, eagles, pinecones, pelicans, crocodiles, caterpillars, snakes, all first created by Sarah in clay and then carved for her by her local masons. She herself described the architecture as 'early Saxon or modified Lombardic' but it is not categorisable. The official list entry, which only grants it a Grade II* status, carefully skirts round any stylistic description, mentioning 'romanesque' in passing (Fig 10.10).

She was deeply attached to her younger sister Katherine (1788–1835) and was heartbroken when she died early, at 47. A mausoleum in the churchyard was commissioned, with a life-size statue of the departed inside that startles the unprepared visitor.

The two-storey Pompeiian Cottage was built *c* 1830 by Sarah as a replica of a house she had seen excavated at Pompeii. This was built for the village schoolmaster, and would presumably imbue him with the true understanding of classical worth.

Sarah Losh's styles varied: at Langarth, Brisco, she built a Tudor-style house, long before Messrs Barrett, Bovis and Wates rediscovered the genre, and also designed and decorated the tiny and well-hidden sandstone wellhead at St Ninian's Well in the same village. The inscription is no longer legible.

Sarah Losh was an original in the most complimentary meaning of the word. After a century and a half of obscurity, her genius is beginning to be recognised. A best-selling biography of her by Jenny Uglow, *The Pinecone*, was published in 2013, and the once overlooked church of St Mary now welcomes architectural pilgrims along with Christian worshippers.

Annie Jane Lawrence

What connects Kodak and Lenin? A mutual admiration for Letchworth Garden City. Letchworth in Hertfordshire was the vision of the dynamic Ebenezer Howard, a typical Victorian steam-engine in trousers, an idealogue impassioned by his concept of garden cities – 'All the advantages of the most energetic and active town life with all the beauty and delight of the country'. Supported by the equally idealistic George Dickman and George Davison, the successive UK heads of Kodak, the town was founded in 1903, and quickly became a magnet for the sort of people whom George Orwell, who lived nearby, described as 'the typical Socialist with vegetarian leanings, every fruit juice-drinker, nudist, sandal-wearer, sex-maniac, Quaker, quack, pacifist, and feminist in England'. Vladimir Lenin came to see this socialist utopia for himself in 1907.

Fig 10.11

The Cloisters, Letchworth: You can't stop a woman with a plan and a pot of gold.

[© Gwyn Headley/fotoLibra]

Capitalist American Kodak finally tired of the radical socialism of its UK boss and after 27 years let Davison go. Instead of retiring to Letchworth he moved to Harlech, North Wales, where he built a fabulously luxurious home that became known by the locals as Tŷ Kodak – Kodak House.

One of Howard's earliest converts was Miss Annie Jane Lawrence (1863–1953). Miss Lawrence would have been perfect source material for Richmal Crompton. You can picture Just William and the Outlaws sniggering through a gap in the hedge at the loopy lady with the lorgnettes and the flowing white gown earnestly conducting a class of eurhythmics.

Annie came to Letchworth to build an open-air school for philosophy students. The design for **The Cloisters** came to her in a dream, and as a rich Quaker she could afford the exorbitant £20,000 it cost to fulfil. She employed the architect William Harrison Cowlishaw, who obligingly incorporated staircases open to the air and going nowhere, clearly inspired by a hallucination of the Palazzo Contarini in Venice, plus a towering octagonal belvedere and a concrete roof. Despite its size, the building is largely one storey; the current manager suspects that what few first-floor rooms there are were created by subsequent owners inserting false floors. The whole confection is one of the most bizarre buildings in Britain, both an affront and a delight to the eyes (Fig 10.11).

Annie was 42 when she started building. Her uncle had been Lord Mayor of London and her brother became a Labour peer. As a young woman she had worked in the slums of east London and The Cloisters was to be her contribution to improve the welfare of her fellow man, her principal intent being the study of 'how thought affects action, and what causes and produces thought'. Clement Attlee, 20 years her junior, had the same transformative revelation in the East End; his resulted in the National Health Service.

Despite being partially deaf, Annie loved music. There were four electric organs in the building, all connected via a system of pipes and louvres so there was music wherever one went. She gave regular concerts at The Cloisters. One of her favourite ensembles was the London Concert Orchestra, consisting of 40 unemployed musicians.

The building was constructed around a semicircular recessed parade of colonnaded arches, known as the Cloister Garth, which bears a remarkable resemblance to the apse in Sarah Losh's church at Wreay. From its vaultings, hammocks were lowered by pulleys for the students to sleep on, thus justifying the 'open air school' appellation. This lasted for three years until the Hertfordshire winters put a stop to it.

By the 1930s, Annie's dream was turning into a nightmare, a ruinously expensive building to maintain and to try to keep the dream alive. She became so desperate to rid herself of her folly that she offered to give away the building, including with it a dowry of £20,000. At that time £20,000 was the entire development cost of the Supermarine Spitfire. The Cloisters was requisitioned by the services at the start of the World War II, and an army occupation is seldom beneficial to the fabric of a building. After the war she tried to donate it to the local council, almost certainly the worst choice of custodian for any building, and in 1948 she was finally successful in persuading the Freemasons to take it over. Annie died in 1953 and The Cloisters is now a wedding and conference venue.

The Freemasons have not treasured their architectural heritage. The Cloister Garth has been bricked up and roofed over, and where it opened onto the gardens, it has been blocked off by a rectangular brick box as a dining/recreation room. Another large rectangular room has been added on the east side, and Annie's bathing pool has been filled in. The original sinuous, curved building design has been severely compromised, and to insult it further, the building was listed Grade II* in 1979, which means the hideous excrescences added in the 1950s and 1960s are also listed by default, and cannot be altered. It was built with little concern as to the cost of maintenance, and a Grade II* listing brings with it obligations but no subvention. It is a lose-lose situation, brought about in the main by imperfectly crafted legislation.

But there's nothing else like it in the country. And the socialist, feminist paradise of Letchworth Garden City now returns a male Conservative MP.

Gazetteer

County/Authority	Location	Folly
Cumbria	Brougham	Countess Pillar
	Wreay	St Mary's Church Pompeiian Cottage
Derbyshire	Chatsworth	The Hunting Tower
Devon	Exmouth	A La Ronde Point In View
Hertfordshire	Letchworth	The Cloisters

11 Remembrance of things past: mausolea, monuments, memorials and memories

Second only to the urge to reproduce is the need to be remembered. The reward is a kind of eternal life – 'Their Names Shall Live On'. Sadly, the great majority of our names don't. You can cover your egregious tomb with praiseworthy inscriptions, but if your descendants have forgotten how to read your language or your signs, all they will know is that that's where Mr Squiggle is buried.

The permanence of remembrance is the goal. In business we propose ideas and then demur, pleading that it's not 'set in stone' or 'cast in bronze'. Yet stone is a powerful statement of remembrance. For 2,000 years and more, the Great Pyramids of Giza glistened in the desert, with their mirror-like coatings of limestone. Then some religious fanatic decided the stone would come in useful for building a couple of mosques, so he stripped the covering, turning the most spectacular buildings ever created by man into quarries.

Essentially, it's all about keeping records. In our lifetimes we have listened to recorded music on 78 rpm records, 45s, 33 rpm, reel-to-reel tapes, 8 track, compact cassettes, CDs, MP3 and M4a (we just missed the wax cylinder). There will be new formats by the time this book is published. We still keep many of the records, but we can no longer hear them. Languages change and evolve, as does writing. There is no language of record, although Latin has had a fairly long run. Then there's the medium. Base metal rusts and decays, precious metal is stolen and melted down, stone is friable, machines become obsolete, data degrades. Who has a cassette player in their car nowadays? Carve your immortal words on the wrong kind of stone and they could be gone within a hundred years. Blockchains have been devised as permanent, enduring, inviolable records of transactions, notoriously supplying provenance and trust for cryptocurrencies such as Bitcoin, stored in servers from Anchorage to Zanzibar. When someone or something manages to crack one, the cryptocurrency's value will evaporate as quickly as a 1970s TV star's reputation.

Size counts, of course. Make a big enough pile of stones and even if your name is incomprehensible or illegible, posterity will know that someone of immense importance lay here. Who was greater than Khufu? Or was that Cheops?

King Mausolus, determined to be remembered for all time, built himself a tomb so vast that it became, along with the Pyramids of Giza, one of the seven Wonders of the Ancient World. Unfortunately, nothing now is left of it except a large hole in the ground in the middle of the modern Turkish holiday resort of Bodrum. But we can see for ourselves today just how massive and impressive the tomb was, because American Freemasons have kindly built a life-size replica of it on 16th Street NW in Washington DC, the House of the Temple of the Scottish Rite (Fig 11.1). It is an undeniably impressive burial chamber for the provincial governor of a vassal state of Persia. Mausolus achieved nothing of particular renown, but he donated his name to the world – every tomb larger than it need be is called a **Mausoleum**.

Sometimes the deceased's earthly remains lie inconveniently in some corner of a foreign field, in which case the accepted convention is to build a monument

as memorial. The Maiwand, or the Forbury Lion in Reading, Berkshire, is a war memorial, not a folly, but is mentioned here because (a) it is a very fine sculpture indeed and (b) the folly is that those who don't pay attention to their history are doomed to repeat it, as Santayana might have said. For this is a war memorial to the 329 men of the 66th Berkshire Regiment of Foot who were killed in the Second Anglo-Afghan War, 1878–80. Guess who won that one? Why didn't our politicians ever come down to Reading, pause a moment to pay their respects at the Maiwand Lion and realise that by going into Afghanistan we were always going to get our arses kicked, just as we did in the 19th century?

We commemorate great men and women with statues in our cities. An undercurrent of resentment has recently arisen among people who disagree with the attitudes and opinions shown by our ancestors. Yes, they may have been horrible men who did horrible things, but so did everyone else at the time, including the so-called victims. They are remembered for the great works they did. There are periodic reassessments of the right to be commemorated; there aren't many statues of Adolf Hitler still standing. Students at Oxford campaigned vigorously to have a statue of Cecil Rhodes removed, despite the benefices and scholarships he bestowed on the university. It is the duty of students to protest, but iconoclasm is an attempt to rewrite history, if not to erase, then to sanitise our cruel and vicious past. Far better to create than destroy; why not erect new statues to the honour of the people they respect, if anyone? In Madrid's Buen

Retiro park is a statue of Satan, the world's only public monument to the Devil. He has his legions, and they walk among us.

The English are famously fond of animals, and some of the celebrations and commemorations of their lives can be read in Chapter 9. Here we are concerned to see how these strange ancestors of ours transitioned to the afterlife.

Eighteenth-century England was almost entirely Christian. There were a few Jews in the larger cities, and maybe a handful of Muslims, mainly pirates, keeping very quiet. Any other religion was seen at best as a curiosity and at worst a threat to our civilisation that needed to be stamped out immediately. So the passage between life and death was the same for everybody; we all sang from the same hymn book. After death, we all faced the Day of Judgement. The righteous went to heaven and the sinners went to hell. Simple. There is no Purgatory or Limbo in the Church of England.

So all funeral rites and rituals were the same? Not a bit of it. As always, it all depended on how rich you were. Your options varied from a pauper's grave to a towering mausoleum, and it's the towering mausoleum that interests us here.

In the past we were fortunate enough to see many of the follies in this book in the perfect state of decay, mummified buildings where you could make out the features but knew beyond any shadow of doubt that they were dead. The mausoleum at Seaton Delaval in Northumberland and the Rockingham Mausoleum at Wentworth Woodhouse in West Yorkshire linger in the memory; wet, soot-blackened stone, emptiness, decay. One is spruced up and restored now, thank heavens, but we have a tinge of regret that the old horrors of a darkling winter afternoon cannot be revisited.

Rockingham Mausoleum

When we first saw the **Rockingham Mausoleum** it was, quite frankly, dangerous. A mausoleum is supposed to commemorate a life, not inflict death and injury on hapless visitors. Nothing was stable, the obelisks on each corner of the site shifted in the wind and the central cenotaph looked as if it would collapse at any minute. It was held together by iron clamps because of subsidence from the coal mining underneath. Thanks to the Fitzwilliam Wentworth Amenity Trust, the mining has stopped, the structure has been stabilised and a visit is now relatively safe.

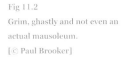

Fig 11.2

Grim, ghastly and not even an actual mausoleum.

[© Paul Brooker]

We do not know of an uglier mausoleum in England. Granted, the design (by Yorkshire's favourite architect John Carr, of course) was inspired by the Mausoleum of the Julii at St Remy de Provence, near Arles, France, dating from 40BC, but not everything from antiquity is a model of beauty (Fig 11.2). The massive Doric rusticated base contains a statue of Charles Wentworth, the 2nd Marquis of Rockingham and prime minister at the time of his death in 1782, by Nollekens. The next stage has four round-headed arches surrounding a sarcophagus, while the top stage is a Corinthian monopteros. The sarcophagus is empty, because this is not actually a mausoleum, it is a cenotaph. It was built between 1784 and 1793 for William Wentworth Fitzwilliam in memory of his uncle who died of influenza, and his body was actually laid to rest in York Minster.

Seaton Delaval

The mausoleum at **Seaton Delaval** in Northumberland is even larger. It is a huge building with a cautionary tale attached. The Delavals were so much of what we expect of rip-roaring, bodice-ripping 18th-century black squires it's a wonder they weren't all named Sir Jasper. Sir Francis Delaval's occupation was baldly described in the *Dictionary of National Biography* as 'Rake'. So notorious was his behaviour that his younger brother, John Hussey Delaval, took over as head of the family and owner of the Seaton Delaval estates.

His son, young John Delaval, was born into rank and privilege. Pre-Weinstein stories of his behaviour say he was 'paying his addresses' to a laundry maid; perhaps now we would be allowed to describe it as attempted rape. The laundry maid was having none of it, and she kicked him in the testicles so hard that she killed him. Her name has been lost to history, but architectural writer H Avray Tipping unkindly described her as a 'buxom slut'. It is unclear how he discovered her chest size when her name is unknown, and surely a slut would not have defended her honour so efficiently. A little overexcitement from Mr Tipping, we feel. It is horrible to imagine what probably happened to her in those grim days past – if, indeed, she even existed, for there is now some doubt that young John would have been capable of doing much beyond coughing. He was a sickly home-schooled child, and his death at 20 took place in 1775 at the hot springs in Bath, far from Seaton Delaval, where he had been sent for a cure. How better to be remembered – as a weak, sickly consumptive or a rampant young bull?

Fig 11.3
The Seaton Delaval Mausoleum is slightly less minatory now it has lost its skeletal dome.
[© Jeff Veevers/fotoLibra]

Jack's body was brought back to Doddington in Lincolnshire for burial, Doddington Hall being a secondary house of the Delavals. His father painted the interior of St Peter's Church entirely black for the funeral, and it stayed black for 30 years. In a recent restoration of the church the layer of black paint was uncovered. They knew how to mourn in those days.

Ten years earlier, Sir John Hussey Delaval had set about the construction of a gigantic mausoleum at Seaton Delaval for his family and, as with the Rockingham Mausoleum, this is a mausoleum without a burial, as the Bishop of Durham and Sir John had a disagreement about consecration fees and so permission to bury young Jack in it was denied. The building is a complete ruin. It is a fine piece of classical architecture by an unattributed architect, although there is a record of the cost – £1,742 11s 0d – and when we first saw it there were still remnants of the high dome, now collapsed or removed (Fig 11.3). Seaton Delaval is one of those strange houses that looks perfectly habitable, but is in fact a ruin.

John the younger's body remains interred in the south aisle of the church at Doddington.

The Dashwood Mausoleum

The **Dashwood Mausoleum** at West Wycombe in Buckinghamshire is hexagonal, open and unroofed. It is a very large and prominent structure, flint with Portland stone pilasters, dominating St Lawrence's Church to its west, indeed big enough to enclose it. Built for Sir Francis Dashwood, whom we met in the chapter on grottoes, it was designed by John Bastard from faraway Blandford. The Bastards were talented Dorset jobbing builders who were influenced by the great Thomas Archer, and who may have had a hand in Sturt's Folly at Horton in Dorset. This is a remarkable mausoleum, unlike

Fig 11.4
West Wycombe Mausoleum with the Golden Ball of St Lawrence's Church behind. [© Scott A McNealy/fotoLibra]

any other in England, listed Grade I and as intact as the day it was built in 1764. As a family the Bastards were noted for their excellent joinery, but young John was a master mason based at Marylebone in London, securing commissions as diverse as the Middlesex Hospital and Stoneleigh Abbey in Warwickshire, distance no object. Hexagonal buildings are not common; there's a church hall at Burwell in Lincolnshire, the Library at Leigh Park in Hampshire and the odd garden shed, but generally it is a wilful plan, conferring few advantages other than idiosyncrasy. The inspiration must surely have come from Dashwood rather than Bastard, for it was built with a legacy of £500 from the diarist and minor politician George Bubb Dodington, Baron Melcombe, for Sir Francis 'to build an Arch or Temple at whichever of His Lordship's Seats was likely to remain the longest,' and although a folly is usually built regardless of expense, Dashwood's mausoleum came in with a fiver to spare at £495 (Fig 11.4).

Fuller's Follies

Mad Jack Fuller (1757–1834) – a fine name – was an MP and Sussex squire. All his buffoonery masked a man of intelligence, discernment and even some finesse. But it may have been the other way round. With John 'Mad Jack' Fuller you never knew. He is the eccentric's eccentric. Fuelled by a wealthy enough background as landowners and ironmasters (hugely augmented by inheriting the Jamaican plantations of his uncle Rose Fuller when John was 20 years of age) and by a supreme confidence in himself and in his county, Fuller set out on a chequered career. His estate of Rose Hill in the small village of Brightling, East Sussex, was to become one of those archetypal settings where the squire lorded it over his surroundings and fellow men, adding follies to emphasise his independence, his unique frame of mind, and his near total power. Benevolent and autocratic like so many country squires, Fuller, for all of his adult life, exuded eccentricity.

His first interest was in the military, becoming a captain in the Sussex militia in 1779, when he was 22. In that year the novelist and friend of Dr Johnson, Fanny Burney (1752–1840), described him: 'Captain Fuller ... has an estate of £4000 or £5000 a year, is but just of age, has figure, understanding, education, vivacity, and independence, and yet voluntarily devotes almost all his time, and almost all his attention to a company of light infantry'. Apparently, she rather liked him, for here she goes again in another letter: 'Mr. Fuller, a very intimate young friend of Mr. Thrale, who is Captain of a Company belonging to [the Sussex militia], Dined with us. He is a Young man of a very large Fortune, remarkably handsome, and very gay, sensible, unaffected and agreeable'.

Burney's circle included Hester Thrale (1741–1821), who mentions him two years later (in the beginning of 1781) in her diaries:

[S]he [her daughter Hester 'Queeney' Thrale (1764–1857)] doats on a Flasher ... Jack Fuller seems her Favorite: Jack Fuller of all People! wild, gay, rich, loud, I wonder how a Girl of Delicacy can take a Fancy to Jack Fuller of Rose-hill? no proposal however has been made, nor do they often meet; but I rather think She likes a boisterous Character.

And again, in a letter of that same year to Burney: 'Captain Fuller flashes away among us. How that boy loves rough merriment! the people all seem to keep out of his way for fear'.

Fuller was, as stated by Burney, a good friend of Hester's husband, the very wealthy London brewer Henry Thrale. And it must have been a few years after that Fuller was in pursuit of Hester Thrale's other daughter Susannah Arabella Thrale (1770–1858). Apparently, she refused him and Fuller possibly never got over it, as he never married. There is a rather nasty version of the story, given in October 1790 in a letter from Florence by the spendthrift and 'nagging' Henrietta Henckell Hare (1748–1826): 'Our neighbour of Rose Hill has been lately I hear refused by Miss Susan Thrale and is so very angry with her that he has brought down a woman of the Town to Tunbridge Wells on purpose to distress her by following her everywhere. If this is a fact I think him a great Fool'.

After a stint as MP for Southampton from 1780 to 1784, serving as a High Sheriff for a year in 1796 and becoming a captain in his own Brightling Yeomanry Cavalry (disbanded in 1802), Fuller turned into a more or less serious politician only later, as MP for Sussex from 1801 to 1812. He claimed to want to represent only the county's interests, and refused a peerage. 'I was born Jack Fuller and Jack Fuller I will die'. Fuller by now was a rather rotund gentleman nicknamed Hippopotamus (his other epithet was 'Honest Jack'), who liked his tipple, and was noted for making outrageous comments in Parliament. Hansard frequently adds 'laughter' or 'cries of Order! Order!' to his reported speeches or interruptions. During this period he spoke 123 times in Parliament, and was rather keen on brewing interests (he would be, wouldn't he), inoculation, the Walcheren expedition, the navy, the militia, the Poor Bill, Roman Catholic Emancipation (against), and slavery (all for it, no surprise, considering his Jamaican possessions, although he claimed to be in favour of the gradual abolition of slavery, but not too hastily, please).

By 1810 things came to a head when Fuller, probably drunk, insulted the Speaker, 'The insignificant little fellow in the wig!' and was escorted from the House by the Serjeant-at-Arms, to spend some time (two days in fact) reflecting on his hasty comments in The Tower. This didn't end Fuller's parliamentary career, for he slogged on another two years. But the fun had gone out of it. He started building his follies, first innocuously enough by placing a Coade stone Gothick summer house in the park (1803, marked 'COADE SEALY LONDON') and a pedestal on which stands a cast iron vignette consisting of a cannon, flames and an anchor, probably in celebration of Trafalgar (1805), while a companion piece marking the grave of a favourite horse has disappeared. A tale tells of Fuller's butler being killed by firing a dud cannon in 1805, again in honour of Trafalgar. In 1806 a visit by Humphrey Repton is recorded, providing Rose Hill (later Brightling Park) with one of his famous Red Books, showing the before-and-after plans of the grounds. But the recommendations weren't followed up, except for a hint or two.

Returning to 1810, that was when Fuller started his building campaigns. He took in hand the young Greek Revivalist architect Robert Smirke (1780–1867) whom Howard Colvin calls 'the favoured architect of the Tory establishment'. But Fuller was first and foremost a small-c conservative. A none-too-remarkable yet beautiful garden building was the result, the Rotunda Temple (1810–1812), although Mad Jack was said to have conducted orgies there involving scantily clad nymphs (Fig 11.5). The orgies were, in reality, probably only drinking

sessions with his cronies. A more serious building was the Observatory of 1810–1818, again by Smirke, which also contained a camera obscura from which J W Turner appears to have surveyed the surroundings for his Sussex sketches and engravings partly funded by Fuller.

The Observatory is said to owe something to Fuller's acquaintance with the famous astronomer William Herschel (1738–1822), albeit that this might be a confusion with his astronomer son John (1792–1871). It reveals yet another side of Fuller's proclivities: his interest in the arts and the sciences. He co-funded part of Michael Faraday's (1791–1867) scientific career, in the end even instigating, a year before his death, the Fullerian Professorship of Chemistry at the Royal Institution, as well as the 1834 Fullerian Professorship of Comparative Anatomy and Physiology. Before that he was one of the Institution's great benefactors, earlier donating, in effect, £1,000 (a loan, which he never asked to be repaid) to the Royal Institution, although his obituary states his total benefactions to the Royal Institution amounted to £10,000.

Science morphed with public-mindedness when Fuller paid for the construction of the unnecessarily picturesque Belle Tout lighthouse near Beachy Head. In 1822 he appears to have witnessed the wrecking of the East Indiaman *The Thames* on the Sussex coast. Fuller paid for a temporary structure, in use by 1828. In the next year construction started on the stone lighthouse, to the designs of James Walker (1781–1862), a Scottish lighthouse specialist, and William Hallett (dates unknown), operable in the year of Fuller's demise, in 1834. In 1822 or thereabouts, another of Fuller's maritime benefactions was launched, the Eastbourne lifeboat called *The Samaritan*. Apparently Fuller was officially the owner, but left it in his will to the Eastbournians. Again, this was brought on by the wrecking of *The Thames*. An earlier, very different act of benevolence, was practised by Fuller in the aftermath of the Napoleonic Wars, which was a time of great distress for both labourers and laid-off soldiers and sailors roaming the countryside. Fuller provided work for the local unemployed by having a wall built, encompassing his estate, over four miles long. He also paid quite well.

The arts were mentioned, and Fuller appears not to have been interested only in the visual arts and architecture, but there was music too. He erected the plaque and profile portrait to the composer ('Auld Lang Syne') William Shield (1748–1829), Master of the King's Music, who appears to have been a personal friend. The monument is in Brightling church, dated 1830, by Henry Rouw the Younger (1770–1852). It was supposed to adorn Westminster Abbey, but the then Dean was offended by the term 'gentleman' in the wording of the plaque, so Fuller withdrew to home ground. Fuller left provisions in his will for Shield, but the latter died earlier, and he in his turn left 'To John Fuller, Cipriani's original drawing of Dr. Arne and a large prospect of the city of Rome'. Dr Arne was the now almost forgotten Thomas Augustine Arne (1710–1778) who composed 'Rule Britannia' – of course a favourite with the rabidly patriotic Fuller. Another of Fuller's musical connections was John Braham (c 1774–1856) a then famous tenor and composer, who wrote some soul-stirring stuff, especially maritime-related songs, and seems often to have performed at Fuller's London town house. On another level we still have the barrel organ (by W A A Nicholls, a London maker) Fuller donated in 1820 to Brightling church. He had earlier presented nine fagots, or bassoons, to the church. The peal of bells was also donated by Mad Jack, and were named after Wellington's battles. Another monument (sculptor unknown) in the church relates to yet another friend of Fuller's, the medical doctor Primrose Blair, Physician to the Fleet, who died in 1819: 'He was a man most eminent in the skill of his profession, and one of inflexible integrity'.

Then there is the saving of Bodiam Castle, another act of public spiritedness. The 14th-century castle was in danger of being demolished in order to sell off the stone as building material, still a valuable commodity at the time. In 1829 Mad Jack bought the castle at auction for £3,000 and carried out some

Fig 11.6
Fuller's pyramid in Brightling churchyard. [© Andy Coleman/fotoLibra]

Fig 11.7
The Sugarloaf from a distance.
[© Richard Broady/fotoLibra]

Fig 11.7
The Sugarloaf from a distance.
[© Richard Broady/fotoLibra]

Fig 11.8
Dallington Church Spire from
a distance. [© Andy Coleman/
fotoLibra]

preservation and restoration work. He never intended to make use of it; it was purely meant to safeguard it as a monument to Sussex and the nation.

We have allowed ourselves to digress from Fuller's follies, but not without reason. The man has marked the stages of his life by specific actions. We can roughly subdivide his biography into (1) the public life *c* 1775–1810; (2) folly-building 1810–1820s; and (3) charity and public benevolence 1820–1834.

It is the middle part that concerns us now. Three other buildings were ascribed to Robert Smirke, but although the 65ft obelisk or **Needle** on Brightling

Down looks good enough, it is not exactly a design or in a material (rough stone) one would credit to a reputable architect. It appears to have been erected around 1808, and possibly refers to the Battle of Trafalgar, although there is no inscription. That the pyramid and the Sugar Loaf were, as is sometimes suggested, designed by Smirke, is even less likely, but in the case of the pyramid – who knows. **The Pyramid**, built in 1810–11, is the quintessential Fuller folly (Fig 11.6). It lives in the churchyard, not surprisingly, and is substantial enough not to be just an incongruous funeral monument. At 25 feet high and with a nicely proportioned portico, it has that lived-in feeling, and so it should, for Mad Jack is seated in there, in an iron chair, in front of a bottle of port and a roasted chicken, with glass strewn on the floor so that the Devil would cut his hoofs when coming to claim his due. Or so the tale was always told. But upon opening up the tomb some years ago, Fuller turned out to be entombed in the conventional way.

The story also goes that he got permission for this strange building by promising the Revd Mr Hayley to move the local pub The Green Man from its position directly opposite the church to a more inconvenient location. And indeed, one could (until it closed some time ago) find The Fuller's Arms in an awkward corner of the village. But alas, on 15 November 1810 Hayley makes a note in the parish register that Fuller wanted to build 'his Edifice' and start removing 'the old Post and rail fence and erecting a stone wall', and he, Hayley, would be satisfied if the new wall would be constructed at the squire's cost. Fuller, according to the note, also threw in 'a couple of substantial stone pillars & an iron gate way'. No mention of the pub. Conspiracy theorists please note: there may of course have been a nondisclosure clause in the contract.

The **Sugar Loaf** (probably erected in the 1810s or 20s) provides perhaps the best folly story, and one is even tempted to believe it. One evening a dispute arose (whether in London or on home turf is not known) among Fuller and a few friends about whether one could see the spire of nearby Dallington church from his dining-room window at Brightling. The bets were on, Fuller of course claiming that one could. Next morning: no spire, no nothing. Although Dallington church is close by Brightling Park, it lies hidden in a fold of the downs. In order to win the bet, Mad Jack immediately had a cone erected on the spot where he claimed one could see the Dallington spire. So sometime later when his cabal visited again, Fuller won his bet (Fig 11.7).

Strange story, because what church spire looks like an old-fashioned sugar loaf? (Sugar used to be sold in hard cones). Go to Dallington and check the spire's shape: in profile it has exactly the form of Fuller's folly (Fig 11.8). And another thing: in 1961 the folly was restored (a very commendable action at a time when follies were widely detested) and the restoration report mentions the original structure consisted of 'nothing more than stones held together by mud', which strongly suggests that the Sugar Loaf had indeed been put up in a hurry.

The final folly is the 25ft Hermit's Tower, located in a copse just outside the village. The tale that it was intended as an abode for a hermit to be hired (no hair or nail clipping allowed, no ablutions or speaking) remains unsubstantiated. And why put a hermit in a tower? Usually we find them in rustic huts. On the other hand, the tower seems to have none of the views claimed – one couldn't see Bodiam Castle from it, nor other Fuller hot spots. No date, but again it will belong to the period 1810–1830.

Mad Jack Fuller was a legend in his own lifetime. One of those magazines of gossip and anecdote so prevalent in the period, *The Olio, Or, Museum of Entertainment*, for example, in 1833 (a year before Fuller's demise) proffers the much-embellished story about Fuller's sojourn in prison after insulting the Speaker. But by 1834 it was another, more serious, periodical that sums up the case for Fuller. Many of the details relative to Fuller's life appear in his obituary in *The Gentleman's Magazine*, compiled, to be sure, by someone who was well acquainted with the man and his reputation. 'Mr. Fuller had died extremely rich' it states. 'Mr. Fuller was distinguished through life by much eccentricity; but it was mingled with a kind heart, that displayed itself in deeds of princely munificence'. His burial took place in the aforementioned pyramid and among, no doubt, other bequests and mementoes, he had arranged in advance for a bronze medal to be given to attendants at his funeral, sculpted by the best *medailleur* of the age, Willam Wyon (1795–1851). Fuller turns out to have been a worthwhile client of Wyon's. His death medal (of which we proudly own a copy) is stated by Nicholas Carlisle's *Memoir of the Life and Works of William Wyon* (1837) to be 'an admirable portrait of John Fuller, Esq., modelled from the life' (Fig. 11.9). And indeed, Wyon produced, in 1828, a Royal Institution medal paid for by Fuller, for 'Chemical Discoveries', and in 1830, again for Fuller, a medal with a view of Bodiam Castle, 'Sold to Visitors of the Castle ... in aid of the Sea Bathing, Infirmary Hastings' – yet another of the man's benevolences, for the establishment of which he provided £200 in 1822.

His own funeral monument is of course in Brightling church, a bust by F L Chantrey (1781–1841), one of the Regency period's foremost sculptors, of 1819. Presumably Rouw's plaque beneath it (stressing Fuller's honesty) is of a later date. But it is Christopher Wren's famous epitaph in St Paul's that would serve best for Fuller as well: 'Si monumentum requiris, circumspice' – go to Brightling and look at the follies.

Gazetteer

County/Authority	Location	Folly
Bristol and Avon	Stoke Gifford	Sarcophagus
	Warmley	Warmley Gardens Follies
Berkshire	Reading	Maiwand Lion
Buckinghamshire	Fawley Court	Mausoleum
	West Wycombe	Mausoleum
Cornwall	Pentillie Castle	Pentillie Tower Mausoleum
Cumbria	Burgh by Sands	King Edward I Monument
	Conishead	Braddyll Mausoleum
	Striding Edge	Gough Memorial
	Thirlmere	Brothers Parting
	Wreay	Sarah Losh's Follies
Derbyshire	Birchen Edge	Nelson Monument Wellington Monument
	Codnor	Jessop Memorial
Devon	Great Torrington	Waterloo Monument
Dorset	Portesham	Hardy Monument
Durham	Whickham (Tyne and Wear)	Long John Monument
East Sussex	Brightling	Pyramid Mausoleum
	Brighton	Sassoon Mausoleum
	Cade Street	Cade Monument
	Patcham	The Chattri
Gloucestershire	North Nibley	Tyndale Monument
	Seven Springs	Thames Monument
Hampshire	Botley	Botleigh Grange Mystery Monument
	Hurstbourne	Hurstbourne Monument
	Portsmouth	Victoria Park Monument
Herefordshire	Hereford	Nelson Column
Isle of Wight	Bembridge	Yarland Monument
	Totland	Tennyson Monument
Kent	Cobham	Darnley Mausoleum
	Doddington	Alexandra Oldfield Monument
	Westerham	Wolfe Cenotaph
Lancashire	Parbold	Parbold Bottle
Lincolnshire	Brocklesby	Mausoleum Holgate Monument
	Woodhall Spa	Wellington Memorial
Liverpool and Manchester	Liverpool (Merseyside)	Mackenzie's Pyramid Nelson Memorial Wellington Monument Sefton Park Monument
London	SW7	Albert Memorial
	Mortlake	Burton's Tent
	Teddington	Shoemaker Stone
	Twickenham	Pope's Grotto Marble Hill Grotto Pope's Other Grotto
Norfolk	Holkham Hall	Leicester Monument

County/Authority	Location	Folly
North Yorkshire	Castle Howard	Mausoleum
	Ebberston	Aelfrid's Memorial
	Kirkleatham	Turner Mausoleum
	Sledmere	Waggoners Monument
Northamptonshire	Naseby	Battle Memorials
Northumberland	Newcastle-upon-Tyne (Tyne and Wear)	Grey's Monument
	Seaton Delaval (Tyne and Wear)	Mausoleum
Nottinghamshire	Milton	Newcastle Mausoleum
Oxfordshire	Mapledurham	Old Palm
Somerset	Athelney	King Alfred's Monument
	Butleigh	Hood Monument
	Cheddon Fitzpaine	Hestercombe Mausoleum
South Yorkshire	Sheffield	Monuments
	Wentworth Woodhouse	Rockingham Mausoleum
Staffordshire	Sandon	Perceval Shrine
	Shugborough	Shepherd's Monument Cat's Monument
	Trentham	Sutherland Monument Mausoleum
Suffolk	Elveden	War Memorial
	Hadleigh	Taylor Monument
Surrey	Box Hill	Labellière's Grave
	Epsom	Amato Tomb
Warwickshire	Leek Wootton	Gaveston Cross
	Meriden (West Midlands)	Cyclists' Obelisk
	Southam	Dispensary Monument
	Stretton-on-Dunsmore	Departure Monument
West Sussex	Stanmer	Frankland Monument
West Yorkshire	Otley	Bramhope Monument
Wiltshire	Etchilhampton	Lydeway Monument

12 The poor man at the gate: scrap shacks and *jardins imaginaires*

Follies are seen as typically British and Irish eccentricities. We display a quiet sense of pride in our ancestors' aberrations. Journalists assume that they are solely a British construct and express surprise when they discover there are follies to be found in almost every country in the world, even North Korea. The difference is that the English love and appreciate their follies, they're happy for them to be called follies and they can laugh at themselves, a quality shared by few other nations, if any.

There's one type of folly, however, where the English lag far behind the rest of the world, so much so that they don't even have an English name and we have to refer to them as *jardins imaginaires* – dream gardens. These are gardens where horticulture takes a back seat to sculpture, preferably home-made. The message of the garden is conveyed through the sculptures, and in case you didn't get it the first time, they are repeated again. And again. And again.

In the USA, when planning restrictions weren't as totalitarian as they are today, people built their houses with whatever came to hand. In the ghost town of Rhyolite, Nevada, most of the houses were built from empty beer bottles. It was the only building material available. 'It's very difficult to build a house with lumber from a Joshua tree', a local advised us. These became generically known as 'scrap shacks' – shacks they undoubtedly were, and they were largely constructed from scrap.

In more ordered England, scrap shacks are not permitted. After all, there is a building code. Yet every year a tabloid newspaper discovers a scrap shack in someone's back garden or even filling the gap between two semi-detached houses, and the puzzled, innocent occupants are led away to be instructed in the baffling rules of their new country's planning permissions.

Mr Fairnington's Cement Menagerie

English planning permission and local authorities are the reason we have so few *jardins imaginaires* and scrap shacks. It's simply not allowed. Even so, a few brave souls have evaded the suffocating hand of bureaucracy. Inevitably they are on a much smaller scale than we can find abroad, apart from one epic example: Mr Fairnington's **Cement Menagerie** in Branxton, Northumberland (Fig 12.1). We suspect the reason for its survival is that it's right on the Scottish border and distant memories of border reivers and the battle of Flodden Field (which actually took place in Branxton) have led the local authorities to tread circumspectly.

Its name tells what it is. It is a menagerie of full-size animals, made from cement and concrete by John Fairnington, ostensibly for the amusement of his son Edwin, who had cerebral palsy. Fairnington began work in 1961, after he retired from his joinery workshop, and continued for nearly ten years. He finished when Edwin died in 1971. Edwin may not have been the only begetter of the garden, as a text on a path reads 'This garden is to the memory of Mary

which she loved for 28 years to 18 September 1963'. In 1971 he dedicated a memory corner to his dead son and stopped work, aged 88 (Fig 12.2).

There are many more texts to be found in the garden, as well as over 300 life-size cement animals. There are few visitors to the remote garden, and at dusk on a dull day there are few more otherworldly experiences to be found in England than to stand here alone among 300 silent creatures. There are zebras, sheep, a camel, rhinoceroses, seals, an ostrich, an elephant, people – including Rabbie Burns, Winston Churchill and Lawrence of Arabia (the film came out in 1962) – horses, a crocodile, cows, pigs, deer, garden gnomes and birds, all staring blindly at Fairnington's house. A stiff drink is required.

Trevor Wynne-Jones

It's well known that the greatest job satisfaction to be had is as an Anglican priest. But other vocations can embed the initiate as firmly as faith. Many builders and developers go to the office or site early in the morning, do their honest day's toil then come home and watch telly or play golf or go on cruises. Others have more pressing calls on their time.

In 1966 young Trevor Wynne-Jones bought an acre of land in Wraysbury, near Windsor in Berkshire. He knocked down the asbestos shack standing in the middle of the plot and went to work as a property developer. He became very successful, and instead of frittering his money away on golf or cruises, he improved his house and garden. Constantly. When he bought the site it was called **Dutch Gardens**, after a Dutch smallholder who had lived there,

Fig 12.3
Steps down to the basement,
Dutch Gardens.
[© Gwyn Headley/fotoLibra]

but Wynne-Jones preferred Venice. Next to his house and garden, he had a passion for La Serenissima, visiting two or three times a year. And gradually over time he is recreating the city of canals in watery Berkshire. There's nothing directly copied – there's no scale model of the Rialto Bridge or St Mark's Campanile – it's just the essence of water and bridges and seclusion, hard to find in today's overcrowded Venice, or indeed in Wraysbury, but still achievable. Water tumbles through the garden, unlike the sedate and fetid *canali* of the original, crossed with small bridges, stepping-stones and large bridges, rushing round the house at the heart of the site. The house itself is still a work in progress, half-completed bathrooms and bedrooms, one massive, monumental, impressively over-engineered staircase leading to the basement, constructed from one huge Polish tree and fabricated on site in his permanent underground workshop (Fig 12.3), but Wynne-Jones has only been going for a little over 50 years so far and there's lots more to do. An amphitheatre is next up. We can't wait.

George Burt

Another builder who couldn't stop when five o'clock came around was George Burt of **Swanage** in Dorset. Together with his uncle John Mowlem he built up one of the most successful public works building contractors of the 19th and 20th centuries, responsible for contracts ranging from paving Blackfriars Bridge to refronting Buckingham Palace, building New Scotland Yard, Admiralty Arch, the Lloyds building, Battersea Power Station, London City Airport and many more iconic London buildings.

Coming from a quarrying and stone merchant background, Burt was fascinated by carved stone and building fragments, and as the company's work in London involved a substantial amount of demolition in building a brave new city, he hoarded pieces that appealed and had them re-erected in his native Swanage. He combined several attributes that are rare in the folly canon: he was an astute businessman yet a full-blooded eccentric; he was a philanthropist and pedant; he was tall, rich and handsome yet still spoke like a peasant. He was sufficiently well-regarded to be made Sheriff of London in 1878. The buildings he tore down in the City were shipped down to Swanage as ballast before the boats were laden with Purbeck stone for the return journey, a sensible and economic move. Burt added a florid porch ('overwhelmingly undisciplined', commented Pevsner) from London's Mercers' Hall to Swanage's Town Hall, removed the Wellington Clock Tower from the south end of London Bridge and re-erected it on the seafront (without the clock), built himself the rather louche Purbeck House using bits of Billingsgate Market, added an obelisk to Ballard Down, built Durlston Castle with its educative geographical inscriptions as a restaurant, had a gigantic 40-ton stone globe brought down from Greenwich where it had been carved (Fig 12.4), and peppered the streets with London bollards. He built a new Anglican church and, just to be on the safe side, a new Methodist one as well. When he and his uncle were lads, Swanage had a population of 200. Through their efforts and their gifts of buildings, it became a major Victorian seaside resort.

Uncle John Mowlem's contribution was a war memorial to a sea battle that may or may not have been fought in the vicinity, perhaps between King Alfred

Fig 12.4

The Great Globe itself. [© David
Young/fotoLibra]

and the Danes, or maybe someone else, about a thousand years earlier. Or whatever.

The firm of Mowlem was founded in 1822 and flourished for 184 years. In 2006 it was taken over by a company called Carillion who took less than 12 years to hose it all up against a wall, going bankrupt in 2018.

Leo Tolstoy

The hardest commandment to follow was passed down by Jesus: 'A new commandment I give unto you, That ye love one another'. Even God didn't go that far when he handed down the tablets to Moses, although it can be seen carved on the tablets at Buckland Beacon (see Chapter 13). Human beings find it very hard to love each other unconditionally. The best we can hope for is tolerance or acceptance. Over the centuries there have been countless attempts to set up communities where equality and fair play rule, and almost all of them implode when the charismatic leader – for they all require a leader – departs or dies. There is always a religious or ideological subtext to feed the human desire for the truth, the way and the light. The great Russian novelist Leo Tolstoy was a deeply committed Christian, and he distilled Christ's teachings into a neat package based on the teachings in the Sermon on the Mount:

> Love your enemies
> Do not be angry
> Do not fight evil with evil, but return evil with good
> Do not lust
> Do not take oaths

Initially he was thrilled when his ideas found widespread acceptance and approval, but his pleasure soon turned to concern when he realised that he'd created a new band of disciples following a so-called Tolstoyan Movement. His response was that '[this] is a great and gross error. There has not been, nor is there any "teaching" of mine'.

But he was powerless to prevent the momentum. Tolstoyan communities sprang up around the world, and not all of them withered and died. In Miserden, Gloucestershire, the **Whiteway Community** was set up in 1898 by a Quaker journalist, Samuel Veale Bracher, with support from Aylmer Meade, the translator of *War and Peace*. They bought a 41-acre site and ceremoniously burnt the deeds as a rejection of the concept of private property, just as the followers of Mrs Girling did in Sway. They embraced pacifism, vegetarianism, anarchism and many other -isms but passed on electricity and mains water until the 1950s. Amazingly enough, to we metropolitan liberal élitists, the colony is still going, perhaps not as austerely as originally conceived but still aware of its origins and traditions. As nobody owned the land, settlers had to build their own houses, eschewing the advice of architects, which accounts for its appearance in these pages. The colony consists of undistinguished houses off muddy tracks flanking a minor road. Polite notices request colonists to clear up after the 43 dogs that share the colony. The modern world has caught up with them in that the houses are now privately owned, and when put on the market they fetch the same as any scrap shacks in Stroud would (Fig 12.5).

Fig 12.5

Whiteway Colony: it's hard to photograph an ideology. [© Gwyn Headley/fotoLibra]

Last Brothers/Corpusty

What the Last brothers John and Roger have done at **Corpusty Mill Garden** in Norfolk is what we would really like to see everyone do: this is not the neo-neo-classical that for the last few decades has been so popular with careful architects and timid home-owners alike, but many of the Last's new follies are done in the Gothick taste (although admittedly they fabricate classical buildings as well). This is not outsider art, or obsessive monomania; this is architecture (and gardening) as a pastime, admittedly an all-absorbing one. The Lasts were professional men, Roger a BBC producer and John a marine biologist; this five-acre garden at their parent's home was a weekend pleasure.

They started in 1974, before follies became fashionable anew, with a ruinated belvedere, some 15ft high, built of rough local stone and with a narrow Gothick entrance, cross arrow slits and some good painted decoration inside, built on a water meadow of the river Bure, which is prone to flooding (Fig 12.6). A three-chambered grotto followed, decorated by river gods (as a precaution?) and fossils (Fig 12.7). Then came the Gothick Greenhouse, which looks like one of the Rendlesham lodges on the rebound, and contains a Victorian reredos from a demolished church. Next came the classical, or rather the Palladian: a pavilion of flint accentuated by greyish-blue brick, with a domed roof, classical statue and busts and two side pavilions that act as repositories for compost. A small grotto

Fig 12.6
The Gothic Ruin at Corpusty
Mill Garden. [© Roger Last]

Fig 12.7
The Grotto at Corpusty Mill
Garden. [© Roger Last]

is at the back (Fig 12.8). The Gothic bits and pieces introduced by the Earl of Orford in the 19th century at Mannington provided the Last brothers with yet another building, The Ruin, which was built in 1985, in which a stone archway from Mannington was set in a flint wall, and yet another sham ruin screen was built from local stone.

Of course, they couldn't stop and more buildings were erected, among them a classical garage at John Last's house in Pakefield, Lowestoft, an Apollo set in the pediment and with squat fluted columns, the moulds of which were borrowed from architect Peter Foster. John died in 1990, but Roger continues his odyssey, building a 250ft-long **Gothick flint wall** with busts of Hadrian, Augustus and Septimius Severus as a memorial to him (Fig 12.9).

A recent addition leaps beyond Gothick stone and rubble – a needle-sharp stainless steel cone called **The Spire**, a contemporary eyecatcher, 21ft high, between the river Bure and the lake (Fig 12.10). Most builders of imaginary gardens have no concept that others may be doing similar work. But the Last brothers were educated men and knew precisely what they were doing. 'We didn't plan to build follies, but, in effect, that's what we did,' said Roger.

Fig 12.8

The interior of the Corpusty Mill

Garden grotto. [© Roger Last]

Fig 12.9

Roger Last peering through the
memorial wall. [© Alan Terrill]

Fig 12.10

The Spire at Corpusty Mill
Garden. [© Roger Last]

Jardins Imaginaires

Jardins imaginaires are by their nature personal and ephemeral, and much
has been lost. Some survive through their overarching ambition, like Mr
Fairnington's concrete menagerie in Branxton, Nek Chand's amazing rock
garden in Chandigarh, India, and Helen Martin's Owl House in Nieuw Bethesda,
South Africa. One lost English example will serve: **Woolmer Green** in
Hertfordshire used to be on the A1 between Welwyn Garden City and Stevenage,
but now the road has been upgraded and it runs to the west of the settlement,
a roadside village that is several furlongs away from being picturesque. A
woodcarver named Harry Macdonald lived here, having come down from

Fig 12.11
The Rectory Garden Centre:
'Everything in the garden has been
given us or reclaimed from skips –
we haven't bought a single thing'.
[© Paul Brooker]

Bradford to find work in the 1930s. He rented a warehouse on the Great North Road, but work was no easier to come by until he had an inspiration – why not carve a life-size policeman and stick it on the side of his shack? It worked – traffic stopped, commissions came in. He was slightly handicapped by his 'utter and complete ignorance of drawing and anatomy' but it didn't hold him back – he carved men, women, birds, animals, festooned the workshop and its garden with bizarre creatures, and the visitors kept pouring in. During World War II an army lorry crashed into the garden after the driver fell asleep at the wheel, rolling over a couple of times and throwing him out. The driver came round to be confronted with a cow jumping over the moon, peacocks, giraffes, ducks and a witch striding high in the sky, and immediately concluded he was dead. After the war the cottage started doing teas and coffees, and it became an attraction for miles around. When Harry died in 1971 the developers moved in and his life's work was erased.

Another sad loss is happening as we write: Arthur Mead was a quiet, gentle man who lived in the village of **Stoke Goldington** in Buckinghamshire. He lived by himself and he was good with his hands, capable of anything from grotto building to icon painting. A path across a field behind his house ended in a small wood, a little less than an acre, and Arthur bought the wood. This was around the time the Folly Fellowship was founded, in 1987. Arthur bought

the present writers' 1986 book on follies – and inspiration struck. He created a *jardin imaginaire* in his private wood, with seats, inscriptions, a grotto (complete with stuffed hermit), a pond and a select arboretum. On the gateposts he inscribed the logo of the Folly Fellowship and he dedicated his detached garden to the new charity. And when Arthur died he left his beloved plot to the Folly Fellowship, whose charitable remit is 'to preserve, protect and promote follies, grottoes and garden buildings', in the certain knowledge it would be safely looked after. But the man living next to Mead's Wood wanted a larger garden, so he approached the Folly Fellowship, which sold him the wood for £10,000. The carvings, inscriptions and logos were torn down, and Arthur Mead's unprotected *jardin imaginaire* lives on only in the memory.

The surviving **Rectory Garden Centre** in Ashton in Makerfield, Greater Manchester (formerly Lancashire), was built from nothing by Kevin Duffy, a keen banjo player who in 1975 bought a house next to an allotment and started selling plants (Fig 12.11). 'Everything in the garden has been given us or reclaimed from skips – we haven't bought a single thing', he claimed. 'From the beginning the idea was to build a lot without buying anything, and we haven't bought a thing'. He has certainly built a lot, mainly staying on ground level and never being tempted to climb up the tower route. His sham church has amazed him by becoming a genuine place of stillness and reflection, where people light candles of remembrance. There are black and white tea rooms, castellated gateways and many, many statues of urchins, musicians, horsemen, angels, clothed mannequins and even a 1960 Ford Popular, perhaps the least desirable classic car (Fig 12.12).

Duffy leaves us with a question which could be applied to many folly sites: 'Is it Art, or is it just a pile of rubbish?' Mr Duffy – it's a *jardin imaginaire*.

Gazetteer

County/Authority	Location	Folly
Berkshire	Wraysbury	Dutch Gardens
Buckinghamshire	Milton Keynes	Concrete Cows
	Stoke Goldington	Arthur Mead's Follies (gone)
Cornwall	Morwenstow	Hawker's Hut
	St Merryn	Prynn's World
East Sussex	Brighton	Mayhew's Folly
Gloucestershire	Whiteway	Whiteway Colony
Hampshire	Weyhill	Jardin Imaginaire
Kent	Rolvenden	Gnome Garden
Leicestershire	Measham	Mr Talbot's Gothic Cathedrals (demolished)
Lincolnshire	Greatford	Folly Garden
Liverpool and Manchester	North Ashton	Rectory Garden Centre
London	N14	Miniature Buildings
	Enfield	Jardin Imaginaire
Norfolk	Corpusty	Last Follies
Northumberland	Branxton	Cement Menagerie Garden
Nottinghamshire	North Clifton	Pureland Garden
Somerset	Dunster	Jardin Imaginaire (demolished)
	Frome	Jardin Imaginaire
Staffordshire	Cheadle	Hales View Farm
	Consall	Consall Hall Gardens
Suffolk	Westleton	The Barn Gardens

13 | Golli-Gosperado: a miscellany of curiosities

If everything always slotted neatly into place, there'd be no room for folly. By definition, a folly cannot be a team player, yet we have lovingly shoehorned our selections into the last 12 chapters by type and style. A grotto is fairly unmistakable, as is a tower, but inevitably there will be follies that blur boundaries and even some that question the definition of structure. There has to be a place for them, a bottom drawer of unrelated objects too precious to throw out but perhaps not fascinating enough to keep on permanent display. Here they are: dip in at will, because you will almost certainly find something you can lose your heart to.

Giocchi d'Acqua is the Italian for 'Water Games', not a phrase in common usage in England. The English pride themselves on their sense of humour, but getting unexpectedly soaked with water in this climate is not as amusing as it might be in torrid Italy, which is why this particular practical joke has never quite caught on in this country. In fact, we know of only three English examples: the long demolished grotto at Roxford in Hertfordshire, the Forbidden Corner at Tupgill, North Yorkshire and the Trick Tree at Chatsworth in Derbyshire, seat of the dukes of Devonshire. Properly called the **Willow Tree Fountain**, the original dated from 1693 when it was made of brass by a Mr Ibeck, who is known for nothing else. It actually does resemble a willow tree in winter. As a 13-year-old princess, Queen Victoria delightedly called it 'the squirting tree', and 13 is about the latest age when one finds this sort of thing amusing.

Fig 13.1
White Nancy has also appeared as a plum pudding and a Waterloo medal.
[© Gwyn Headley/fotoLibra]

Celia Fiennes, who travelled through England at the turn of the 17th and 18th centuries, visited Chatsworth and wrote:

> There is another greene walk and about ye Middle of it by ye grove stands a fine Willow tree, the Leaves, Barke and all looks very naturall, ye roote is full of rubbish or great stones to appearance and all on a Sudden by turning a sluice it raines from Each Leafe and the branches like a shower, it being made of brass and pipes to Each Leafe, but in appearance is Exactly like any Willow.

Through England on a Side Saddle in the Time of William and Mary was written in 1702 but not published until 1888. There was another *Giocchi d'Acqua* at the long-demolished Roxford grotto; see Chapter 6.

A liking for follies goes along with a taste for the inexplicable. How do you explain something like **White Nancy** in Cheshire (Fig 13.1)? Why would anyone want to explain it? Much loved by the local community, it is generally a white blob on the top of Kerridge Hill, a ridge overlooking the town of Bollington. We say 'generally' because at the time of great public celebrations it gets painted in every which way – at Christmas it might become a giant plum-pudding; at Armistice Day a huge poppy; on royal anniversaries and jubilees a colourful patriotic flag; a commemoration of singer Mark E Smith of The Fall; or the Manchester Peace Bee; or sometimes simply a huge St George's Cross. But basically it's white, and occasionally disfigured with graffiti.

Bollington was a cotton town, so is it so remarkable that the shape of White Nancy resembles a cotton boll? It was built to commemorate the battle of Waterloo, as well as being an eyecatcher and summerhouse, by John Gaskell Jr of nearby Ingersley Hall in 1817. It wasn't rendered and whitewashed until George V's Silver Jubilee in 1935. Before White Nancy was built there was an ordnance beacon on the site, so '-nance' could be the origin of Nancy. John Gaskell (no relation to the novelist Mrs Gaskell) was a landowner and property developer. Descended from tenant farmers and workers on the Legh family's grand estate at Lyme Park, the Gaskells assiduously worked their way up the social ladder: John's father built Ingersley House in 1774 as a pleasant three-bay Georgian house; John Jr tripled it in size and renamed it Ingersley Hall. White Nancy was a trifle, an eyecatcher, a whim for him. Now there's even a beer and a goat's cheese named after it.

George Durant/Tong

A creature of the Middle Ages, dark, crepuscular, evil, George II Durant (1776–1844) wasn't a person you would like to meet. Durant was an utterly nasty man, the antithesis to a basically good egg like Mad Jack Fuller. And yet he built follies like no one before or after him. Although many buildings have bitten the dust through neglect, vandalism and destruction by officialdom, there is still a selection of them to be seen in the village of Tong and in the other dependencies of George Durant, squire of **Tong**, Shropshire.

The story starts with the father, George I Durant (1731–1780), a vicar's son from Hagley. And it was here at Hagley in 1756 that the young Durant started an affair with the much older Elizabeth Rich (1716–1795), the second

Fig 13.2
Tong Castle. Today the M54
motorway runs straight through
the middle of this. [Gwyn Headley
collection]

wife of the top-ranking politician (Chancellor of the Exchequer), writer and
co-creator of Hagley Hall and grounds, George Lyttelton (1709–1773). She was
something of an accomplished portrait painter, but according to Hester Thrale
(1741–1821) 'her indiscretions made an unhappy household'; though she
possessed 'good talents [Elizabeth] was little esteemed by any one, though had
been pretty'. By the way, Hester Thrale was possibly not well disposed to Durant
(and by implication to Elizabeth Rich) as in 1765 he, Durant, stood against her
husband in the Southwark elections. Lyttelton's brother wrote the following in
a letter about the affair: ''tis generally said her ladyship was caught abed with
the young man ... her infernal temper has left her so few friends that I don't
hear of a single person who speaks in her favour'. An even-handed account was
published in the introduction to Lyttelton's poems in the 1797 edition: 'In 1749,
[Lyttelton] sought happiness in a second marriage with Elizabeth Rich. It is said
the experiment was unsuccessful. They seperated by mutual consent'.

By 1757 George I Durant was given a position as clerk, and in 1762 he
was nominated paymaster to the army under Lord Albermarle's expeditionary
force to Cuba and was present at the 'rape of Havana'. Before that, in 1758, he
had already been deputy paymaster of the expedition to Guadeloupe, which
was a rather doubtful prerogative, as when someone tried to influence one of
the London government officials to have his son placed with the Guadeloupe
expeditionary force, he received the following answer: 'the money is to be
issued in Spanish silver [obviously not much good], and what is more, the
climate to which they are destined not very healthy ... so Durant of the Office
goes'. Sounds like Durant was expendable. But four years later he made his
fortune in the Cuba affair, skimming off the payroll and making deals here,
there, everywhere. Because of it, Durant appears to have become a very wealthy
slave-owner indeed. On his return he was able to buy the village of Tong, and
set about tearing down the medieval Tong Castle, having Capability Brown
erect a Gothico-Moorish extravaganza instead (Fig 13.2). George had in 1773
eventually married Maria Beaufoy (1755–1832), the daughter of a Quaker
Lambeth vinegar merchant, stood against the aforementioned Thrale, and

conceded defeat, became a Freemason and Grand Master of the Shropshire Lodge, and died in 1780.

On his tours through Britain John Byng, later Viscount Torrington (1743–1813), visited Tong Castle in 1792 and was none too pleased. 'This place purchas'd by Mr. D. has been rebuild in a most overgrown taste; and would require a very large fortune to keep up. How people can build these pompous edifices without a sufficiency of surrounding estate is wonderful!' Poor Byng, who had to do without the Durant fortune, discovered Tong's secret: 'no library! Your hasty wealth thinks not of that. – Every part of this magnificent house is cover'd by pictures – from Xties [Christie's] – and other auctions, of dying Saints, naked Venuses, and drunken Bacchanals – disgusting to every English eye that has not been harden'd by Italy.' Horrified, Byng recapped: Tong, 'cover'd by filthy, naked or dying pictures!'

But it is high time we reluctantly join George II Durant. Even more of a cad than his father, he took possession of the castle in 1797. His personal fiefdom measured some 2.5 × 3 miles and apart from Tong itself took in the hamlets of Tong Norton, Tong Forge and Tong Havannah (yes, named after the origin of the family's wealth), and consisted of about 400 to 500 inhabitants. George II Durant was the owner of the castle, the demesne, the village and appendages; he was the local Justice of the Peace, he terrorised the inhabitants, drove his family to insanity and was responsible, directly and indirectly, for the death of some of them. The whiff of lunacy must have lingered long at Tong. The Revd J E Auden (1860–1946), vicar of Tong from 1896 to 1913, left notes saying that in Durant's time (1) a child was born that had great resemblance to a bear and (2) at Tong Hill Farm a child was born with fully grown wings, it took flight from its cot and circled the room. 'It was made away with'.

Shortly after George became the master at Tong, a servant, Mary Lee, was found murdered near one of the estate's lakes. Durant as JP organised a trial by ordeal, and had the male population of Tong parade past the victim as she would no doubt produce a nosebleed when her murderer passed by. Poor Mary Lee's nose didn't bleed on the occasion. We wonder whether Durant himself also had to walk past – obviously not.

By 1799 Durant had married into a family of landed gentry of long standing, his wife being Marianna (Mary Anne) Eld (1775–1829) of nearby Seighford Hall, a black-and-white manor house. Durant gave her the rather doubtful pleasure of siring 14 children with her. In 1817, she decided to investigate the smoke coming out of a chimney in a part of Tong Castle that had never been lived in. She found Durant's mistress in residence, who had already brought up three children there. Marianne immediately left for Seighford Hall and never returned. She filed for divorce. The case was taken up in 1820 and took seven years. The transcripts of the proceeding make for quite candid and very disturbing reading:

Mr. Durant is charged with having formed, in 1807, an adulterous connection with Mary Bradbury, and with having had three children by her; the first born in July, 1808; the second in March, 1810; the third in December, 1811; and he is alleged to have acknowledged and supported these children. He is also charged with having formed another adulterous connection with Elizabeth Cliffe, by whom he had a child born on the 19th of June, 1809; both these persons were nursery maids in his family. In 1816 he is charged with an adulterous connection with Mary Dyke, his dairy maid; of that connection no child was born which he acknowledged, but it is alleged that in June 1816, he was seen with her in the criminal act. In 1818 he is charged also with an adulterous connection with Jane James, a Labourer's wife, and on the 4th of November with having been caught in the act on the floor of her cottage. In 1820 there is a similar charge with another labourer's wife, of the name of Starkey; and, on the 26th of April 1820, it is asserted that he was caught in the act in a room in the cottage called White Oak Lodge.

These 'connections' took place in the direct surroundings of the castle, stables, brewhouse, laundry, henhouse, a wall, under the trees of the drive, but also in the worker's cottages. Quite often servants physically had to pull Durant off a chambermaid, and they were very angry that further adulteries took place in a room opposite the nursery.

Things didn't even stop there. In all Durant produced at least 32 bastards in the village. He insisted upon being their godfather and naming them: Napoleon Wedge, Columbine Cherrington, Louis Quatorze James, Cinderella Greatback, Luther Martin, Richard Coeur de Lion Chesney. His own children also sported equally ludicrous names: Francis Ossian, Hope, Anguish, Cecil Augustus Caesar, May Osmond Alonzo and one whose sex we couldn't assess: Bruce Emma (there were two Bruces among Durant's children). He usually acknowledged the illegitimates and paid for their education. Durant was in the habit of locking up any fractious children in the so-called Demon Hut, a small windowless building to the south of the castle. On the inside its walls were painted with fluorescent paint depicting hideous monsters and demons, so that children would eventually leave the hut half-mad, or perhaps poisoned by the radioactive paint. The Demon Hut seems to have been the catalyst for the lifelong guerilla warfare waged by the male children against their father.

Before we carry on, first a word or two about the Tong follies. Durant's venery wasn't his only enthusiasm. He built follies like a madman. Most of them bear the imprint of his insane soul. South of the castle drive he erected a sham ruin in 1816, the Convent Lodge, in which a poor dear was made to dress up as a door-keeping nun. On its walls he had some verses applied from Thomas Moore's popular *Irish Melodies* (1808 onwards). A long wall showing heraldic and semireligious imagery led to a hermitage occupied by an ornamental hermit (see Chapter 1). Also on the Convent Wall he erected a stone pulpit-cum-summerhouse, a copy of the medieval one at Shrewsbury Abbey, from which Durant chatted to his neighbours and passers-by. Not that many of them would have anything to do with the man. In 1821 he had decided to ruin the view of a neighbour of his, John Bishton of Kilsall Red House. They had been engaged in an argument concerning Durant's many water features draining the water from Kilsall. Exactly within the line of view from Kilsall Durant had the so-called New Buildings erected, a three-storey farmhouse looking like an early high-rise, in order to spoil Bishton's view. It did. Disgusted, Bishton withdrew to nearby Neach Hill. George Durant built around 50 follies on and near his estate, as many as he had children. His tenants, in effect his subjects, had to endure anything Durant threw at them.

The birth and burial registers of the parish provide their addresses: Pigeon House, The Louvre, Pavilion Cottage, Rosary Lodge, The Piazza, The

Phoenix. Some had to share their cottages with the pigeons, others lived in cottages that were bedecked with Durant's extravagant decorations. A row of houses on the estate was situated in what was called Hell Hole, changed by Durant's placing a placard with the new name: PARADISE. The village of Tong and its surroundings must in its heyday have looked like a crash between a lunapark and a lunatic asylum; partly it still does, if one knows where to look.

The village's craftsmen also had to endure Durant's particular brand of humour. The joinery, which also made coffins, was labelled 'IN MORTE LUCRUM' and 'GARDE A VOUS', the smithy was indicated by several melancholy observations but also with 'Strike with the iron hot'. The village school became 'Ecole des Belles Lettres', and was also given the local prison cell as an adjunct. North and south of his demesne Durant had gates erected made from the jaw bones of a whale. One carried the label 'MORS IANUA VITAE' (Death – the Gate of Life) and 'POST TOT NAUFRAGIA PORTUM' (a safe haven after so many storms). Their shapes and labels of course referred to the female pudendum so familiar to Durant.

White Oak Lodge, where Durant bothered Starkey, the wife of a labourer, had been built by Durant in 1818 and was also known as Acorn Lodge. Later he built a pyramidal pig sty and a Tudor cowshed with 'ROWS OF COWS'. Those rows of cows are to be taken with a pinch of salt; there's hardly enough room to swing a calf.

Of course, Durant didn't only bother neighbours, tenants and employees – he also annoyed the animals. The kennels, next to a castle gate, were surmounted by aeolian harps. The wind playing eerily through these instruments drove the dogs berserk. Even the castle's coal bunker got its inscription: 'MAUSOLEUM'.

The key to Durant's programme of folly building remains elusive. His obsessions appear to be nobility, religion and above all death and decay. He does have a personal iconography, but we couldn't make head or tail of it. There were three pyramids in total at Tong (one has disappeared, as well as an 'Egyptian Cottage' decorated with the reliefs of an Egyptian man and woman) – do they refer to Freemasonry, or are they *memento mori* in the form of mausolea? And what do the imprints on the 1842 Egyptian Aviary at Vauxhall Farm mean? There is a list of these glazed tiles on this pyramid (some can still be seen today), under the motto 'AB OVO'. Are they only jokey references to sayings and proverbs, or do they have a wider meaning?

The third pyramid was on an island; we last saw it around 1980. In fact, it was an Egyptian loo and carried labels like 'PARVA SED APTA' (small but comfy) and 'SOLITAR'. By the time we visited again in 1986 it had, like so many buildings at Tong, been vandalised and destroyed. A farmer told us the story: 'They knocked that privy down; lads that came to live in the village. Oh, dem were awful. Real buggers, them; just knocked it down. Used to have a slanting door and holes in the roof for ventilation'.

Durant certainly felt the need to parody the nobility. At the end of August 1839 a three-day mock medieval tournament was held by Lord Eglinton, at Eglinton near Kilmarnock, Scotland. It attracted enormous publicity and the crowds (up to 100,000) swamped the area, but rain fell throughout the whole event. The Whigs had a great time making fun of it. Ian Anstruther wrote its history, *The Knight and the Umbrella: An Account of the Eglinton Tournament*

1839 (1963), but even Anstruther wasn't aware that barely two weeks later, on September 16, Durant ridiculed the whole affair by having his own aptly named Acquatic Tournament, held on Tong Lake, in honour of Eglinton's watery disaster. Three to four thousand visitors came – not bad; and luckily it also rained most of the time.

All of Tong was decorated, as said, by typical Durant devices: crosses, shields, lozenge-shaped brick patterns and so on. This is also visible on the Offoxey Road, leading some three miles to another Durant outpost, Bishop's Wood. The farms, the walls, the Old Bell Inn are emblazoned in the same style. This road was built for Durant in 1815. Part of the lands through which it spear-headed towards the hamlet was church land, the rent of which was meant for the poor of the parish. In order to obliterate any memory of this fact, Squire Durant made away with the old notice board in church saying so, and had it destroyed. The then vicar was forced to submit to this and noted, 'the squire has this day sown damnation to his own soul and to mine also'.

Durant had remarried after the death of his divorced wife, to a governess, Celeste Lefevre/Lefebvre (*c* 1800–?). She hated living in the castle, and although Durant imported snails and frogs from France to satisfy her French palate, she chose to live at another Durant possession, Childwick Hall near St Albans, in their London town house and in France. She bore him seven children, which brought the sum total of Durants, legitimate or not, to 53.

His legitimate sons mostly seemed to hate him, although his daughters appear to have adored their father. Son Ernest built a gallows in the park, with an effigy of his father dangling from it. On becoming an adult he went to live nearby at Neachley Grange, on Bishton's estate, his father's old enemy. Each and every day Ernest walked by Tong Castle on the hour Durant and his new wife dined, and played two ditties on his flute: 'Home Sweet Home' and 'Poor Mary Anne', the last of course in reference to his dead mother. Ernest himself died in 1846 and was laid to rest in the tomb in Tong churchyard, which had been specially reserved for estranged Durant offspring. The rest were buried in church or at St Chrysostom's Cemetery (see below). By 1844 Ernest was bequeathed half-a-crown, but he refused to accept it, and at his own funeral the coin was put on his casket. Heir apparent, George Stanton Eld, was in 1822 sent to France to search for the Durant roots. They were thought to be from the Chateau Virginie near Caen, which appears to be codswallop, as were their supposed family ties to Louis XIV. The son saw the genealogic quest as an occasion to distance himself from his father, asked for even more funds, and on becoming 21, travelled to Brussels and married. He returned to England, but not to Tong. He was kept by his mother's family at Seighford Hall and by the Bishtons. He died young.

Another son, Anguish Honor Augustus, teamed up for a while with Ernest and made several illegal forays into the castle grounds, destroying goods and insulting people. Anguish, however, remained quite sane and later invented Sweep's Patent Chimney Brushes.

Son Frank trained for priest's orders, but like Ernest and Anguish, patrolled the castle grounds and was noticed in Durant's diary, 22 January 1832: 'Mr. Robinson preached a very good sermon. Fine. Maria rode round the wood and the kitchen garden. I walked by her. We saw Frank in the road by the Convent and heard he was sent back by the Bishop from the Ordination without getting priests' orders'. Frank is also buried separately outside Tong church. Another vicar in the family was Leonard Henry St George, one of the bastard sons by Mary Bradbury. He became vicar of Tong in 1839, but relations with his father soon cooled off, and Leonard left Tong after preaching his last sermon: 'Is thine eye evil because I am good?'

When Durant's pigs proved one day to have been poisoned, there were more than enough suspects: sons, neighbours, servants, mistresses, tenants. Death was the family friend at Tong. Most of the Durant children died young, very young or relatively young. In many cases the cause of death was rather sinister or at least peculiar. Mark died when seven, after (1) being forced to swim Castle Pool by his brothers when overheated or (2) his father insisted upon him learning to swim, threw him in Castle Pool, and he drowned. Mark was buried at midnight. One of the onlookers got so overworked by the scene of the strange, torch-lit ceremony, that she died of a heart attack.

Durant went from one funeral to another, in the meantime trying out new medications for the ailments of his dogs, his many children, and his wife. In 1823 he erected a large red-sandstone Maltese cross (one of the Durant emblems) and had it inscribed with verses by Byron, Thomas Moore and Walter Scott. It became the resting place for unbaptised children. In 1833 Celestine was buried here, a daughter who, according to Durant, died at birth due to a mistake by the midwife. His diary:

> Celeste was delivered of a female child, which I have no doubt was strangled at Birth. It came out with its feet first and I saw them move but she was dead ten minutes before the head came out. The Midwife denies it came feet first. She certainly killed the little girl, but it was very small for 7 months, as Celeste calculated, but the hair which I kept was and the nails and hands quite perfect [sic] ... Mr. Dean made a neat coffin and we took it to be buried at Chrysom's Cemetery at 11 at night.

Belle Durant died aged 28. Her father had forbidden her engagement. Belle took a bag of cherries and choked on a stone. Bruce Emma Durant died in his or her nineteenth year in Paris and lies in Père Lachaise. Eliza Durant in 1831 went with her parents to Liverpool in order to evade the burial at Tong of the male heir, George Stanton Eld Durant. On the hour of the funeral Eliza was attacked and bitten by a mad dog in the streets of Liverpool. She was paralysed for the rest of her life. Eliza had detested her brothers, and in turn they saw her misfortune as punishment for her father.

May Osmond Alonzo Durant, another son, was reported to be the best-looking man in Shropshire, but he was a bit strange, and his life ended at 45 in Ramsgate, 'found dead in a dyke'. Another strange man was the subsequent heir to the Durant fortune, George Charles Selwyn, the son of George Stanton Eld. On coming to Tong at 16 years of age, after the death of his grandfather, his mother ordered another colour livery for the servants and had some of the buildings where George II Durant carried out his excesses demolished. He was given to cross-dressing. The comedy ended in June 1872 when George Stanton Eld, last of the Durants, jumped out of a window at the Star and Garter Hotel in Richmond, having married just a month before.

George II Durant himself died in 1844. A newspaper report:

George Durant died from ossification of the Heart, a disease from which
he had long suffered. When he felt that he could not much longer survive
he sent for a Master Carpenter from Shifnal and gave him instructions to
prepare his coffin from a plan which he had committed to writing. When the
coffin was finished it was brought to Tong Castle, and by the dying man's
instructions taken up into his room. On seeing it he wept for some time, but
on becoming calm expressed his approval of the work.

And that night, on 29 November 1844, George Durant, tyrant, thief, philanderer,
murderer and eccentric, did die. As soon as they heard of his death, two of
his surviving sons took to their horses, drove at full speed through the village,
shouting 'The old man is dead at last, the old man is dead at last!' Twenty-nine
men from the village were collected, two caskets of gunpowder were taken from
the castle cellars, and at midnight, under the direction of Ernest and Augustus,
the whole crowd set off to Knowle Hill, to the Divorce Monument, a curious
three-storey building with two octagonal pillars on top, each measuring about
75 feet, completed by an offensive inscription in Latin celebrating his divorce.
A family living in the lowest storey was given a few minutes to gather their
belongings, and the gunpowder was put in place. The explosion could be heard
far and wide.

There aren't many follies left at Tong, but enough survive to get the feel
of the place. The castle itself was blown up in 1954 by the 213 Field Squadron
Royal Engineers as an exercise. The castle gates were removed to Blakenhall,
Wolverhampton, where they now greet visitors to Apostle Kenneth Njume's
Word and Fire Ministries International church. In the 1970s many Durant
follies were destroyed to make way for the M54 motorway, which in 1982 was
driven right through the remains of the castle. Vandals occupy themselves with
the remainder.

Graffiti

There is a fundamental human need to write on walls. Graffiti used to be
assiduously carved over a period of time, but now we have far less time and
use aerosol spray cans. In the past if you were rich enough and idle enough
you could pay a local to carve your graffiti for you – in 1825 on the Temple of
Hatshepsut at Medinet Habu in Luxor, Egypt, the architect Joseph Bonomi
had his name carved on the wall, along with his fellow travellers James Burton,
some unfortunate whose name has been obliterated, and Charles Humphreys.
Clearly the English aren't the only ones who have trouble with Welsh names:
the hapless Egyptian carver rendered it 'HUMHREYS'. Burton had become an
Egyptologist after being sacked by Pasha Mohammed Ali, who had employed
him to find coal in the Egyptian desert. He was unsuccessful, and the Pasha
remarked that Burton 'couldn't find a butterfly even if it were on the nose of his
horse'.

The Wirral is a strange prepuce of land between Wales and Lancashire
bordered by the Dee and the Mersey, containing settlements such as Hoylake,
Birkenhead, Tranmere, Port Sunlight and Bebington. A Liverpool saying has
it that 'Rome wasn't built in a day ... but Birkenhead was'. In the foyer of the

library in **Bebington** is a curious survival, fragments of a wall surrounding a long-vanished house.

```
    AR
       UBB
 I
    NGS
 TONEF
     ORAS
   SE
 S
```

This is completely incomprehensible, though it may once have made sense. It was the home of Thomas Francis (1762–1850), and it was peculiar enough to attract the attention of passing American novelist Nathaniel Hawthorne:

> In the village of Bebington we saw a house built in imitation of a castle, with turrets in which an upper and under row of cannons were mounted. On the wall there were eccentric inscriptions cut into slabs of stone, but I could make no sense of these. We peeped through the gate and saw a piazza beneath which seemed to stand the figure of a man. He appeared advanced in years, and was dressed in a blue coat and buff breeches, with a straw hat on his head. Behold too, a dog sitting chained. Also close behind the gateway, was another man seated. All were images, and the dwelling with the inscriptions and queer statuary was probably the whim of some half crazy person.

One of the inscriptions, 'SUBTRACT 45 FROM 45 THAT 45 MAY REMAIN' might be computed as follows: subtract 123456789 (the digits add up to 45) from 987654321 (the digits add up to 45) and the remainder is 864197532 (the digits add up to 45).

Another read 'FROM 6 TAKE 9, FROM 9 TAKE 10, FROM 40 TAKE 50, AND 6 WILL REMAIN'. SIX has to be spelled out and everything else must be in Roman numerals, so S without IX (9) equals S; IX (9) without X (10) equals I; XL (40) without L (50) equals X; hence SIX. The things we do for you.

The house was demolished many years ago, and the remains of the inscriptions are built into the foyer wall of Bebington Library.

Curios

There is an even smaller puzzle in North Yorkshire: visitors to Yarm, a peninsula on the River Tees, are puzzled when locals enthuse about **Yarm Castle**, because they can't see it. All they can see is the mighty railway viaduct slicing right through the centre of town, the biggest structure imaginable, built out of seven million bricks. If you happen to travel down West Street looking for the castle and you can't find it, pay closer attention to Number 28, Commondale House. There it is in plain view, still intact, on top of a wall outside the house. For Yarm Castle is no shambling ruin but a 2-foot-high model castle, built in 1882 by 18-year-old David Doughty, and later in the 20th century his son Henry added Yarm Town Hall beside it. The windows are made of coloured glass and apparently it can be lit from inside (Doughty later became the manager of the Yarm Gas Company) but we have never been fortunate enough to be in Yarm after dark. Residents of Yarm (Yarmists?) are fiercely proud of their little folly and it appears in every account of the town.

Men of the cloth are taught to condemn folly. In Ecclesiastes the Preacher harps upon folly – 'Then I saw that wisdom excelleth folly, as far as light excelleth darkness' – so when the Revd R S Hawker (1803–1875), rector of **Morwenstow** in Cornwall, embellished his rectory it was the most natural thing imaginable to enhance his rectory with replica towers of all the local churches he liked – the towers of Stratton, Whitstone and North Tamerton, except for the tower above the kitchen, which is a copy of his mother's tomb (Fig 13.3). They can't have been follies because they were practical additions, serving as the chimneys for the rectory. Hawker was a Cornish patriot, dimly remembered today for his stirring anthemic poem 'And Shall Trelawney Die?' but in his youth he was given to bizarre pranks such as sitting on the breakwater at Bude dressed as a mermaid and combing his seaweed hair. He dressed flamboyantly in bright colours and made sure his many cats and dogs attended morning service. Aged 19, he married a 41-year-old woman and lived in peace, affection and harmony with her for 40 years until her death, whereupon he married a 20-year-old and fathered three children with her. Hawker also introduced the Harvest Festival to the Anglican calendar.

Another West Country rector, the Revd Edward Atkyns Bray (1778–1857) of Tavistock, felt impelled to improve the **Cowsick** (Fig 13.4) (unhappy name!) valley in Devon by providing mental as well as visual stimulation to visitors. His intention was to inscribe a treasury of classic poetry on the rocks in the river, honouring over 50 great poets and writers such as Chaucer, Scott, Wieland, Ann Radcliffe, Ossian, Esau, Spenser, Burns, and Dante – an eclectic selection and

Fig 13.3

Hawker's Chimneys.

[© Gwyn Headley/fotoLibra]

one that may not have stood the test of time (Ossian was unmasked as a fraud and forgery in the 18th century). He made his selection, over 2,000 words of it, generally the poet's name followed by a couplet:

> TO TALIESIN
> How boiled his blood! How thrilled the warrior's veins!
> When roused to vengeance by thy patriot strains.

> TO LA FONTAINE
> He taught the beasts that roam the plains
> To speak a moral to the swains

before realising that the boulders wouldn't provide a suitably flat surface for the carver, nor was Dartmoor granite the easiest material to work with. It would have taken over a century to fully implement his scheme.

Relatively undeterred, he simply modified his plans by dropping the couplets and justifying himself as follows:

> As the name alone of Theocritus or of Virgil could not fail to communicate to a poetical mind a train of pleasing associations, I did nothing more, at first, than inscribe upon a few rocks 'To Theocritus,' 'To Virgil,' etc. This of itself, in so wild and solitary a scene as Dartmoor, was not without its effect: it seemed to people the desert; at any rate one might exclaim, 'The hand of man has been here!'

Years of water and wild weather have worn away the words; when we visited we could only find 'TO MILTON' and 'TO SHAKESPEARE', although 'TO SPENCER' [*sic*] and 'TO HOMER' are said to remain legible (Fig 13.4).

Fig 13.4
TO SPENCER. It became too
fatiguing to incise every poet's
name, risking spelling mistakes.
[© Julia K Rich/fotoLibra]

The Ten Commandments

The Whitley brothers, William and Herbert, came to Devon from Liverpool in the 1900s. Their father Edward was a solicitor, Mayor of Liverpool and Conservative MP first for Liverpool, then for Everton in the 1880s. The family firm, Greenall Whitley, founded in 1762, was an acquisitive brewer, buying up rival brewers and closing them down, until 1991 when they decided to quit brewing and concentrate on running pubs and hotels. It is now called the De Vere Group. Consequently, William and Herbert were men of leisure. William bought the Buckland estate and Herbert the Primley estate in Paignton, where he founded a private zoo, which became Paignton Zoo, now owned by the Whitley Wildlife Conservation Trust. William's son Herbert worked hard towards the creation of the Dartmoor Commons Act of 1985, giving public right of access in perpetuity to all the commons. Through his legacy we are able to stroll freely over Buckland Beacon and admire his father's great work.

William Whitley may never have been gainfully employed, but he was a passionate Protestant. In 1927 a bill for a new Book of Common Prayer came before Parliament. This outraged a great many conservative Anglicans, as it was seen as the Romish camel's nose under the tent; it contained revised texts proposed by the English Church Union and the Alcuin Club, both Anglo-Catholic groups. To their relief, Parliament rejected the proposal, and to commemorate the victory, Mr Whitley decided to have the Ten Commandments carved on flat tables of stone on the top of Buckland Beacon.

He employed a local sculptor, W A Clement, to engrave the words (Fig 13.5). Work started on 23 July 1928, and was completed on 31 August. Clement stayed up on the Beacon during that time. At night he slept in a cowshed, on wire netting covered in blankets he had to bring himself, while as for his food, a loaf of bread was left on the roadside wall each Thursday.

The first four commandments are on the left-hand slab, followed by the dates December 15 1927 – June 14 1928, the dates of the readings of the bill.

Fig 13.5
The Ten Commandments were
literally carved in stone.
[© Julia K Rich/fotoLibra]

Underneath are words from a hymn by John A Wallace, 'There Is An Eye That Never Sleeps':

JOB 33 V 14

BUT THERE'S A POWER, WHICH MAN CAN WIELD
WHEN MORTAL AID IS VAIN,
THAT EYE, THAT ARM, THAT LOVE TO REACH
THE LISTENING EAR TO GAIN
THAT POWER IS PRAYER.

The sculptor added his initials – A. C.

On the second slab are carved the remaining six commandments. A large empty space was left over, so Clement suggested to Whitley that he should add an eleventh commandment, along with the third verse of 'O God Our Help in Ages Past'. So the wording reads:

DEUTERONOMY 4 vv 2 6-8
A NEW COMMANDMENT
I
GIVE UNTO
YOU
THAT YE LOVE ONE ANOTHER
JOHN 13 v 34

and then

BEFORE THE HILLS IN ORDER STOOD,
OR EARTH RECEIVED HER FRAME,
FROM EVERLASTING THOU ART GOD,
TO ENDLESS YEARS THE SAME.

Down in the village of Buckland Mr Whitley kept himself busy after the death of his mother in 1929: the face of the church clock, instead of reading I, II, III, IIII, V and so on, reads A R R E H T O M M Y D E. It's not too hard to decipher. Every quarter hour the church clock chimes 'All things bright and beautiful.'

A few years later he commissioned Mr Clement again:

1282 FT
BUCKLAND BEACON
A BEACON FIRE – ONE OF A CHAIN
WAS LIT HERE BY THE PARISHIONERS
OF BUCKLAND-IN-THE-MOOR
IN CELEBRATION OF THEIR
MAJESTIES SILVER JUBILEE
MAY 6TH 1935
AND ALL THE PEOPLE SHOUTED
AND SAID GOD SAVE THE KING

Julie's House

The Landmark Trust was founded to restore interesting small buildings, funding the restoration by letting the places out for holiday rentals. A large proportion of their restored buildings are follies, and the charity has proved extremely popular among the upper-middle-class cognoscenti. Applying the same principle but slightly more recherché is Living Architecture, which builds its holiday shacks from scratch using noted architects and designers, the best-known of whom is Grayson Perry with his Julie's House in Manningtree, Essex (Fig 13.6).

Julie's House, or A House for Essex, is a tribute to 'single mums in Dagenham, hairdressers in Colchester, and the landscape and history of Essex' (Fig 13.6). Essex-born Grayson Perry, no stranger to publicity, is often to be seen on television promoting his latest work wearing a floral print dress harking back to the 1950s; this is his alter ego Claire. His popularity increases. Julie's House is quite a sight: there is nothing else like it anywhere. Designed by Perry with FAT Architects, it has been 'designed to evoke the tradition of wayside and pilgrimage chapels. It belongs to a history of follies, whilst also being deeply of its own time'. Compact and colourful, its exuberance catches the eye quicker than an Instagram puppy.

Fig 13.6

Julie's House – just for fun.

And some income.

[© Denise Anne Darbyshire]

Fig 13.7

Julie was a fictional Essex girl.

[© Denise Anne Darbyshire]

Gazetteer

County/Authority	Location	Folly
Buckinghamshire	Burnham	Brookend Dairy
	Dropmore	Aviary
	Stowe	Chinese House
	Waddesdon	Aviary
	West Wycombe	Golden Ball
Cambridgeshire	Six Mile Bottom	Windmill Folly
Cheshire	Bollington	White Nancy
	Peckforton	Elephant and Castle
Cornwall	Morwenstow	Morwenstow Vicarage Chimney
	St Ewe	Garden Jokes
	Werrington Park	Sugar Loaves
Cumbria	Coniston Water	The Labyrinth Ednam's Staircase
	Kirklinton	Privy Dovecote
	Lower Holker	Garden Pulpit
	Netherby	Fortified Salmon Coop
Derbyshire	Calke Abbey	Trompe l'Oeil Door
	Chatsworth	Trick Tree
	Crich	Derby Assembly Rooms
	Sudbury	Deerfold
Devon	Buckland-in-the-Moor	Buckland Beacon Ten Commandments
	Hartland	Highford Farm
	Saltram	Amphitheatre
	Two Bridges	Cowsick Valley Inscriptions
Dorset	Swanage	Burt's Follies
Durham	Bishop Auckland	Deer House
	Burn Hall	Cow House
	Coatham Mundeville	Hallgarth Deer House
	Darlington	Morton Park Mallard
	Gateshead (Tyne and Wear)	The Angel of the North
	Shildon	Pigeon Palace
Essex	Clacton-on-Sea	Moot Hall
	Fingringhoe	Bear Pit
	Manningtree	Julie's House
	Southend	Crow Stone
Gloucestershire	Tetbury	The Folly
Hampshire	Hurstbourne	Hurstbourne Monument
Herefordshire	Elton	Chicken Run
	Hereford	Urn
	Pembridge	Bottle Dome Giant Cuckoo Clock

County/Authority	Location	Folly
Hertfordshire	Driver's End	Node Dairy
	Great Amwell	Inscription
	King's Langley	Ovaltine Dairy
Kent	Grain	London Stone
	Greatstone-on-Sea	Listening Device
	Knole	Birdhouse
	Mereworth	Aviary
Lancashire	Barrowford	Waterloo Plantation
	Hornby	Claughton Hall
	Lancaster	Music Room
	Parbold	Parbold Bottle
Leicestershire	Belvoir Castle	Dairy
Lincolnshire	Wootton	Castellated Pigsty
Liverpool and Manchester	Bebington (Merseyside)	Mr Francis's Inscribed Wall
	Dunham Massey (Greater Manchester)	Deer Shelter
	Maghull (Merseyside)	Maghull Folly
London	E9	Stone Poem
	EC2	Turkish Kiosk (now the Victorian Bathhouse)
	SE18	Rotunda
	SE26	Dinosaurs
	WC2	Trafalgar Square Globular Lights and Police Station
Norfolk	Raveningham	Raveningham Milestone
Northamptonshire	Geddington	Boughton House Chinese Tent
Northumberland	Alnwick	Tree House
	Sunderland (Tyne and Wear)	St Peter's Sculpture Project
North Yorkshire	Ebberston	Aelfrid's Memorial
	Grewelthorpe	The Kitchen
	Little Ribston (NY)	Butler
	North Grimston (NY)	Horseshoe Piles
	Ripley Castle	Swiss Village
	Yarm	Yarm Castle
Nottinghamshire	Scarrington	Horseshoe Pile
Oxfordshire	Buckland	Ice House
	Headington	Headington Shark
	Watlington	White Mark
Shropshire	Acton Round	Castellated Tractor Shed
	Cross Houses	Bus Shelters
	Lydbury North	Dacha
	Pitchford	Pitchford Tree House

County/Authority	Location	Folly
	Tong	Durant's Follies
South Yorkshire	Barnsley	The Imaginary City
Staffordshire	Biddulph	Giant Frog
	Longton Hall	Pottery Follies
	Mapleton	Necessary House
	Shugborough	Shepherd's Monument Chinese House
Suffolk	Cavenham	Water Organ
Surrey	Cobham	Tartar Tent
	Witley	Underwater Ballroom
Tyne & Wear	Sunderland	Red House
West Sussex	Milland	Ivy Folly
Wiltshire	Amesbury	Chinese Temple
	Bromham	Tree House
	Malmesbury	Hannah Twynnoy's Grave
Worcestershire	Rous Lench	Postbox

Bibliography

This bibliography lists the publications essential to understanding and researching the folly in its manifold manifestations. For a full bibliography we refer the reader to our editions of *Follies: A National Trust Guide, Follies: A Guide to Rogue Architecture*, and *Follies Grottoes & Garden Buildings*.

We have not included the numerous 18th- and 19th-century county histories, old tourist guides and guides to gardens and/or follies, or articles and books concerning one specific folly or architect. Extensively used were the volumes of The Royal Commission on Historical Monuments, The Victoria County Histories, The Shell County Guides, Arthur Mee's *The King's England* series, *Country Life, Garden History*, and *The Journal of Garden History*. We should like to acknowledge our special debt to Barbara Jones's *Follies and Grottoes*, Nikolaus Pevsner's *The Buildings of England*, the *Dictionary of National Biography*, and Howard Colvin's *Biographical Dictionary of British Architects: 1600–1840. The Follies Newsletter*, and *Follies Magazine* were also helpful. Online we recommend www.fabulousfollies.net run by Ray Blyth; the Folly Fancier Group on Facebook: https://www.facebook.com/groups/447186618695453/; the Folly Flâneuse: https://thefollyflaneuse.com and the Folly Fellowship: http://follies.org.uk.

We have decided not to mention the many travel diaries etc. this book is also based on, with one glorious exception: John Byng's *The Torrington Diaries*, 5 volumes, London 1934–1938/Marlow s.a. The same goes for biographies, again with one exception: Aubrey's *Brief Lives*, although we want to sneak in another reference tool: http://www.historyofparliamentonline.org.

To set the scene for the 18th- and 19th-century garden folly, we recommend the following sources and the subsequent studies into the tastes and eccentricities of the age, as well as architectural pattern or model books and books on the design and furnishing of the landscape garden:

Anon, *Eccentric Biography*, London 1803.

Burke, Edmund, *A Philosophical Inquiry into the Origin of Our Ideas of the Sublime and the Beautiful*, London 1773 (ed. pr. 1756).

Chambers, William, *A Dissertation on Oriental Gardening*, London 1772.

Dearn, T D W, *Designs for Lodges and Entrances to Parks, Paddocks, and Pleasure Grounds, in the Gothic, Cottage and Fancy Styles*, London 1823 (ed. pr. 1811).

Decker, Paul, *Chinese Architecture, Civil and Ornamental*, London 1759.

Decker, Paul, *Gothic Architecture Decorated*, London 1759.

Elsam, Robert, *An Essay on Rural Architecture*, London 1803.

Gandy, John, *The Rural Architect*, London 1805.

Gilpin, William, *Essays on Picturesque Beauty*, London 1794.

Halfpenny, William, *New Designs for Chinese Temples*, London 1750.

Halfpenny, William and John, *Rural Architecture in the Chinese Taste*, London 1752.

Halfpenny, William and John, *Rural Architecture in the Gothic Taste*, London 1752.

Hall, John, *Essay on the Origin, History and Principles of Gothic Architecture*, London 1813.

Hogarth, William, *The Analysis of Beauty*, London 1753.

Knight, Richard Payne, *The Landscape: A Didactic Poem*, London 1794.

Knight, Richard Payne, *An Analytical Inquiry into the Principles of Taste*, London 1805.

Langley, Batty, *New Principles of Gardening*, London 1728.

Langley, Batty, *Gothic Architecture Improved*, London 1747.

Lightoler, Thomas, *The Gentleman and Farmer's Architect*, London 1774.

Loudon, John Claudius, *An Encyclopaedia of Gardening*, London 1822.

Loudon, John Claudius, *An Encyclopaedia of Cottage, Farm and Villa Architecture and Furniture*, London 1833.

Mason, George, *An Essay on Gardening*, London 1795.

Mason, William, *The English Garden: A Poem*, 3 vols, 1772–1783.

[Middleton, Charles], *Decorations for Parks and Gardens*, London [1790].

Morris, Robert, *The Art of Architecture: A Poem*, London 1742.

Morris, Robert, *Rural Architecture*, London 1750.

Morris, Robert, *The Architectural Remembrancer*, London 1752.

Over, Charles, *Ornamental Architecture in the Gothic, Chinese and Modern Taste*, London 1758.

Overton, Thomas Collins, *Original Designs of Temples* [later editions: *The Temple Builder's Most Useful Companion*], London 1766.

Papworth, John Buonarotti, *Rural Residences*, London 1818.

Plaw, John, *Ferme Ornée; or Rural Improvements*, London 1795.

Pocock, W F, *Architectural Designs for Rural Cottages*, London 1807.

Price, Uvedale, *An Essay on the Picturesque*, London 1794.

Le Rouge, Georges Louis, *De jardins anglo-chinois à la mode / Détail de nouveaux jardins à la mode*, 21 vols, Paris 1775–1789.

Soan[e], John, *Designs in Architecture; Consisting of Plans, Elevations, and Sections, for Temples, Baths, Cassines, Pavilions, Garden-Seats, Obelisks and Other Buildings; for Decorating Pleasure-Ground, Parks, Forests, &c. &c.*, London 1778.

Timbs, John, *English Eccentrics and Eccentricities*, London 1875.

Walpole, Horace, *Works*, 8 vols, London 1798–1825.

Wilson, G H, *The Eccentric Mirror*, 4 vols, London 1806–1807.

Wilson, Henry and James Caulfield, *The Book of Wonderful Characters Memoirs and Anecdotes of Remarkable and Eccentric Persons in All Ages and Countries*, London [1873].

Wright, Thomas, *Arbours and Grottos: a facsimile of the two parts of 'Universal Architecture' (1755 and 1775)*, London 1979.

Wrighte, William, *Grotesque Architecture*, London 1790 (ed. pr. 1767).

Follies, styles, shapes and forms, including more or less recent studies into the tastes of the age:

Barnes, Richard, *The Obelisk: A Monumental Feature in Britain*, Kirstead 2004.

Beamon, Sylvia P and Susan Roaf, *The Ice-Houses of Britain*, London 1991.

Campbell, Gordon, *The Hermit in the Garden*, Oxford 2013.

Carrott, Richard G, *The Egyptian Revival: Its Sources, Monuments, and Meaning 1808–1858*, Berkeley 1978.

Casson, Hugh (ed), *Follies*, London 1963.

Casson, Hugh (ed), *Monuments*, London 1963.

Clark, Kenneth, *The Gothic Revival*, London 1928.

Coffin, David R, *The English Garden: Meditation and Memorial*, Princeton 1994.

Conner, Paul, *Oriental Architecture in the West*, London 1979.

Curl, James Stevens, *The Egyptian Revival*, London 1982.

Curtis, R A (ed), *Monumental Follies*, Worthing 1972.

Darley, Gillian, *Villages of Vision*, London 1975.

Davis, Terence, *The Gothick Taste*, Norwich 1974.

Dobai, Johannes, *Die Kunstliteratur des Klassizismus und der Romantik in England*, 3 vols, Bern 1974–77.

Elffers J and M Schuyt, *Fantastic Architecture*, London 1980.

Elliott, Chris, *Egypt in England*, Swindon 2012.

Head, Raymond, *The Indian Style*, London 1986.

Hipple, Walter John Jr, *The Beautiful, The Sublime & The Picturesque in Eighteenth-Century British Aesthetic Theory*, Carbondale 1957.

Hitching, Claude, *Rock Landscapes: The Pulham Legacy*, Woodbridge 2012.

Hussey, Christopher *The Picturesque: Studies in a Point of View*, London 1927.

Jones, Barbara, *Follies and Grottoes*, London 1953.

Jones, Barbara, *Follies and Grottoes*, London 1974 (new, augmented edition).

Lambton, Lucinda, *Beastly Buildings: The National Trust Book of Architecture for Animals*, London 1985.

Macaulay, James, *The Gothic Revival 1745–1845*, Glasgow 1975.

Miller, Naomi, *Heavenly Caves: Reflections on the Garden Grotto*, London 1982.

Crook, J Mordaunt, *The Greek Revival: Neo-Classical Attitudes in British Architecture 1760–1870*, London 1972.

Mowl, Tim and Brian Earnshaw, *Trumpet at a Distant Gate: The Lodge as Prelude to the Country House*, London 1985.

Rawlinson, Guy, *Prehistory, Romantic Antiquarianism and Landscape Design: The Development of Megalthic Follies*, diss. Manchester 1991.

Robinson, John Martin, *Georgian Model Farms*, Oxford 1983.

Rowan, Alastair, *Garden Buildings*, Feltham 1968.

Piggott, Stuart, *Ruins in a Landscape: Essays in Antiquarianism*, Edinburgh 1976.

Sirén, Osvald, *China and Gardens of Europe*, New York 1950.

Steegman, John, *The Rule of Taste from George I to George IV*, London 1936.

Thacker, Christopher, *Masters of the Grotto: Joseph and Josiah Lane*, Tisbury 1976.

Watkin, David, *Thomas Hope and the Neo-Classical Ideal*, London 1968.

Wiebenson, Dora, *Sources of Greek Revival Architecture*, London 1969.

Woodbridge, Kenneth, *Landscape and Antiquity*, Oxford 1970.

A short listing of the major publications on follies and garden buildings in other countries and British regions (for comparison's sake). There are by now also quite a few books on follies by county or area – too many to list here.

Buxbaum, Tim, *Scottish Garden Buildings: From Food to Folly*, Edinburgh 1989.

Headley, Gwyn, *Architectural Follies in America*, New York 1996.

Headley, Gwyn and Wim Meulenkamp, *Follies of Wales*, London and Harlech 2016.

Howley, James, *The Follies and Garden Buildings of Ireland*, New Haven and London 1993.

Lancaster, Clay, *Architectural Follies in America or Hammer, Saw, Tooth & Nail*, Rutland 1960.

Meulenkamp, Wim, *Follies: bizarre bouwwerken in Nederland en België*, Amsterdam/Antwerp 1995.

Nyreröd, Anna-Lisa, *Lusthus: till bruks och till syns*, Stockholm 1979.

Index